The
EVERYTHING®
Learning French Book
2nd Edition

Dear Reader,

French is much more than a language—it's a culture and a way of being. Learning French is a journey. It carries with it its own idiosyncrasies, its own expressions, its own logic, and its own style. In this book, you'll find an insider's guide to the basics of the French language, giving you the knowledge you need to navigate through the French-speaking world.

Whether you're learning French for travel or to impress your friends, this book will help you achieve your goal. Learning French can help you better your English as well, as it causes you to look carefully at the way language is constructed.

As you begin your French journey, don't be critical of yourself if it takes you some time to learn. Take it slowly and don't lose faith. Before you know it, things will fall into place, and you'll be speaking French with ease.

Vive le français !

Bruce Sallee

David Hebert

Welcome to the EVERYTHING® Series!

These handy, accessible books give you all you need to tackle a difficult project, gain a new hobby, comprehend a fascinating topic, prepare for an exam, or even brush up on something you learned back in school but have since forgotten.

You can choose to read an *Everything*® book from cover to cover or just pick out the information you want from our four useful boxes: e-questions, e-facts, e-alerts, and e-ssentials.

We give you everything you need to know on the subject, but throw in a lot of fun stuff along the way, too.

We now have more than 400 *Everything*® books in print, spanning such wide-ranging categories as weddings, pregnancy, cooking, music instruction, foreign language, crafts, pets, New Age, and so much more. When you're done reading them all, you can finally say you know *Everything*®!

QUESTIONS?
Answers to common questions

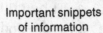

FACTS
Important snippets of information

ALERTS!
Urgent warnings

ESSENTIALS
Quick handy tips

PUBLISHER Karen Cooper

DIRECTOR OF ACQUISITIONS AND INNOVATION Paula Munier

MANAGING EDITOR, EVERYTHING SERIES Lisa Laing

COPY CHIEF Casey Ebert

ACQUISITIONS EDITOR Lisa Laing

DEVELOPMENT EDITOR Elizabeth Kassab

EDITORIAL ASSISTANT Hillary Thompson

Visit the entire Everything® series at *www.everything.com*

THE
EVERYTHING®
LEARNING
FRENCH BOOK
2nd Edition

Speak, write, and understand
basic French in no time!

Bruce Sallee and David Hebert

Adams Media
New York London Toronto Sydney New Delhi

Adams Media
An Imprint of Simon & Schuster, Inc.
57 Littlefield Street
Avon, Massachusetts 02322

An Everything® Series Book.
Everything® and everything.com® are registered trademarks of Simon & Schuster, Inc.

ADAMS MEDIA and colophon are trademarks of Simon and Schuster.

For information about special discounts for bulk purchases, please contact Simon & Schuster Special Sales at 1-866-506-1949 or business@simonandschuster.com.

The Simon & Schuster Speakers Bureau can bring authors to your live event. For more information or to book an event contact the Simon & Schuster Speakers Bureau at 1-866-248-3049 or visit our website at www.simonspeakers.com.

Manufactured in the United States of America

20 19 18 17 16 15 14 13

Library of Congress Cataloging-in-Publication Data has been applied for.

ISBN 978-1-59869-412-3

Contents

Top Ten Things You'll Accomplish
Through Reading This Book

1. You will feel a lot more confident visiting France, Québec, Sénégal, Guadeloupe, or the many other countries where French is spoken.

2. You'll be able to go to Paris and order a *café* with ease.

3. You'll be able to watch French language television on the Internet or via satellite.

4. You'll be able to go to the many French-speaking areas of the United States, like Lewiston, Maine, with its many Franco-Americans, or Miami, Florida, with its large Haitian population, and speak to the locals.

5. You'll learn a thing or two about the English language as you learn French.

6. French is an international language, and being able to use it at work will make you more international, too.

7. You'll be able to write an e-mail to reserve your hotel room on the beach in Martinique.

8. You can go across the border to Québec and order some of the famous *poutine* (French fries with gravy and cheese)!

9. You can one day read *Les Misérables* in the original.

10. Once you learn one foreign language, the next one will be easier.

Introduction

FRENCH is a part of the language family known as romance languages, so called because they came from Latin (which was spoken by Romans—get it?!). Included in this family are Italian, Spanish, Portuguese, and Romanian; these languages share many similarities because they all come from a common source. Despite the similarities, however, each is distinct and different, and many agree that French is one of the most "romantic" languages of all, even if they are referring more to Champagne than Caesar.

French is spoken around the world, in a vestige of the vast French colonization which began in the seventeenth century and lasted until the mid-twentieth. In North America, you may run across French speakers in Canada or Louisiana. It is widely spoken in Europe, Africa, and the West Indies; even some Asian countries use French as a major language. In short, you'll never know where it may come in handy to know a little bit of French. In this book, we concentrate on standard French, which is sometimes referred to as Parisian French.

In a sense, the French language has its own governing body. The French Academy, or *l'Académie française,* was originally established in 1635 and oversees the development of the language. It registers all official French words; until the Academy approves it, a word isn't officially a part of the language. Despite its efforts to preserve the French language, some expressions still slip in. You'll inevitably be understood if you order *un hamburger* or *un hot-dog* in French, even if the Academy doesn't acknowledge these words.

Chapter 1

Pronouncing and Writing French

In this chapter, you will dive into French, starting with a little speaking and a little writing. You will discover how to pronounce basic French letters, letter combinations, and words, and you will begin writing by focusing on punctuation marks and accents.

The Alphabet

While French and English use the same alphabet, the letters are pronounced differently in French. Learning their pronunciation is important. If you ever have to spell your name out at a hotel, for example, you want to make sure that you're understood.

TRACK 1

Table 1-1
The French Alphabet

a	e	i	m	q	u	y
b	f	j	n	r	v	z
c	g	k	o	s	w	
d	h	l	p	t	x	

Accents

French uses accents, which are pronunciation marks that appear with some letters. There are four accents commonly used with vowels: the *accent aigu*, the *accent grave*, the *accent circonflexe*, and the *tréma*. One mark, the *cédille*, appears under the consonant "c," making it "ç."

The Accent Aigu (Acute Accent)

The *accent aigu* is spelled *é*. It only appears over the letter "e," and is an integral part of a word. The *accent aigu* also provides important clues about where the word fits in a sentence.

TRACK 2

Table 1-2
Accent Aigu

French	English
réveil	alarm clock
médecin	doctor
épicé	spicy

The Accent Grave

The *accent grave* is spelled *è*. The *accent grave* appears mostly on "e" but can appear over the letters "a," "i," "o," or "u"; however, it changes the pronunciation only when it appears above "e."

TRACK 3

Table 1-3
Accent Grave

French	English
très	very
où	where
troisième	third

The Accent Circonflexe

The *accent circonflexe* can appear over any vowel, and it looks like a little hat over the letter, as in *ô*.

Table 1-4
Accent Circonflexe

French	English
forêt	forest
hôpital	hospital

The Tréma

The *tréma* is spelled with 2 dots above a vowel: *ë*. In English, it is known as an *umlaut*. The accent tells you that the second vowel is to be pronounced on its own, distinct from the vowel preceding it.

TRACK 4

Table 1-5
Le Tréma

French	English
coïncidence	coincidence
Jamaïque	Jamaica
Noël	Christmas

The Cédille

The *cédille* appears underneath the letter "c" and looks like a tail: ç. It indicates a soft "s" sound instead of the hard "k" sound the letter "c" would normally have if it appeared before the letter "a" or "o." For example, the French language is referred to as *le français*.

TRACK 5

Table 1-6
La Cédille

French	English
français	French
garçon	boy
leçon	lesson
façon	manner

General Pronunciation Rules

In general, French is pronounced forward in the mouth (rather than in the back, as in English), and in a tense muscular fashion.

Listen for the intonation of a French sentence. In general, you will notice that the voice falls at the end of a statement, and rises at the end of a question.

In addition, French is pronounced with equal stress on each syllable, with a slight increase in stress at the end of a word or word group.

TRACK 6

Paul est fatigué.
Est-ce que Paul est fatigué?
Céline va au café.
Est-ce que Céline va au café?

Les Consonnes Muettes

Sometimes, letters are silent and are not pronounced; this often occurs with letters at the end of words. Here are the letters to watch:

- Words ending in -d: *chaud*, meaning "hot."
- Words ending in -s: *compris*, meaning "included."
- Words ending in -t: *achat*, meaning "purchase."
- Words ending in -x: *choix*, meaning "choice."

The following letters are generally pronounced at the end of a word: "c," "r," "f," and "l." "In French, the letter "h," no matter where it appears in the word, is always silent.

Using Liaison with Articles

When a word ending in a consonant that is normally silent is followed by a word beginning with a vowel sound or an "h," the ending consonant is sometimes pronounced. This is called *liaison*. Some ending consonants actually change their pronunciation when *liaison* occurs: For example, "s" and "x" are pronounced "z" in a *liaison*. "D" becomes "t."

The rules governing *liaison* are complicated; for now, we will just concentrate on the use of *liaison* with articles. Whenever an article that ends in a consonant is used with a noun that begins with a vowel, the final letter joins with the next vowel sound in a *liaison*.

Table 1-7
Liaison and Articles

French	English
un enfant	child
les abricots	apricots
les hommes	men

Pronunciation of Vowels and Consonants

To talk about the particular sounds of a language, we refer to the International Phonetic Alphabet. You will hear the pronunciation of these sounds on the next few tracks. For now, we will concentrate on the sounds that present the most challenges for an English speaker.

French Vowels and Semi-Vowels

French vowels are pronounced with none of the diphthong sound of their English counterparts (in other words, the gliding sound between two vowels). Listen to the difference between the French /a/ and the English "a" in the name Ann(e).

TRACK 9

Ann   Anne

TRACK 10

Table 1-8
French Vowels and Semi-Vowels

Ipa Symbol	Letter or Letter Combination	French Word
/a/	a	chat, ça va, campagne
ə	e	regarder, acheter, rester
ɛ	e, è	veste, père
/e/	e, é	les, Céline, Valérie
/i/	i	ici, Philippe
/u/	ou, où	vous, toujours, où
/y/	u	tu, étudie
/w/	ou, o (before i)	oui, chouette, loin
/j/	i, ill	bien, maillot de bain
(ø)	eu	peu, euro
(œ)	eu, œu	sœur, neuf
/o/	o, au, eau	vélo, chaud
ɔ	o	mort, donner

- /a/: The French "a" is always pronounced like the "a" of the English word "ah."
- /y/: This sound, which does not exist in English, is pronounced as if you were pronouncing the /i/ of Philippe, but with your lips rounded, to form the sound of the word *tu*.

- /w/ and /j/: These semi-vowels do not exist in English. They are pronounced very quickly, as are consonants (thus their status as almost vowels)!

Les Voyelles Nasales

In French, when a vowel is followed by an "m" or an "n," the "m" or "n" is not pronounced and the vowel is pronounced with a nasal sound.

TRACK 11

Table 1-9
Les Voyelles Nasales

IPA symbol	Letter Combination	Word
õ	on/om	*maison, onze*
œ	un/um/in/ain/aim	*un, demain, copain*
ã	en/em/an/am	*enchanté, Henri*

Note that when an ending nasal vowel occurs in a *liaison* (as in the phrase, *un ami*), the vowel is denasalized, and the ending "m" or "n" is pronounced.

ESSENTIAL

French is known for the rolling "r" sound. You can learn to roll your r's, too, with just a little bit of practice. Start to make a "k" sound and hold it. Close your throat a little bit, breathe out slowly, and start to say "raw." Don't worry if it starts to come out as "graw"—keep doing it. Practice this a couple of times a day, and you'll soon sound just like Gérard Depardieu.

French Consonants

In general, French consonants are pronounced crisply, and do not have the aspiration (puff of breath) found in English consonants. Note the difference between the pronunciation of a French and English "t" in the name Thomas.

TRACK 12

Thomas   Thomas

A few consonants and combinations to watch out for in French:

Table 1-10

TRACK 13

Letters	Examples
ch	*chat, chocolat*
gn	*espagnol, ligne*
qu	*qui, quand*
s	*poison*
ss	*poisson*

- "ch": Note that although in general, "ch" is pronounced like "sh," there are a few words in which it is pronounced like "k": Christine, for example.
- "s" and "ss": When found in the middle of a word, "s" is pronounced like a "z," while "ss" is always pronounced as an "s."

The French "r"

The French "r" is more guttural than the English one, made at the back of the throat instead of at the front.

TRACK 14

arrondissement
ravi
rare
projet

Punctuation Marks

Written French looks very similar to English, so reading books in French should feel familiar. For the most part, French uses the same punctuation marks, and they function in much the same way as in English.

Les Crochets (Brackets)

Brackets, called *les crochets*, are often used to show words inserted into quoted text to help explain the original.

Les Deux-Points (Colon)

The colon, called *les deux-points*, is used to introduce another phrase that is related to the previous one. Usually, the following phrase will be an elaboration on a point or something that explains the sentence more clearly. The colon functions the same in both languages.

La Virgule (Comma)

The comma, called *la virgule*, is used in the same way as English uses it, but note that French also uses *une virgule* when indicating an amount of money. For example, 1.25 in English would be 1,25 in French.

Le Point D'exclamation (Exclamation Point)

An exclamation point, called *le point d'exclamation*, is used at the end of a sentence to indicate an element of surprise, excitement, or other intense emotion. The usage between French and English is, for the most part, interchangeable.

Les Parenthèses (Parentheses)

Parentheses, called *les parenthèses*, are used in the same way as in English, usually to refer to an aside statement without interrupting the flow of the sentence. Wrapping a phrase in parentheses indicates that the phrase is meant to elaborate but at the same time be self-sustaining, separate from the phrase that appears around it.

Le Point (Period)

The period, called *le point*, is used at the end of a sentence; any time you use a period in English, you can do the same in French, except when indicating amounts of money.

Le Point d'Interrogation (*Question Mark*)

A question mark, called *le point d'interrogation*, is used to indicate a question. In written French, you will most often see *est-ce que* used to indicate a question; in dialogue, however, you may encounter inversion or even plain sentences that use a question mark (see Chapter 7). In the latter case, the dialogue is intended to be read with intonation; the question mark is your clue.

Les Guillemets (*Quotation Marks*)

French quotation marks, called *les guillemets*, appear slightly different from English ones. Instead of using symbols that look like commas like we do in English, French uses small double arrows that wrap around the quotation, as follows:

Il dit: « je ne sais pas. »   He said, "I don't know."

Le Point-Virgule (*Semicolon*)

A semicolon, called *le point-virgule*, is used to attach a phrase that is loosely related to the previous phrase in the sentence.

Activité 1

TRACK 15

Listen to the speaker's pronunciation. Repeat each word after the speaker.

1. *chocolat*
2. *jamais*
3. *certain*
4. *espagnol*
5. *Thomas*
6. *ennuyer*
7. *salut*
8. *enchanté*

Chapter 2

Using Everyday Expressions

In this chapter, you will start preparing to speak French like a native! Here, you'll discover some everyday expressions that don't necessarily make sense when you translate them word for word into English but will certainly make sense to the French speaker you're communicating with. To aid in that communication, this chapter also helps you understand hand gestures, greetings, and basic numbers.

Useful Expressions to Get By in France

It's not necessary to understand all the complexities of French grammar in order to learn some basic expressions. The following sentences can be memorized in order to get you started speaking French. As you go along in this book, you will be introduced to the grammar in a more systematic way, which will help you understand how these sentences are structured; for now, just have fun trying to communicate with them.

Bonjour. Comment Allez-Vous?
Bonjour. Comment Ça Va?

Both expressions are used to ask "Hello, how are you?" The first is used in formal situations (with colleagues, for example, or people you don't know well), and the second in informal situations (with friends or children).

Notice that in the phrase *comment allez-vous?*, the "t" sound at the end of *comment*, when pronounced, is attached to the beginning of *allez*, making it sound like "tallay." This is an example of *liaison*. The "t" of *comment ça va?*, however, is not pronounced, as it precedes a consonant sound.

To respond to these greetings, you can say *Bien, merci*, or *Ça va bien, merci* or simply *Ça va*.

Comment Vous Appelez-Vous?

This means, "What is your name?" You'll notice that *vous* appears twice. It's a versatile word that can pull double duty. The last *vous* is the subject pronoun, and means "you." The first *vous*, however, is used as a reflexive pronoun, and means "yourself." Jump to Chapter 13 to find out more about reflexive pronouns.

Je M'appelle . . .

This means "My name is . . . ." The literal interpretation takes a circuitous route, translating as "I call myself . . ." or "I am named . . ."

Je Ne Parle Pas Français.

This means, "I don't speak French." *Je* is the French word for "I." You use it whenever you are talking about yourself as the subject of a sentence. *Ne* and *pas* are the French equivalent to "not"; they always appear together in written form, but the *ne* is sometimes dropped in conversational French. The *ne* is just a language pointer to let you know that the subject is going to be in the negative, while *pas* means "not." There are other negative expressions in French, but *ne . . . pas* is by far the most common you'll encounter. *Français*, as you may have guessed, means French.

Parlez-Vous Anglais?

This means "Do you speak English?" It can be used to address one person in the formal address, or it can be used to address more than one person. Note that there's no *liaison* between *vous* and *anglais*.

Où Sont Les Toilettes?

This means "Where is the bathroom?" To get right to the point, you can ask, *"Les toilettes, s'il vous plaît?"* Note that if you were to try and translate this literally into French, you would say *"Où est la salle de bain?"* In French, however, a *salle de bain* is literally the room containing the bath, and often does not have a toilet in it!

Je N'ai Pas Compris.

This means "I didn't understand." Note that it is in the past tense, which you will learn about in Chapter 12. *"Compris"* is the past tense form of the verb *"comprendre,"* which you'll notice is very similar to the English word "comprehend."

Répétez, S'il Vous Plaît.

This means "Please repeat." *S'il vous plaît* is the French way of saying "please." Literally translated, it means "If it pleases you."

Parlez Plus Lentement, S'il Vous Plaît.

This means "Speak more slowly, please."

Je Voudrais . . .

This is how to say "I would like . . . ," and is the polite way of ordering things. You'll find it a useful expression in stores and restaurants.

Pardon, or Excusez-moi.

Both expressions mean, "Excuse me," and are useful when negotiating though a crowd to let people know that you need to pass.

Pronunciation of Common Phrases

In this section, you learned some useful expressions to get you started in French. Listen to the CD for their pronunciation.

TRACK 16

Bonjour. Comment allez-vous?	Hello. How are you?
Bonjour, comment ça va?	Hello, how are you? (informal)
Bien, merci.	I'm well, thank you.
Ça va bien, merci.	I'm well, thank you.
(informal)	
Comment vous appelez-vous?	What is your name?
Je ne parle pas français.	I don't speak French.
Parlez-vous anglais?	Do you speak English?
Je m'appelle . . .	My name is . . .
Où sont les toilettes?	Where is the bathroom?
Je n'ai pas compris.	I didn't understand.
Répétez, s'il vous plaît.	Please repeat.
Parlez plus lentement, s'il vous plaît.	Speak more slowly, please.
Pardon.	Excuse me.
Excusez-moi.	Excuse me.

Colloquial, Idiomatic, and Other Useful Expressions

Idiomatic and colloquial language expresses things in a way that is unique to that language. Idiomatic expressions usually follow a certain pattern of construction, and are very much a part of the grammar of each language. Colloquial expressions are generally not part of the formal language. They often bend the rules of grammar a little bit, or use words in unusual ways, but are so widely recognized within the spoken language that it's acceptable to use them in everyday speech. In English, an example of a colloquial expression is: "To get the skinny (on something)," which means to get the inside information.

Here are a few idiomatic and colloquial expressions in French that you might hear.

TRACK 17

J'ai pas compris.	"I didn't get that."
J'en ai marre.	"I've had it!"
Ce n'est pas la peine.	"Don't worry about it."

Note that although the expression "*J'ai pas compris*" is in the negative, it has omitted the *ne* that we talked about earlier. This is a common omission in spoken, more casual French.

Salutations and Other Expressions

The following vocabulary list includes various words and expressions, including simple greetings. Listen to the CD for their pronunciation.

TRACK 18

Table 2-1
Salutations and Greetings

French	English
à bientôt	see you soon
à demain	see you tomorrow
à tout à l'heure	see you later

à vos souhaits	bless you (after someone sneezes)
au revoir	good bye
bienvenue	welcome
bonne chance !	good luck!
bonne nuit	good night, sleep well
bonjour	hello, good morning, good afternoon
bonsoir	good evening
bravo !	well done!
de rien	you're welcome
enchanté(e)	pleased to meet you
merci	thank you
merci beaucoup	thank you very much
salut !	hi! bye!
santé !	cheers!
tant pis	so be it

Cardinal Numbers

In addition to using the same alphabet (see Chapter 1), French also uses the same numerical symbols. In English, these are known as Arabic numbers; in French, they are called *chiffres arabes*. Math, at least, looks the same in French. The spoken numbers are quite different, though, and you will have to memorize their pronunciation.

Table 2-2
Numbers from Zero to Nineteen

French	English
zéro	zero
un	one
deux	two
trois	three

quatre	four
cinq	five
six	six
sept	seven
huit	eight
neuf	nine
dix	ten
onze	eleven
douze	twelve
treize	thirteen
quatorze	fourteen
quinze	fifteen
seize	sixteen
dix-sept	seventeen
dix-huit	eighteen
dix-neuf	nineteen

The numbers twenty through sixty-nine follow a consistent pattern, very similar to the English way of naming a group of tens—like "twenty"—and following it with another word, such as "one," to form "twenty-one." In written French, the numbers are combined with a hyphen, with the exception of *et un*, which contains two words and translates as "and one." To form numbers between thirty and sixty-nine, simply add the appropriate number after the end of the word for the group of tens.

Table 2-3
Numbers from Twenty to Sixty

French	English
vingt	twenty
vingt et un	twenty-one
vingt-deux	twenty-two

vingt-trois	twenty-three
vingt-quatre	twenty-four
vingt-cinq	twenty-five
vingt-six	twenty-six
vingt-sept	twenty-seven
vingt-huit	twenty-eight
vingt-neuf	twenty-nine
trente	thirty
quarante	forty
cinquante	fifty
soixante	sixty

At seventy, a new pattern emerges. Instead of having a separate word for "seventy," "sixty," and "ten" are combined, to form *soixante-dix*. The numbers eleven through nineteen are used to designate numbers up to seventy-nine. Eighty doesn't have a separate word, either. Instead, it is designated as *quatre-vingts* (when alone; when combined with other numbers, the *-s* is dropped). Note that in written French, eighty-one becomes *quatre-vingt-un*, and does not use the *et* found in the earlier numbers. Ninety is very similar to seventy, combining the *quatre-vingt* of eighty with *dix* to form *quatre-vingt-dix*. The numbers then follow the same progression, up to ninety-nine.

Table 2-4
Numbers from Seventy to Ninety-Nine

French	English
soixante-dix	seventy
soixante et onze	seventy-one
soixante-douze	seventy-two
quatre-vingts	eighty
quatre-vingt-un	eighty-one

quatre-vingt-deux	eighty-two
quatre-vingt-dix	ninety
quatre-vingt-onze	ninety-one
quatre-vingt-douze	ninety-two
quatre-vingt-treize	ninety-three
quatre-vingt-quatorze	ninety-four
quatre-vingt-quinze	ninety-five
quatre-vingt-seize	ninety-six
quatre-vingt-dix-sept	ninety-seven
quatre-vingt-dix-huit	ninety-eight
quatre-vingt-dix-neuf	ninety-nine

At 100, everything starts all over again. The French word for hundred is *cent*; the other numbers are used after it to indicate the numbers between 101 and 199. One hundred and one is *cent un*. One hundred and ninety-nine is *cent quatre-vingt-dix-neuf.*

To indicate more than 100, the appropriate word is inserted before *cent*. When the number is an even hundred, *cent* is used in the plural—it has an unpronounced "s" on the end. For example, 400 is *quatre cents*, and 420 is *quatre cent vingt.*

One thousand follows the same pattern as one hundred, using the word *mille*. Dates also fall into this category, when referring to a year.

Table 2-5
Numbers from 1,000 to 2 million

French	English
mille	one thousand
deux mille	two thousand
deux mille un	two thousand and one
deux mille deux	two thousand and two
dix mille	ten thousand
cent mille	one hundred thousand

cent mille cent dix	one hundred thousand one hundred and ten
cinq cent mille	five hundred thousand
un million	one million
deux millions	two million

Ordinal Numbers

Related to cardinal numbers are ordinal numbers ("first," "second," "third," etc.).

In French, the word for "first" is the only ordinal number that must agree in gender and number with the noun it modifies.

Table 2-6
The Ordinal "First"

Gender	Singular	Plural
Masculine	*premier*	*premiers*
Feminine	*première*	*premières*

The rest of the ordinal numbers don't change to agree with gender, but will still add an "s" to agree with a plural noun.

Table 2-7
Ordinal Numbers

French	English
deuxième	second
troisième	third
quatrième	fourth
cinquième	fifth
sixième	sixth
septième	seventh
huitième	eighth
neuvième	ninth

dixième	tenth
la troisième fois	the third time

You don't have to memorize all of these numbers; you can learn to form them on your own. Ordinal numbers in French are formed using the cardinal number. To form the ordinal form of a number in French, simply drop the *-e* from the end of the cardinal number and add *-ième* to the end. If the cardinal number does not end in *-e*, simply add the *-ième* ending to the word. This works for all numbers but these three: *premier,* which is unique when compared to the other ordinal numbers; *cinquième,* which adds a "u" after the "q;" and *neuvième,* which changes the "f" into a "v."

To abbreviate the ordinal numbers, number 1 is followed by a super-scripted "*er*" in its masculine abbreviated form (1*er*), and a superscripted "*ère*" in its feminine abbreviated form (1*ère*). All others are followed by a small "*e*" (6*e*). You will often encounter these abbreviations in a variety of places: in newspapers, on signs, and in books and magazines.

Table 2-8
Ordinal Numbers Abbreviations

French	Abbreviation
premier (m)	1er
première (f)	1ère
deuxième	2e
troisième	3e
dix-huitième	18e

In this section, you learned French numbers. Listen to Track 17 for the pronunciation of some of the most common numbers.

Table 2-9
Common Numbers

TRACK 19

French	English
zéro	zero
un	one

deux	two
trois	three
quatre	four
cinq	five
six	six
sept	seven
huit	eight
neuf	nine
dix	ten
onze	eleven
douze	twelve
treize	thirteen
quatorze	fourteen
quinze	fifteen
seize	sixteen
dix-sept	seventeen
dix-huit	eighteen
dix-neuf	nineteen
vingt	twenty
vingt et un	twenty-one
trente	thirty
trente et un	thirty-one
trente-deux	thirty-two
quarante	forty
quarante et un	forty-one

quarante-deux	forty-two
cinquante	fifty
cinquante-quatre	fifty-four
soixante	sixty
soixante-neuf	sixty-nine
soixante-dix	seventy
quatre-vingts	eighty
quatre-vingt-dix	ninety
cent	one hundred

Dates

Face it. There are going to be some words you just have to learn to get by in French—little words, like days of the week and months of the year. You may find it helpful to read these word lists out loud a few times, memorizing them by rote, just like students do in school. When said out loud in a series, these groups have a catchy rhythm, so it shouldn't take you long to have them down pat.

Table 2-10
Days of the Week

French	English
lundi	Monday
mardi	Tuesday
mercredi	Wednesday
jeudi	Thursday
vendredi	Friday
samedi	Saturday
dimanche	Sunday

Table 2-11
Months of the Year

French	English
janvier	January
février	February
mars	March
avril	April
mai	May
juin	June
juillet	July
août	August
septembre	September
octobre	October
novembre	November
décembre	December

In written French, days of the week and months of the year are not capitalized.

Activité 2

TRACK 20

Listen to the speaker's pronunciation of the following words or expressions. Repeat each word after the speaker.

1. *quatre-vingts*
2. *Bonjour.*
3. *Comment ça va?*
4. *lundi*
5. *première*
6. *Je n'ai pas compris.*
7. *Je voudrais un café.*
8. *Excusez-moi.*

Chapter 3

Developing a Basic Vocabulary

This chapter helps you master the little words that will add up to big results when you begin speaking to native French speakers. The chapter starts with conjunctions (in English, words such as "and," "or," and "but"), and then moves into a series of basic words and phrases that will help you move toward fluency.

Conjunctions

Conjunctions are words that are used to join parts of a sentence together. In English, common conjunctions are "and," "or," and "but." Here are some common French conjunctions.

donc	so, then, therefore
ou	or
ensuite	next
puis	then
et	and
mais	but

Basic Words to Memorize

The following vocabulary list includes a few basic words you can quickly master. Listen to the CD for their pronunciation.

TRACK 21

Table 3-1
Basic French Words

French	English
oui	yes
non	no
bonjour	hello
excusez-moi	excuse me
s'il vous plaît	please
merci	thank you
merci beaucoup	thank you very much
Pardon?	Pardon me?
Monsieur	Mr.
Madame	Mrs.
Mademoiselle	Miss

You can use a number of different phrases to refer to things and people, depending on the particular situation.

The French Definite and Indefinite Articles

The French articles *le, la, l'* and *les* (definite articles) and *un, une, des* (indefinite articles) accompany nouns and correspond to the English "the" (definite article) and "a" (indefinite article).

Le film est amusant.	The film is funny.
Je voudrais un café.	I'd like a coffee.
J'aime beaucoup les fraises.	I love strawberries.

Gender and Number

There is almost always a noun at the heart of every French sentence. Two properties determine how you should build a sentence: the noun's gender and its number.

Assigning Gender

Unlike English, French nouns have a gender—either masculine or feminine. There is very little rhyme or reason to which nouns are masculine and which are feminine.

French adjectives have both masculine and feminine forms. An adjective's gender must match, or agree with, the gender of the noun it modifies. If you have a masculine noun, use the masculine form of the adjective; if the noun is feminine, the feminine form of the adjective is appropriate.

un homme courtois / une femme courtoise	a polite man / a polite woman
un grand avion / une grande aérogare	a big airplane / a big airport terminal

Singular and Plural

Just as there's a difference in English between "the car" and "the cars," French words change slightly to account for quantity. Unlike English, adjectives change, too. Some adjectives follow simple patterns for matching the number, but some follow very irregular patterns.

Agreement of Adjectives

There are rules for adjectives and their agreement with other words. As a basic rule, to make an adjective agree with a feminine noun, you simply add an "e" to the end of the masculine form (unless it already ends in an "e." You add an "s" to make the adjective plural (unless it already ends in an "s"). This works with the majority of adjectives.

TRACK 22

Table 3-2
Agreement of Adjectives

Masculine	Feminine	English
grand(s)	grande(s)	large, big
court(s)	courte(s)	short, brief, concise
courtois	courtoise(s)	courteous, polite
fermé(s)	fermée(s)	closed
intelligent(s)	intelligente(s)	intelligent, smart
vrai(s)	vraie(s)	true, real, right
français	française(s)	French
amusant(s)	amusante(s)	amusing, entertaining

Consider the following examples:

Il est grand.	He is tall.
Elle est amusante.	She is funny.
Elles sont françaises.	They are French.

Il/Elle Est

In English, we often use the phrase "it is" to describe things. In French, this can be done using either *il/elle est* or *c'est*. Both *il/elle est* and *c'est* mean the same thing—"he is," "she is," or "it is," depending on the construction of the sentence. *Il/elle est* and *c'est* are used in different situations.

Il/elle est is the correct choice in the following circumstances. *Il est* is used when the subject of the sentence is male, either a male person or a male noun. Similarly, *elle est* is used for a female subject.

Using a Single Adjective

When using a single adjective that refers to a specific person or a specific thing, *il/elle est* is the proper construction. The adjective will agree in gender and number with the subject of the sentence.

J'aime ce café. Il est très agréable.	I love this café. It is very nice.
La fille s'appelle Sophie.	The girl's name is Sophie.
J'ai lu ce livre. Il est intéressant.	I read this book. It is interesting.

Referring to a Profession

When simply stating that a person is of a certain profession, the phrase *il est* or *elle est* is used, and the noun appears with no article. (Note that in English, we use an indefinite article with the noun.)

Elle est médecin.	She is a doctor.
Il est pharmacien.	He is a pharmacist.
Il est policier.	He is a police officer.

Referring to Nationalities

When stating that a person is of a certain nationality, *il est* or *elle est* is used with the adjective, without any article. When a nationality is used in this fashion, it is not capitalized, because the word acts as an adjective. Only when a nationality is used as a noun is it capitalized.

Elle est française.	She is French.
Il est anglais.	He is English.

Referring to Religious Beliefs

When you wish to state that a person is of a certain religious belief or denomination, *il est* or *elle est* is used with an adjective, which also appears without an article, like the previous constructions. English normally capitalizes these words, but French does not.

Elle est catholique.	She is Catholic
Il est protestant.	He is Protestant.

C'est

The phrase *c'est* also means "it is." Study its uses in this section, and then compare and contrast it with the previous section on *il/elle est* so you understand the differences between the choices.

With a Proper Name

When you wish to refer to someone using his or her proper name, *c'est* is the appropriate choice, rather than *il/elle est*.

C'est Yvon Lauliac.	It's Yvon Lauliac.
C'est Monsieur Allard.	It's Mr. Allard.

With a Disjunctive Pronoun

C'est is used before disjunctive pronouns in French.

C'est moi.	It is me.
C'est toi.	It is you.
C'est elle.	It is her.

When Referring to a Situation or Idea

C'est is often used with a singular masculine adjective to refer to states of being or ideas.

Oui, c'est vrai.	Yes, that's right.
J'achèterai le livre, c'est certain.	I will buy the book, it's certain.

When Referring to a Noun That Is Modified by Other Words

When a noun is used with adjectives that modify or refine the meaning of the noun, *c'est* is the appropriate choice. Even a single article used with a noun is enough to modify it and make it necessary to use the *c'est* construction.

C'est un livre excellent.	It's an excellent book.
C'est une jolie maison.	It's a beautiful house.

Il Y A

In English, we often use phrases like "there is" or "there are" to refer to the general existence of things. In French, this is done with the idiomatic phrase *il y a*. The French word *y* is an object pronoun. In this construction, it is the rough equivalent of the English "there." Even when *il y a* is used with a plural object, the subject and verb don't change. It doesn't change for feminine objects, either; *il* is still used in the construction, even when referring to something feminine.

TRACK 23

Il y a un bon film au cinéma.	There is a good film at the theater.
Il y a une grande vedette en ville.	There is a big star in town.

You can also use the construction *il y a* as a question to ask if something exists. You could use the phrase *est-ce que* in front of it to form the question, or you can use inversion. When inversion is used, however, the pronoun retains its regular position in front of the verb, so you must insert a "t" in between.

Y a-t-il un bon film ce week-end?	Is there a good film this weekend?
Y a-t-il un médecin dans la salle?	Is there a doctor in the room?

Voilà

Voilà is used to indicate something specific. It is actually a preposition that means "there is," "here is," "there are," "here are," or even "that is." Rather than merely pointing out its existence the way *il y a* does, *voilà* points specifically to the item being indicated when used at the beginning of the sentence. It is like actually pointing to an item with your finger; as a general rule, *voilà* should be used only when pointing your finger would be an appropriate gesture to accompany the statement.

If you look at the following sentences carefully, there isn't actually any verb used. *Voilà* takes the place of both the subject and the verb, being used only with the object of the sentence.

Voilà les enfants.	Here are the children.
Voilà une fenêtre.	There is a window.

Because *voilà* doesn't use a verb, you don't have to worry about agreement with any of the words; any articles must still agree with the nouns, however.

Activité 3

TRACK 24

Listen to each of the following masculine adjectives, then write its feminine form on the lines provided.

1. *grand* _____
2. *court* _____
3. *courtois* _____
4. *fermé* _____
5. *intelligent* _____
6. *vrai* _____
7. *français* _____
8. *amusant* _____

Chapter 4

Understanding Articles

As you learned in Chapter 3, the French articles *le, la, l'* and *les* (definite articles) and *une, une, des* (indefinite articles) accompany nouns and correspond to the English "the" (definite article) and "a" (indefinite article). Articles serve a grammatical purpose by showing how the word is to be treated in the sentence—whether it is referring to a specific object or referring to things in a more general sense. It tells you how the noun fits and relates to the other words in the sentence.

Discovering French Articles

French articles change form depending on their use with masculine or feminine nouns, plural or singular nouns, and nouns that begin with vowels. In English, the definite article can often be dropped or ignored, but in French, articles are very much a necessity to proper communication.

FACT

You can use articles to help you remember the gender of nouns with nouns that begin with a vowel. Because gender is mostly a matter of memorization, the indefinite article will tell you the gender, leaving one less thing to memorize.

The Definite Article

In French, the definite article can take one of four forms:

- *le*: when used before a word with masculine gender
- *la*: when used before a word with feminine gender
- *l'*: when used before a word that starts with a vowel or silent "h"
- *les*: when used to indicate a group or more than one of an item

Referring to Specific Items or People

The definite article is used when referring to specific items.

Le professeur est en classe.	The teacher is in the classroom.
Le chien n'aime pas les chats	The dog doesn't like cats.
La viande n'est pas bonne.	The meat is not good.

Before a Vowel

Whenever *le* or *la* precedes a word starting with a vowel or a mute "h," it becomes *l'*.

l'eau (f)	water
l'écran (m)	screen
l'heure (f)	hour

Before some words with an aspirated "h," the articles *le* or *la* are retained: *Le héros.*

Before Nouns Used in General Sense

The definite article is used to refer to nouns used in a general sense.

J'aime le français.	I love French.
Je déteste le café.	I hate coffee.

Languages

The definite article is used to refer to names of languages, except when they are paired with the verb *parler*, as in "*je parle français.*"

le français	French
l'anglais (m)	English
l'espagnol (m)	Spanish
l'allemand (m)	German
le portugais	Portuguese
l'italien (m)	Italian
le chinois	Chinese
le japonais	Japanese
le russe	Russian

In this section, you learned about the definite article. Listen to the CD for the pronunciation of some of the words and phrases you learned.

TRACK 25

Le professeur est en classe.	The teacher is in the classroom.
Le chien n'aime pas les chats.	The dog doesn't like cats.
La viande n'est pas bonne.	The meat is not good.
l'eau (f)	water
l'écran (m)	screen

l'heure (f)	hour
J'aime le français.	I love French.
Je déteste le café.	I hate coffee.
le français	French
l'anglais (m)	English
l'espagnol (m)	Spanish
l'allemand (m)	German
le portugais	Portuguese
l'italien (m)	Italian
le chinois	Chinese
le japonais	Japanese
le russe	Russian

The Indefinite Article

Indefinite articles are used with nouns that are not specific, and are similar to the English "a," "an," and "some." There are three forms of indefinite articles in French:

- *un*: when used before a word with masculine gender
- *une*: when used before a word with feminine gender
- *des*: when used to indicate a group or more than one of an item

Indefinite articles are used when one is referring in general to an item. *Un* and *une* are equivalent to "a" in English. *Des*, the plural, can mean "some" or "any" in English, and is used with plural nouns of either gender.

The Partitive Article

French also has a unique class of articles, known as the partitive, which is used when the exact quantity of an item is not known. It conveys the sense of "some" or "any."

In French, however, the partitive article is required to convey proper meaning. It is known as the partitive because it describes only a part of the object and not the object as a whole. Whenever the sense of "some" or "any" is inferred in a sentence, the partitive article must be used.

The partitive is formed by combining *de* and the definite article.

- *de + le = du*: when used before singular nouns with masculine gender
- *de + la = de la*: when used before singular nouns with feminine gender
- *de + l' = de l'*: when used before singular nouns that begin in a vowel or silent h
- *de + les = des*: when used before plural nouns of either gender

Suppose you're talking to a friend who invites you over to her place for coffee. You hope she has milk, so you could ask any of the following in English:

Do you have any milk?
Do you have milk?
Do you have some milk?

Because you are only referring to a small amount of all the milk available in the world, "some" is meant, so the partitive is used in French, as follows: *As-tu du lait?*

Suppose you are getting together with your friend to bake a triple-layer cake. Wondering if she has the milk that the recipe calls for, you want to ask, "Do you have the milk?" Because milk is being referred to in a specific sense, the definite article is used, rather than the partitive article: *As-tu le lait?* You aren't asking whether your friend has some milk, or any milk, or enough milk—you're asking whether she has the specific amount of milk that the recipe calls for.

Pay particular attention to the amount when choosing which article to use. If you use a definite article when the partitive is required, native French speakers may become terribly confused, trying to figure out what you mean.

Partitive Article in Negative Expressions

As you may recall from Chapter 2, *ne* . . . *pas* can be used to make an expression negative. It is the equivalent of the English word "not." There are other ways to make a statement negative (see Chapter 8).

When the partitive is used in a negative expression, *de* appears alone, without the definite article. Whether the noun being used in the partitive is masculine or feminine, the only word appearing before it will be *de*.

Masculine: As-tu du lait?	Do you have some milk?
Non, je n'ai pas de lait.	No, I don't have any milk.
Feminine: As-tu de la farine?	Do you have any flour?
Non, je n'ai pas de farine.	No, I don't have any flour.

Naturally, there's an exception. When using *être*, the verb "to be," the proper partitive article is always used, whether the sentence is negative or not. Say your friend asks if there is water in your glass. You answer: *Non, ce n'est pas de l'eau. C'est de la bière.* (No, it's not water. It's beer.) In the negative, notice that *de l'eau* includes both *de* and the definite article: The partitive is used in full because it appears with the verb *être*. If another verb were being used in the negative, only *de* would be used.

Être is the only verb that uses the regular partitive article in a negative expression; all other verbs, simply use *de* alone as the partitive article.

Activité 4

Add the missing article to the following sentences.

1. _____ *professeur est en classe.*
2. _____ *viande n'est pas bonne.*
3. *Je déteste* _____ *café.*
4. *As-tu* _____ *lait?*
5. *Non, je n'ai pas* _____ *farine.*

Chapter 5

Using Nouns

A noun is the grammatical term for a word that designates a person, place, thing, or idea. In French, a noun is known as a *nom*, which also happens to be the same word for "name." That's actually a good way to remember it—a noun is simply the name of a person, place, thing, or idea.

Understanding Nouns

There are two general types of nouns: concrete and abstract. A noun is concrete when it describes something definite, like a person, place, or thing. Ideas and emotions are also nouns, but these are considered abstract.

There are a number of ways to use nouns in a sentence. They can appear as the subject of a verb, performing the action described in the sentence, or they can appear as the object and receive the action of the sentence, either directly or indirectly. Note how *the girl* is used in the following sentences.

- **Subject:** The girl is walking.
- **Direct object:** I found the girl.
- **Indirect object:** I gave the puppy to the girl.

The same noun can be used to convey a variety of different meanings. French, like English, relies on word order and auxiliary words to show how the noun is affected by the sentence.

There are other kinds of nouns, too. Pronouns are words that replace nouns, such as "him" or "her." Pronouns are used in place of a noun; in the first of the preceding examples, the word "she" could replace "the girl," and the word "her" could be used instead as the direct object or indirect object.

Gender of Nouns

One of the biggest differences you'll notice between French and English is the use of gender. Each noun in French has a feminine or masculine gender. This a linguistic trait inherited from Latin, where there could be three categories of gender: masculine, feminine, and neuter. French has only two: masculine and feminine.

The gender designation in French is rather arbitrary. There isn't necessarily much logic as to whether a noun will be masculine or feminine.

There are some general pointers but in the end, the advice is always the same: Memorize the gender of a word as you learn it.

ALERT!

Don't get confused about the concept of gender in French. It refers only to the noun as a word. Although in many instances when referring to a person, the gender will correspond to that person's sex (*une femme, un homme,* for example), in general, gender is a grammatical concept and has nothing to do with the biological sex of the object or person involved. For example, *un professeur* can be either a male or a female teacher, but the word *professeur* is linguistically masculine.

The gender of a noun is important to know; it affects how the word is used and how other words are used along with it.

In this book, nouns are presented with the article (or, if the article is ambiguous, you'll find a small "m" for masculine and a small "f" for feminine nouns).

While there are no rules about determining the gender of nouns, the majority of French words follow a consistent gender pattern. In addition to the noun's article, the ending can sometimes help you determine the proper gender of a noun.

Masculine Nouns

Here are some endings that generally indicate that the noun is masculine. Listen to the CD for their pronunciation.

Table 5-1
Masculine Nouns

TRACK 26

Nouns Ending in *-aire*	
le dictionnaire	dictionary
le propriétaire	owner
le vocabulaire	vocabulary
*la grammaire**	grammar

Nouns Ending in -asme and -isme

le sarcasme	sarcasm
l'optimisme	optimism
le pessimisme	pessimism
le tourisme	tourism

Nouns Ending in -eau

le bateau	boat
le bureau	office
le chapeau	hat
le manteau	coat

Nouns Ending in -et

l'alphabet	alphabet
le billet	ticket
l'objet	object
le sujet	subject

Nouns Ending in -in

le magasin	shop
le matin	morning
le vin	wine

Nouns Ending in –ent

l'accent	accent
l'accident	accident
l'argent	money

Nouns Ending in -*oir*	
l'espoir	hope
le miroir	mirror
le rasoir	razor
le soir	evening

*Exception to this ending.

Feminine Nouns

Here are some endings that generally indicate that the noun is feminine. Listen to the CD for their pronunciation.

TRACK 27

Table 5-2
Feminine Nouns

Nouns Ending in -*ade*	
la limonade	lemonade
la parade	parade
la promenade	walk
la salade	salad

Nouns Ending in –*son*	
la maison	house
la raison	reason
la saison	season

Nouns Ending in -*ance*	
l'assistance	assistance
la balance	scale
la chance	chance
la naissance	birth

Nouns Ending in -ence

la différence	difference
l'essence	gasoline
la science	science
la sentence	sentence
le silence*	silence

Nouns Ending in -ande

la commande	command
la demande	request
la viande	meat

Nouns Ending in -ise

l'église	church
la fraise	strawberry
la surprise	surprise
la valise	suitcase

Nouns Ending in -son

la boisson	drink
la prison	prison
la chanson	song

Nouns Ending in -té

la beauté	beauty
la cité	city
la liberté	liberty
la nationalité	nationality
le côté*	side
l'été*	summer

Nouns Ending in -tié

l'amitié	friendship
la moitié	half
la pitié	pity

Nouns Ending in -ude

l'étude	study
l'habitude	habit
la solitude	solitude

Nouns Ending in -ture

l'aventure	adventure
la ceinture	belt
la culture	culture
la facture	invoice
la nourriture	food, nourishment
la grammaire	grammar

*Exception to this ending.

Some Special Gender Notes

As a rule, most French nouns have a specific gender. Some nouns, however, can use either gender but have two different meanings, depending on the particular gender used.

Table 5-3
Nouns with Different Gender Meanings

Masculine	English	Feminine	English
le livre	book	la livre	pound
le poste	position	la poste	mail, postal service
le vase	vase	la vase	mud, slime

Formation of the Plural

Most French nouns follow fairly simple rules for the formation of the plural: they simply add an "s" to the end of the noun to make the plural form. Other nouns, however, may pose more difficulty. French nouns can have a great variety of endings, and some of the plural forms are made in unique ways.

Nouns Ending in -s, -x, or -z

If the noun already ends in -s, -x, or -z, no change occurs; a plural article is simply used with a word to indicate the plural.

Table 5-4
Nouns Ending in -s, -x, or -z

Singular	Plural	English
le fils	les fils	son(s)
le repas	les repas	meal(s)
le prix	les prix	prize(s) or price(s)
le nez	les nez	nose(s)

Nouns Ending in -ail

Most nouns ending in -ail add an "s" at the end of the word to form the plural.

Table 5-5
Nouns Ending in -ail

Singular	Plural	English
l'éventail	les éventails	fan(s)
le détail	les détails	detail(s)

A few nouns ending in -ail don't follow the regular rules, dropping the -ail and adding -aux to the end instead.

Table 5-6
Irregular Nouns Ending in -ail

Singular	Plural	English
le bail	les baux	lease(s)
le corail	les coraux	coral(s)
l'émail	les émaux	enamel(s)
le travail	les travaux	work(s)

Nouns Ending in -eau

For nouns ending in *-eau*, simply add an "x" to the end of the noun.

Table 5-7
Nouns Ending in -eau

Singular	Plural	English
le couteau	les couteaux	knife/knives
le gâteau	les gâteaux	cake/cakes

Nouns Ending in -eu

For nouns ending in *-eu*, add an "x" to the end of the noun.

Table 5-8
Nouns Ending in -eu

Singular	Plural	English
le jeu	les jeux	game(s)
le feu	les feux	fire(s)

Nouns Ending in -al

For nouns ending in *-al*, the ending is changed to *-aux*.

Table 5-9
Nouns Ending in -al

Singular	Plural	English
l'animal	les animaux	animal(s)
le canal	les canaux	canal(s)

Nouns Ending in -ou

For nouns ending in *-ou*, add an "x" to the end of the word.

Table 5-10
Nouns Ending in -ou

Singular	Plural	English
le chou	les choux	cabbage(s)
le genou	les genoux	knee(s)

Nouns That Are Always Plural

Some French nouns are always used in the plural sense; the singular either doesn't exist or means something different.

Table 5-11
Nouns That Are Always Plural

Plural Noun	English
les gens	people
les mathématiques	mathematics

Family Names

When the noun is a family name, nothing is added. It is used on its own, without turning the noun itself into a plural form; the plural is inferred from the article.

les Tavernier	The Tavernier family
Les Tavernier sont très gentils	The Taverniers are very nice.

Irregular Plurals

Some words undergo a bit of a transformation or even change entirely in the plural sense. These are irregular plurals.

Table 5-12
Irregular Plurals

Singular	Plural	English
l'œil	les yeux	eye(s)
Monsieur	Messieurs	Mr.
Madame	Mesdames	Mrs.
Mademoiselle	Mesdemoiselles	Miss

In these sections, you learned how to form plural nouns. Listen to the CD for the pronunciation of some of the words and phrases found in this section.

TRACK 28

Table 5-13

Singular	Plural	English
le fils	les fils	son(s)
le repas	les repas	meal(s)
le prix	les prix	prize(s) or price(s)
le nez	les nez	nose(s)
l'éventail	les éventails	fan/fans
le détail	les détails	detail/details
le couteau	les couteaux	knife/knives
le jeu	les jeux	game(s)
l'animal	les animaux	animal(s)
le genou	les genoux	knee(s)
l'œil	les yeux	eye(s)
Mademoiselle	Mesdemoiselles	Miss

Activité 5

On the lines provided, write the plural form of each of the following words. Remember to include the article in your response.

1. *le fils* _____
2. *le repas* _____
3. *le prix* _____
4. *le détail* _____
5. *le bail* _____
6. *le couteau* _____
7. *l'animal* _____
8. *l'œil* _____

Chapter 6

Subject Pronouns and Forming Present-Tense Verbs

This chapter gets you into creating full sentences by introducing you to the subject pronouns and verbs, specifically those in the present tense. While forming the verb in the present tense is easier than for the past and future tenses, verbs can still be a challenge. This chapter simplifies the process.

Subject Pronouns

Sentences in French are formed, for the most part, in the same way that they are formed in English. Every sentence must have a subject to do something and a verb to indicate what the subject is doing. You can always find your way around the sentence when you know who's doing what. Sentences can get more complex when other words, like prepositions or direct objects, are added, but if you can identify the subject and verb, the other words fall into place.

There are three kinds of subjects—first person, second person, and third person. The following sentences demonstrate the English subject pronouns in action. Reviewing these will help you better understand the French subject pronouns.

- **First person:** I am going to the store.
- **Second person:** You are going to the store.
- **Third person:** She is going to the store.

Each of the above also has a plural form. In English, the plural forms would be:

- **First person:** We are going to the store.
- **Second person:** You are going to the store.
- **Third person:** They are going to the store.

The French subject pronouns are seen in Table 6-1. Listen to the CD for their pronunciation.

TRACK 29

Table 6-1
French Subject Pronouns

Person	Singular	Plural
1st Person	*je*	*nous*
2nd Person	*tu*	*vous*
3rd Person	*il* (m)	*ils* (m)
	elle (f)	*elles* (f)

Note the following slight differences between the way these pronouns are used in English and French:

- English doesn't have a separate second person form to distinguish between singular and plural. French does, so when formulating sentences, you will have to be careful that you make the appropriate choice. *Tu* is singular, so it is used when talking to one other person. *Vous* is plural and is used for two or more people.
- In the plural, *elles* is only used when referring to more than two female subjects. If all the members of the group to which you are referring are not female or if the sex is not known, *ils* is used as the subject pronoun. It may help to think of *ils* as "they" in general, including but not limited to males, while *elles* can only be used when the pronoun is replacing female subjects.

French has two forms of address, formal and informal. Each has its own way of addressing people: When you are talking to someone you know well (friends your own age, for example), you use the informal, or familiar, *tu*. To address people you don't know well, use the formal *vous* until told otherwise.

Whenever the plural subject pronouns are used with a verb that begins with a vowel, the "s" sound gets tacked on to the beginning of the next word, in a *liaison* (see Chapter 1).

Verb Forms: The Infinitive

You've probably noticed that when you refer to verbs in English, the verb is prefaced by the word "to." "To go," "to be," and "to speak" are examples. The "to" tells you that the verb is being used in a general sense, not tied to a particular subject. Because these verbs don't have a subject or object, they are said to be in the infinitive.

In French, the infinitive has its own form. As a matter of fact, you have likely already learned many infinitive French verbs. The infinitive in French is simply the unconjugated form of the verb you have probably already seen throughout the book. Listen to the CD for the pronunciation of the following infinitives.

TRACK 30

avoir	to have
aimer	to love
être	to be
écouter	to listen
parler	to speak
nager	to swim

FACT

In general, when you use a verb, it will be in a conjugated form. But there is a common use of the infinitive: You will often see signs in French that use the construction *Défense de* + infinitive, to say that something is prohibited. For example, *Défense de fumer* means *Smoking is prohibited.*

Verb Forms: *The Present Tense*

Verbs change slightly to reflect the subject of the sentence. This is known as conjugation—putting the correct form of the verb with the subject. The ending of the verb must always match the subject.

For example, the verb *courir* means "to run." When using it in a sentence, the verb changes slightly for each different subject it takes. If you wanted to say "I run," you would say, *Je cours. Je* is the subject, meaning "I," and *cours* is the properly conjugated form of the verb *courir*. In French, the endings of verbs can also help you determine the gender and number of the subject if you're unsure.

Verb Stems

The stem of the verb is the magic key to French verbs. It is the part of the word that does not generally change when conjugated with various subjects. Constructions in tenses other than the present all utilize the verb stem, adding on special endings to indicate the tense of the verb. (In Chapters 12 through 16, you find out about other verb tenses, so that you can refer to things in the past or in the future.)

In general, to find the stem of a verb, you simply drop the infinitive ending from the infinitive form. Consider the following verbs and note their stems and endings:

Verb	English	French Stem
parler	to speak	*parl-*
habiter	to live	*habit-*

Most of the French verbs you'll encounter follow simple rules for conjugation. The word endings follow a predictable pattern, so you have to memorize only the endings for one verb. You can then replace the endings on other verbs with similar endings without having to memorize all of the forms over and over again.

French also has some irregular verbs, where the verb forms seem to follow no logical pattern at all. These will have to be memorized individually. Fortunately, there are only a few of them.

-er Verbs in the Present Tense

Verbs that end in the infinitive with *-er* are the most common ones in the French language; for the most part, they all follow the same conjugation pattern. This means that you only have to memorize the word endings one time—after that, you can just use the endings of the verbs you already know to come up with the appropriate ending. Verbs that end in *-er* use the following endings when conjugated in the present tense.

Table 6-2
Endings of -er Verbs

Person	Singular	Plural
1st Person	*je* (I) *-e*	*nous* (we) *-ons*
2nd Person	*tu* (you) *-es* (informal)	*vous* (you) *-ez*
3rd Person	*il/elle* (he/she) *-e*	*ils/elles* (they) *-ent*

Here is how the verb *parler* looks when conjugated. Listen to the CD for the pronunciation.

Table 6-3
The Verb Parler (to Speak)

Singular	Plural
je parle	*nous parlons*
tu parles	*vous parlez*
il/elle parle	*ils/elles parlent*

TRACK 31

Some of the verb endings have distinct sounds, such as *parlons* and *parlez*. The other endings are actually silent, so they all sound the same. You must rely on the subject pronoun to determine what is going on in the sentence. Even though the endings aren't pronounced, however, it's still important to know the spelling of the proper endings, because they are required in written French.

As you've probably gathered, *je parle* means "I speak," *tu parles* means "you speak," *il parle* means "he speaks," and so on. In English, we have a few different ways of speaking in the present tense. For example, in English, we can say:

I speak.
I am speaking.
I do speak.

All these sentences, in essence, mean the same thing. All are conjugated in the first person singular, present tense. They indicate an action is occurring to a subject (I), and describe what that subject is doing: speaking. In English, stylistic factors usually determine which of the three choices is used; French uses fewer words to say the same thing. Any or all of those English meanings can be conveyed by saying *Je parle.*

ALERT!

Remember that the verb *parler,* when used with the name of a language, does not take a definite article. You say « *Je parle français,* » not « *Je parle le français.* »

Here are a few other -*er* verbs you should know. Listen to the CD for their pronunciation.

TRACK 32

aimer	to like, to love
étudier	to study
arriver	to arrive
placer	to place, to put
désirer	to desire, to want
porter	to wear, to carry
écouter	to listen
rester	to remain, to stay
entrer	to enter, to come in
retourner	to return, to go back

The beauty of most -*er* verbs is that they are all conjugated alike. In order to conjugate a verb ending in -*er,* you simply have to cut off the "er" of the infinitive form to get the stem. After you have the stem, you can tack on the appropriate ending.

Stem-Changing –er Verbs

There are a few verbs whose stems also change when conjugated, and they're covered in this section. These changes always affect the spelling and often affect the pronunciation.

Verbs Ending in -cer

For verbs ending in *-cer*, the "c" changes to a "ç" when used with *nous* to maintain the soft "s" sound. Other forms follow the regular *-er* conjugation pattern.

Table 6-4
The Verb Commencer (to Begin)

Singular	Plural
je commence	nous commençons
tu commences	vous commencez
il/elle commence	ils/elles commencent

Verbs conjugated like *commencer* include:

épicer	to spice
annoncer	to announce
prononcer	to pronounce

Verbs Ending in -ger

Verbs ending in *-ger* add an "e" before the *-ons* of the *nous* form in order that the "g" sound remain soft.

Table 6-5
The Verb Manger (to Eat)

Singular	Plural
je mange	nous mangeons
tu manges	vous mangez
il/elle mange	ils/elles mangent

Verbs conjugated like *manger* include:

changer	to change
charger	to load
voyager	to travel

Verbs with an *É* + Consonant + *Er*

For *-er* verbs with an *é* + consonant + *er*, in order to aid pronunciation, the accent changes to an *accent grave* (see Chapter 1) in all cases except for *nous* and *vous*. Note that this only affects the accent closest to the ending of the stem.

Table 6-6
The Verb Préférer (to Prefer)

Singular	Plural
je préfère	*nous préférons*
tu préfères	*vous préférez*
il/elle préfère	*ils/elles préfèrent*

Verbs conjugated like *préférer* include:

insérer	to insert
espérer	to expect, to hope

Verbs Ending in *-eler*

For verbs ending in *-eler*, the stem changes to include a double "l"; this affects all conjugation forms but *nous* and *vous*.

Table 6-7
The Verb Appeler (to Call)

Singular	Plural
j'appelle	*nous appelons*
tu appelles	*vous appelez*
il/elle appelle	*ils/elles appellent*

Verbs Ending in -*eter*

Verbs ending in -*eter* are very similar to *appeler*; these verbs double the "t" in all cases but *nous* and *vous*.

Table 6-8
The Verb Jeter (to Throw)

Singular	Plural
je jette	nous jetons
tu jettes	vous jetez
il/elle jette	ils/elles jettent

Verbs conjugated like *jeter* include:

projeter	to project
rejeter	to reject, to throw back

Verbs Ending in -*ayer*

For verbs ending in -*ayer*, to form the new stem, simply turn the "y" into an "i" in all cases but *nous* and *vous*.

Table 6-9
The Verb Payer (to Pay)

Singular	Plural
je paie	nous payons
tu paies	vous payez
il/elle paie	ils/elles paient

Verbs conjugated like *payer* include the following:

effrayer	to frighten
rayer	to delete, to scratch, to erase

Verbs with a Mute *e*

In verbs that have a mute *e* in the next-to-last syllable, the mute *e* changes to an *è* in the singular forms and the 3rd person plural.

Table 6-10
The Verb Peser (to Weigh)

Singular	Plural
je pèse	nous pesons
tu pèses	vous pesez
il/elle pèse	ils/elles pèsent

Verbs like *peser* include the following:

lever	to lift

Verbs Ending in *-oyer*

In verbs ending in *-oyer*, like verbs ending in *-ayer*, the "y" changes to an "i" in all cases but *nous* and *vous*.

Table 6-11
The Verb Nettoyer (to Clean)

Singular	Plural
je nettoie	nous nettoyons
tu nettoies	vous nettoyez
il/elle nettoie	ils/elles nettoient

Verbs conjugated like *nettoyer* include:

employer	to employ
noyer	to drown
envoyer	to send
renvoyer	to return

Verbs Ending in -*uyer*

Verbs ending in -*uyer* follow the same pattern as the other verbs with endings that include a "y," using an "i" to form the endings in all forms but *nous* and *vous*.

Table 6-12
The Verb Appuyer (to Support)

Singular	Plural
j'appuie	nous appuyons
tu appuies	vous appuyez
il/elle appuie	ils/elles appuient

Verbs conjugated like *appuyer* include:

ennuyer	to annoy
essuyer	to wipe

-re Verbs in the Present Tense

There are two more regular verb forms: verbs that end in -*re* and verbs that end in -*ir*. Like the -*er* verbs, each group follows a predictable pattern. There are, of course, some exceptions for each group, but these irregular verbs also tend to follow similar conjugation patterns when compared to each other, so it should be relatively easy to recall the forms. You'll learn about verbs ending in -*ir* in the next section of this chapter.

Regular verbs ending in -*re* use the following endings:

Table 6-13
Endings of -re Verbs

	Singular		Plural	
1st Person	je	-s	nous	-ons
2nd Person	tu	-s	vous	-ez
3rd Person	il/elle	–	ils/elles	-ent

Note that the third person singular form merely uses the stem of the verb alone; no extra endings are added. To create the third person singular form in written French, you need only remove the *-re* ending and use the stem alone with the proper subject or subject pronoun. Listen to the CD for the pronunciation of the verb *vendre* (to sell).

TRACK 33

Table 6-14
The Verb Vendre (to Sell)

Singular	Plural
je vends	*nous vendons*
tu vends	*vous vendez*
il/elle vend	*ils/elles vendent*

A number of verbs, as follows, are conjugated like *vendre*. Practice conjugating the verbs using different subject pronouns until they become natural to you. Listen to the CD for the pronunciation of these verbs.

TRACK 34

défendre	to defend, to protect
descendre	to go down, to get off
fondre	to melt, to dissolve
mordre	to bite
pendre	to hang, to hang up, to suspend
perdre	to lose, to waste
rendre	to return, to give back, to repay
répondre	to respond
tordre	to twist, to wring, to contort

Here are some examples of *-re* verbs in action.

Le caissier vend les billets.	The cashier is selling the tickets.
Les policiers défendent la ville.	The police protect the city.

When a "p" appears at the end of an *-re* verb stem, a "t" is added to the ending in the third person singular. This is an issue of pronunciation—it would be very difficult to pronounce a "p" at the end of a word, so a "t" is added but not pronounced, as follows:

interrompre:	to interrupt
Il interrompt le film.	He is interrupting the film.
rompre:	to break, to snap, to break off.
Il rompt le pain.	He breaks off the bread.

ALERT!

There aren't a whole lot of verbs that end in *-pre*, but you should still know how to use them. Adding the "t" in the third person singular ending also occurs in written French, so remember to make the change when writing, too.

-ir Verbs in the Present Tense

There is one last type of regular French verbs, those that end in *-ir*. You'll probably find yourself using these words a lot, so it shouldn't take you too long to get used to the conjugation patterns. Listen to the CD for the pronunciation of the verb *finir* (to finish).

TRACK 35

Table 6-15
The Verb Finir (to Finish)

Singular	Plural
je finis	*nous finissons*
tu finis	*vous finissez*
il/elle finit	*ils/elles finissent*

Here are some French verbs ending in *-ir* that follow the same pattern as *finir*. You can simply form the stem of the verb by dropping the *-ir* ending and replacing the properly conjugated ending as usual. Listen to the CD for the pronunciation of these verbs.

TRACK 36

accomplir	to accomplish, to achieve
accueillir	to welcome
agir	to act
applaudir	to applaud
bâtir	to construct, build
choisir	to choose
faillir	to fail
fleurir	to blossom, to bloom
fournir	to provide
garantir	to guarantee
mourir	to die
obéir	to obey
rafraîchir	to refresh

Irregular Verbs

Irregular verbs do not follow the patterns for *-er*, *-re*, and *-ir* verbs. Instead, they have their own patterns that you must memorize for each verb.

Avoir, Être, Faire, *and* Aller

Two of the most used irregular verbs, *avoir* and *être*, are an integral part of the French language, as they often get used in conjunction with other verbs when complex sentences are formed. *Avoir* means "to have" and *être* means "to be." *Faire* (to do, to make) and *aller* (to go) are also common irregular verbs.

Table 6-16
The Verb Avoir

Singular	Plural
j'ai	nous avons
tu as	vous avez
il/elle a	ils/elles ont

Table 6-17
The Verb Être (to Be)

Singular	Plural
je suis	nous sommes
tu es	vous êtes
il/elle est	ils/elles sont

Another commonly used irregular verb, *faire*, means "to make" or "to do."

Table 6-18
The Verb Faire (to Make, to Do)

Singular	Plural
je fais	nous faisons
tu fais	vous faites
il/elle fait	ils/elles font

The verb *faire* can be used with the infinitive form of another verb to indicate the sense of "to have something done" or even "make something happen." This is often used when you are having something done by someone else, especially when the person doing it isn't important to the meaning. The someone is inferred. Whenever you aren't doing something yourself, you can use this phrase.

The verb *faire* is used in many expressions in French, such as the following:

faire un voyage	to take a trip
faire attention	to pay attention

Aller is another word that is used extensively in the French language. It means "to go," and like the other verbs that get constant usage, it is irregular.

Table 6-19
The Verb Aller (to Go)

Singular	Plural
je vais	*nous allons*
tu vas	*vous allez*
il/elle va	*ils/elles vont*

Irregular Verbs Ending in -oir

Irregular verbs ending in *-oir* don't really make much sense at first glance. Some of the singular endings of words end in "x," while others end in "s," and none of the endings seem to have any inherent logic. With practice, you'll get used to the endings. These verbs tend to be some of the most widely used words in the French language, so you'll get lots of practice with them.

In addition, you can use some of these verbs with an infinitive to create new and complex sentences, expanding immensely your ability to speak French. As you read over the lists, pay attention to the third person plural ending; it is usually formed differently from the other plural conjugations. It is actually more similar to the singular endings of the conjugated verb. Consider the following irregular verbs ending in *-oir*.

Table 6-20
The Verb Vouloir (to Want, to Wish, to Will)

Singular	Plural
je veux	nous voulons
tu veux	vous voulez
il/elle veut	ils/elles veulent

Table 6-21
The Verb Pouvoir (to Be Able To)

Singular	Plural
je peux	nous pouvons
tu peux	vous pouvez
il/elle peut	ils/elles peuvent

When the verb *pouvoir* is used with an infinitive verb, it takes on the sense of the English "can," as in the following examples:

Je peux voir.	I can see. I am able to see.
Nous pouvons y aller.	We can go. We are able to go.
Ils peuvent payer les billets	They can pay for the tickets. They are able to pay for the tickets.

FACT

The verb *devoir* can also carry the meaning of "ought" when translated into English; many people use the word "should" to indicate this case, too. Using *devoir* is almost like saying you "must" do something, but just a little bit softer in meaning. For example, *Je dois voir le film* can mean "I should see the film," "I ought to see the film," or "I have to see the film."

Table 6-22
The Verb Voir (to See)

Singular	Plural
je vois	nous voyons
tu vois	vous voyez
il/elle voit	ils/elles voient

Table 6-23
The Verb Recevoir (to Receive, to Get)

Singular	Plural
je reçois	nous recevons
tu reçois	vous recevez
il/elle reçoit	ils/elles reçoivent

Table 6-24
The Verb Devoir (to Have To, to Owe)

Singular	Plural
je dois	nous devons
tu dois	vous devez
il/elle doit	ils/elles doivent

Table 6-25
The Verb Savoir (to Know)

Singular	Plural
je sais	nous savons
tu sais	vous savez
il/elle sait	ils/elles savent

Irregular Verbs Ending in -ir

Some of the following irregular -ir verbs can be used with nouns after them to indicate the object that the verb refers to. This is known as a direct object; you will learn more about these in Chapter 9.

Table 6-26
The Verb Courir (to Run)

Singular	Plural
je cours	nous courons
tu cours	vous courez
il/elle court	ils/elles courent

Table 6-27
The Verb Dormir (to Sleep)

Singular	Plural
je dors	nous dormons
tu dors	vous dormez
il/elle dort	ils/elles dorment

Table 6-28
The Verb Obtenir (to Obtain)

Singular	Plural
j'obtiens	nous obtenons
tu obtiens	vous obtenez
il/elle obtient	ils/elles obtiennent

Table 6-29
The Verb Offrir (to Offer)

Singular	Plural
j'offre	nous offrons
tu offres	vous offrez
il/elle offre	ils/elles offrent

Table 6-30
The Verb Ouvrir (to Open)

Singular	Plural
j'ouvre	nous ouvrons
tu ouvres	vous ouvrez
il/elle ouvre	ils/elles ouvrent

Table 6-31
The Verb Partir (to Leave, to Depart)

Singular	Plural
je pars	nous partons
tu pars	vous partez
il/elle part	ils/elles partent

Table 6-32
The Verb Servir (to Serve)

Singular	Plural
je sers	nous servons
tu sers	vous servez
il/elle sert	ils/elles servent

Table 6-33
The Verb Sortir (to Go Out)

Singular	Plural
je sors	nous sortons
tu sors	vous sortez
il/elle sort	ils/elles sortent

Table 6-34
The Verb Tenir (to Have, to Hold)

Singular	Plural
je tiens	nous tenons
tu tiens	vous tenez
il/elle tient	ils/elles tiennent

Table 6-35
The Verb Venir (to Come)

Singular	Plural
je viens	*nous venons*
tu viens	*vous venez*
il/elle vient	*ils/elles viennent*

Idiomatic Expressions with Avoir

In Chapter 2, you learned about idiomatic expressions—expressions that have meaning only in a particular language. Some phrases using *avoir* have unique translations that don't quite parallel the English usage. Many of these phrases will seem foreign to you, as English uses the verb "to be" for most of them. *Avoir* means "to have" or "to hold," so you may need to spend some time becoming familiar with these expressions.

It is relatively easy to remember these idiomatic expressions when translating from French to English, because they don't make a whole lot of sense if translated literally. When moving from English to French, however, extra caution is needed, as you can easily fall into a trap if you accidentally translate the English words literally to form a French sentence. This can seriously alter the meaning, so pay close attention.

Avoir can be used with different words to describe a variety of physical conditions. In some cases, English has its own verb that functions as the equivalent of the expression; in others, it uses an adjective.

Avoir Chaud

Literally, it looks like "to have hot," which does not make sense in English, but the meaning is "to be hot" or "to feel hot." Note that to say "It is hot (outside)," you need to use the verb *faire: Il fait chaud.*

Avoir Froid

This means "to feel (be) cold." As seen above, to say "It is cold (outside)," you need to use the verb *faire: Il fait froid.*

Avoir Faim

Literally, this means "to have hunger," which makes sense in English, but sounds absurd. Instead, in French, this expression means "to be hungry."

Avoir Soif

This construction, which means "to be thirsty," closely resembles "hunger," so you should find it easy to remember the two of them.

Avoir L'Air

The literal translation of this expression (which means "to seem") is "to have the air," which is very close to "seem" in English.

Avoir Sommeil

You can use this phrase, which means "to be sleepy," when you want to indicate that someone is tired or sleepy, including yourself.

Avoir . . . Ans

You can use this phrase when you want to indicate that you are a particular age. Literally, it means "to have years," as in *J'ai trente ans*, or in other words, "I am thirty years old."

Avoir Mal

This expression is used to describe an ache or pain and is followed by the preposition *à* and a noun with a definite article to indicate the source of the pain. An example is *Il a mal à la tête*, which means "He has a headache."

Avoir Tort

There is no separate verb for "wrong." Instead, this idiomatic expression is used, and it means "to be wrong."

Avoir Raison

This phrase is the opposite of *avoir tort* and means "to be right."

Avoir Besoin de

Literally, this phrase would translate as "to have a need for." When translating into English, a close approximation is "to need." The phrase *J'ai besoin de lait* means "I need milk."

Avoir Peur de

When translating this expression, which means "to be afraid," you can also use the verb "to fear."

Avoir Honte de

Honte means shame, so it literally means "to have shame about" something. A more common translation is "to be ashamed of something."

Avoir Envie de

In the English equivalent of this expression that means "to feel like," "feel like" is often followed by a word ending in "-ing," like "reading." After the French idiomatic expression, the infinitive of the verb is used: *Je n'ai pas envie de manger* means "I don't feel like eating."

Avoir Lieu

You can use this phrase to describe the beginning of almost any event—it means "to take place."

Avoir de la Chance

Chance means luck; you can wish someone "good luck" by saying *Bonne chance!* In order to say that someone is lucky, use this idiomatic expression: *il a de la chance.*

Avoir L'occasion de

In English, this phrase usually means "to have the opportunity." It can also be translated as "to have the chance," but be sure not to confuse it with *avoir de la chance.*

The Present Participle

In English, you often use verb forms that end in "-ing" to describe actions; sometimes, these are used as verbs or adjectives, while other times they are used as nouns. We refer to these words as present participles.

In French, the present participle is based on the stem of the *nous* (us) form of the present indicative conjugation. To form the present participle, simply drop the *-ons* ending from the present conjugation of the *nous* form and replace it with *-ant*.

Table 6-36
Present Participles

Infinitive	Nous Form	Present Participle	English
parler	*parlons*	*parlant*	speaking
courir	*courons*	*courant*	running
voir	*voyons*	*voyant*	seeing
vouloir	*voulons*	*voulant*	wanting
étudier	*étudions*	*étudiant*	studying
prendre	*prenons*	*prenant*	taking
entendre	*entendons*	*entendant*	hearing
travailler	*travaillons*	*travaillant*	working

Fortunately, there are only three irregular present participles: *avoir*, *être*, and *savoir*.

Table 6-37
Irregular Present Participles

Infinitive	Present Participle	English
avoir	*ayant*	having
être	*étant*	being
savoir	*sachant*	knowing

The most common use of the present participle in French is with the word *en* ("by," "while," or "in") to indicate simultaneous events or cause and effect. In this case, it is called a gerund. Consider the following sentences:

Je lis le journal en regardant la télévision.	I am reading the paper while watching television.
Je gagne de l'argent en travaillant au McDo.	I earn money by working at McDonald's.

This construction will often appear at the beginning of a sentence to set the mood or context of the sentence:

En lisant, j'ai beaucoup appris.	By reading, I learned a great deal.

When used in this fashion, the present participle is tied to the subject of the verb. Be careful when translating from English that the participle actually relates back to the subject; English is notorious for "dangling participles," which are participles that don't clearly relate back to a source. Try to determine exactly what is meant in the sentence and translate accordingly.

When translating from French to English, simply choose the form that makes the most sense within the context of the sentence. The preposition *en* can carry any of the three meanings, so use whichever seems appropriate to you to complete the meaning of the sentence.

Note that in English, we often use the present participle "-ing" form of a verb as the past participle in the present, but we also use it to form other compound tenses. Consider the following examples.

I am speaking to the man.
I will be going to Paris.

Take care not to confuse the French past participle with the English present participle: Don't automatically assume that every time you see a word ending in "-ing" in English that the present participle will be used in French. The present participle form in French is to be used only for events that are truly taking place in the present.

Present Participle as a Noun

The participle in English can also be used as a noun. Consider the following examples.

Speaking is my favorite pastime.
I love singing.

Each of these "-ing" words is technically being used as a noun, even though they appear to be verbs. "Speaking" is the subject of the sentence; only things can be subjects, so a special construction is required. In English, this is accomplished using the participle; when used in this fashion, it is known as a gerund. Therefore, the participle can be the subject of the sentence or the object, as with "singing." In French, a gerund is represented by the infinitive of the verb, instead of using a participle:

Parler est mon passe-temps favori.　　　Speaking is my favorite hobby.

Don't worry about the fancy linguistic terms, though. To determine the difference between a participle and a gerund in English, see how it's being used. Whenever you come across a participle in English, run through the following points to determine what function it serves in the sentence:

- Is the participle being used as a verb in a compound construction? Remember that in English, we can say both "I walk" and "I am walking." When translating the latter into French, the verb is conjugated in the present indicative, as the present indicative conjugation encompasses the English present participle in such constructions.

- Is the participle being used as a noun? Does it appear as the subject or object of the sentence? If so, it is a gerund, and a participle is not used in French. Instead, an infinitive is used.

- Does it have the sense of "by," "while," or "upon" doing something? If so, you are required to use the construction using *en*, as discussed earlier.

Activité 6

Complete the blanks with the correct form of the verb in parentheses.

1. *J'_____ soif. (avoir)*
2. *Vous _____ très vite ! (courir)*
3. *Nous _____ très heureux. (être)*
4. *Ils _____ leur devoir. (finir)*
5. *Vous _____ travailler plus. (devoir)*
6. *Est-ce que tu _____ la littérature anglaise? (étudier)*
7. *Je te _____ mon cousin André. (présenter)*
8. *Vous _____ français? (parler)*

Chapter 7

Asking Questions and Giving Orders

This chapter helps you ask questions in a variety of ways (something you may need to do a lot of if you're traveling to a French-speaking country!) and give orders or imperatives, such as telling someone to "fetch me that French dictionary."

Est-ce que

In French, there are a few different ways to ask a question. The most common are *est-ce que*, inversion, and intonation.

Est-ce que is placed at the beginning of sentences as a sort of marker to let listeners know that a question is coming. You can use *est-ce que* at the beginning of any declarative sentence to turn it into a question.

Declarative sentence: Paul est ici.	Paul is here.
Question: Est-ce que Paul est ici?	Is Paul here?

Intonation

Another way to ask a question is simply to raise your voice at the end of a sentence. This is called intonation. Intonation is usually combined with other ways of asking a question; most French speakers will ask questions with intonation even when the other methods are used, too. In informal situations, intonation can even be used on its own to turn a regular sentence into a question without changing the word order or adding a phrase like *est-ce que*.

Paul est ici?   Is Paul here?

Inversion

Inversion involves changing the word order in the sentence, putting the verb before the subject pronoun. English does the same thing. For example, "You are going to the store" is a declarative statement. To create a question, you may ask, "Are you going to the store?"

"You," the subject pronoun, appears first in the declarative statement, immediately before the verb, "are." In an inverted question, however, the verb begins the statement and the pronoun directly follows the verb.

Habitez-vous en France?   Do you live in France?

In order to ask a question using inversion, the subject and object are reversed. In written French, a hyphen is placed between the two words to indicate their relationship. In spoken French, anytime you hear a verb come before the subject, remember that you're being asked a question. Listen to the CD for the pronunciation of the questions seen below.

TRACK 37

Est-ce que Paul est ici?
Paul est ici?
Habitez-vous en France?

Asking Questions about People

In English, we often begin questions by asking "who" or "what." These are known as interrogative pronouns. French uses a similar set of interrogative pronouns that ask questions about people or things. *Qui* (who, whom) is the French interrogative pronoun used to ask questions about people.

Qui *as the Subject of the Sentence*

You can use *qui* to ask a question about someone by using it as the subject of the sentence. When used in this construction, the sentence does not need to be inverted, nor does *est-ce que* need to be used. *Qui* looks after the question for you; simply place it at the beginning of the sentence and follow it with a verb conjugated in the third person singular.

Qui est ici?   Who is here?
Qui est venu hier soir?   Who came last night?

You may also encounter the phrase *qui est-ce qui* used to start a question. This is just a longer way of doing things.

Qui *as the Direct Object of the Sentence*

Qui does not have to be the subject of the sentence; it can also be used as the object. When used in this way, the question must be formed a little differently. The proper subject and verb must be used, along with one of the traditional ways of forming a question, either *est-ce que* or inversion of the subject and verb. *Qui* is placed at the beginning of the sentence even though it is technically the object.

Qui regardes-tu?	Who are you looking at?
Qui est-ce que tu regardes?	Who (whom) are you looking at?

Both of the above sentences actually mean the same thing; the only difference is in the form of the question.

Qui Used with a Preposition

When *qui* is used in a question with a preposition, the preposition is placed at the beginning of the sentence, with *qui* immediately following it. The rest of the sentence is then formed in the same way as if *qui* were simply appearing as the object in *est-ce que* or inversion form.

À qui avez-vous parlé?	Who have you spoken to?
À qui est-ce que tu as besoin de parler?	Who do you need to talk to?

When *qui* is used with a preposition, it appears as the object and may also translate as "whom" in English. The above sentences could also be translated as "To whom have you spoken?" and "To whom do you need to talk?"

Pronunciation of Qui

In this section, you learned about asking questions about people using interrogative pronouns. Listen to the CD for the pronunciation of the expressions you learned.

TRACK 38

Qui est ici?	Who is here?
Qui est venu hier soir?	Who came last night?
Qui regardes-tu?	Who are you looking at?
Qui est-ce que tu regardes?	Who are you looking at?
À qui avez-vous parlé?	Who have you spoken to?

À qui est-ce que tu as besoin de parler?   Who do you need to talk to?

Asking Other Kinds of Questions

When you're not asking specifically about a person, use one of the following interrogative pronouns to ask about actions, ideas, situations, and things.

Qu'est-ce qui *as the Subject of the Sentence*

Qu'est-ce qui is used to begin a question with "what," when the "what" being discussed is the subject of the sentence.

Qu'est-ce qui se passe dans le livre?   What happens in the book?
Qu'est-ce qui t'a plu dans le film?   What did you like in the film?

Because it is used as the subject of the sentence, the verb must be used in the third person singular. Any pronouns you see between this phrase and the verb will be object or reflexive pronouns, not subject pronouns; don't let them confuse you into thinking that they are the actual subject. (See Chapters 9 and 13.)

Que *as the Object of the Sentence*

Many times in English, the "what" that begins the section is actually the direct object. Consider the following English examples:

What did you do last night?
What are you doing at the hospital?
What did you take to the game?

In all of these sentences, "what" is the direct object. "You" is the subject. Be careful not to get them confused, because the direct object interrogative pronoun takes a different form in French. *Que* is used as the interrogative pronoun, which translates in this case as "what." It must be used with either the *est-ce que* or inversion form.

Qu'est-ce que tu vas faire demain?   What are you going to do tomorrow?

The word *que* doesn't always mean "what"; you will also encounter *que* in different contexts where it has other meanings. You will learn more about this in Chapter 9.

Quoi *as the Object of a Preposition*

When you are creating sentences with prepositions, *quoi* is used as the object of the preposition to say "what." Its form follows the same pattern as *qui*, with the preposition appearing at the beginning of the sentence, immediately followed by the interrogative pronoun. The rest of the sentence is constructed normally, using either *est-ce que* or inversion to complete the question.

À quoi penses-tu?   What are you thinking about?
De quoi est-ce que Phillipe a parlé?   What did Philippe talk about?

The majority of these uses will be idiomatic, as English verbs are often handled differently than when it comes to using prepositions. Refer to Chapter 6 for more information on verbs that use prepositions with their objects.

Qu'est-ce que c'est? is a very common French phrase; when pronounced, it is completely run together. It's pronounced a lot shorter than it looks, and if you try to pronounce it like it reads, you may not be understood.

Other Uses of Qu'est-ce que

Qu'est-ce que can also be used to ask other kinds of questions, such as "What is that?" In French, this is done using variations of the French phrase *Qu'est-ce que c'est?* which means "What is it?" This construction can be used to ask for more information about something when followed with a noun, or can ask for a general definition when used with a pronoun.

Qu'est-ce que c'est que ça?	What is that?
Qu'est-ce que c'est qu'une	What is a correct response
réponse vraie à la question?	to the question?
Qu'est-ce que c'est que le titre?	What is the title?

Using the Interrogative Adjective Quel

In Chapters 9 and 10, you can learn a number of pronouns and adjectives. There is another adjective, *quel*, meaning "what" or "which," that you can also use to ask questions in French. As an adjective, it must agree in gender and number with the noun it is modifying. Table 7-1 includes the available forms.

Table 7-1
Forms of Quel

Gender	Singular	Plural
Masculine	*quel*	*quels*
Feminine	*quelle*	*quelles*

Simple Questions

Quel can be used to begin the sentence and ask the question "what" or "which." The verb *être* is used, and the noun that *quel* modifies is placed immediately following the verb.

Quel est ton nom?	What is your name?
Quelle est ta couleur préférée?	What is your favorite color?

Quel Modifying the Subject

Quel can also be used to modify the subject of a sentence. When this happens, *quel* begins the sentence. It is placed immediately before the noun that's acting as the subject of the sentence. *Quel* forms the question for you; you do not need to add *est-ce que* or use inversion in this construction.

Quelle tarte veux-tu?	Which pie would you like?

Quel Modifying the Object

Quel can also modify the object of a sentence. Simply place *quel* at the beginning of the sentence and place the noun it modifies immediately after it. Either *est-ce que* or inversion can then be used to complete the question.

Quel homme est-ce que vous avez vu?	Which man did you see?

Quel Modifying the Object of a Preposition

When *quel* is used to modify a noun that's being used as the object of a preposition, the preposition is placed at the beginning of the sentence, with the proper form of *quel* immediately following it. The noun being modified is then placed directly after *quel*, with inversion or *est-ce que* being used to complete the question.

Other Interrogative Expressions

Here are a few additional interrogative expressions that can be used in French to ask questions about location, time, manner, number, or cause. Normally, they are placed at the beginning of a sentence and used with *est-ce que,* inversion, or intonation to complete the question.

À quelle heure?	At what time?
Combien?	How much?
Combien est-ce que tu as payé ce chemisier?	How much did you pay for this blouse?
Combien de	How many
Combien de romans as-tu achetés?	How many books did you buy?
Comment	How
Comment allez-vous aujourd'hui?	How are you doing today?

Où	Where
Où est la salle de bain?	Where is the bathroom?
Pourquoi	Why
Pourquoi n'allons-nous pas à Paris?	Why are we not going to Paris?
Quand	When
Quand est-ce qu'il arrivera?	When will he arrive?

Pronunciation of Questions

In this section, you learned how to ask various kinds of questions using interrogative pronouns. Listen to the CD for the pronunciation of some of the expressions you learned.

TRACK 39

Qu'est-ce qui se passe dans le livre?	What happens in the book?
Qu'est-ce que tu vas faire demain?	What are you going to do tomorrow?
Qu'est-ce qu'il a fait hier soir?	What did he do last night?
À quoi penses-tu?	What are you thinking about?
De quoi est-ce que Phillipe a parlé?	What did Philippe talk about?
Qu'est-ce que c'est?	What is it?
Qu'est-ce que c'est que ça?	What is that?
Quel est ton nom?	What is your name?
Quelle est ta couleur préférée?	What is your favorite color?
Combien est-ce que tu as payé ce chemisier?	How much did you pay for this blouse?
Combien de romans as-tu achetés?	How many books did you buy?
Comment allez-vous aujourd'hui?	How are you doing today?
Où est la salle de bain?	Where is the bathroom?
Pourquoi n'allons nous pas à Paris?	Why are we not going to Paris?
Quand est-ce qu'il arrivera?	When will he arrive?

Giving Orders: The Imperative Verb Form

In English, we can tell people what to do by saying things like "go to the store" or "bring me a drink." Because it's a direct order to someone, there doesn't really need to be a subject pronoun, because you know who's supposed to do what in the conversation. In French, this operates much the same way and is done using the imperative form of the verb.

The imperative form of the verb is based on the present-tense conjugation. There are three possibilities using the imperative form. The first two use either the *tu* or the *vous* form of the verb, and the third uses the *nous* form. To form the imperative, simply drop the subject pronoun from the construction, which turns it into an order.

Tu Form

The *tu* form of the verb is used when you are giving an order to one person with whom you are very familiar. If you want to give an order to someone you don't know very well, use the *vous* form instead. For verbs ending in -*er*, when the verb is used in the imperative, the "s" is dropped from the end of the *tu* form in written French. In spoken French, the "s" in the tu form isn't pronounced anyway, so you shouldn't notice much of a difference. This happens only with verbs ending in -*er*, however. The "s" is maintained at the end of the word in verbs ending in -*ir* and -*re*.

Porte la chemise rouge.	Wear the red shirt.
Finis le livre.	Finish the book.

Vous Form

The *vous* form of the verb is used when giving an order to a group of people that does not include yourself. In addition, it is used as a polite form when speaking with someone to whom you should show deference and respect.

Téléphonez à votre maman.	Call your mother.
Finissez le repas.	Finish the meal.

Nous Form

The *nous* form of the verb is used form sentences such as "Let's go to the mall." This form of the imperative collects everyone together and makes them a group. Because you are included in the group, the *nous* form of the verb is used. If you are telling someone else to go and do something, and you are not included in the action, use the *vous* form.

Restons ici.	Let's stay here.
Partons maintenant.	Let's go now.

Irregular Imperative Verb Forms

The imperative can be used with irregular verbs. This section shows the forms of the four most common irregular verbs. Familiarize yourself with them so that you can recognize them on sight. If you forget about one of the forms and don't recognize it when you come across it, the fact that it is used without a subject pronoun should jog your memory.

Être

The forms of *être* are completely irregular. Instead of using the present indicative conjugation, the following forms must be used:

- **Tu form:** *Sois courageux!*
- **Nous form:** *Soyons patients et attendons qu'ils reviennent.*
- **Vous form:** *Soyez prudents!*

Avoir

Like *être*, *avoir* also has unique formations in the imperative.

- **Tu form:** *aie*   *Aie confiance, je suis là!*
- **Nous form:** *ayons*   *Ayons la conviction de nos opinions.*
- **Vous form:** *ayez*   *Ayez le courage de le lui dire.*

Faire

Faire is unique in that even though it's an irregular verb, it follows the regular conjugation pattern, using the present indicative conjugated form.

- **Tu form:** *fais*   *Fais tes devoirs avant d'aller rejoindre tes amis.*
- **Nous form:** *faisons*   *Faisons preuve de bon sens!*
- **Vous form:** *faites*   *Faites savoir à vos parents qu'ils sont invités.*

Aller

Aller forms the imperative much like the regular *-er* verbs, dropping the "s" from the end of the *tu* form. When the *tu* form *va* is used with an object pronoun such as *y*, it takes an "s," to form *vas-y*.

- **Tu** form: *va*   *Va lui en parler*
- **Nous** form: *allons*   *Allons voir ce qui se passe à la gare!*
- **Vous** form: *allez*   *Allez parler à votre cousine.*

Pronunciation of Imperatives

In this section, you learned how to use imperatives. Listen to the CD for the pronunciation of some of the expressions you have learned.

TRACK 40

Porte la chemise rouge.	Wear the red shirt.
Finis le livre.	Finish the book.
Apprends la leçon.	Learn the lesson.
Restons ici.	Let's stay here.
Partons maintenant.	Let's go now.
Lisons quelque chose.	Let's read something.
Téléphonez à votre maman.	Call your mother.
Finissez le repas.	Finish the meal.
Lisez le journal.	Read the newspaper.

Activité 7

Unscramble the following phrases to create a logical sentence.

1. *tu / fais / qu'est-ce que /?*

_____

2. *voulez / un / est-ce que / vous / café /?*

_____

3. *journal / le / lisez / .*

_____

4. *vous / parlez- / anglais /?*

_____

Chapter 8
Negating Words and Phrases

If you've read other chapters in this book, you've probably seen *ne . . . pas* used to make negative statements. It is equivalent to the English "not"; it is probably the most common negative expression you will encounter. Naturally, there are more. *Ne* is almost always a part of the construction, but other words can be used in place of *pas* to create negative expressions.

Negative Expressions

To create a negative in the present tense, *ne* is placed before the verb and *pas* is placed immediately after:

Tu ne parles pas français.	You don't speak French.

If the verb begins with a vowel, the "e" is dropped from *ne* and an apostrophe is used:

Je n'ai pas de lait.	I don't have any milk.

Some other common negative expressions include the following. For each one, place the *ne* before the verb, and the expression after it.

Ne ... jamais

Ne . . . jamais means "never," as in the following:

Il ne va jamais à l'opéra	He never goes to the opera.
Nous n'avons jamais raison.	We are never right.

Ne ... rien

Ne . . . rien means "nothing," as in:

Je n'ai rien.	I have nothing; I don't have anything.

Ne ... personne

Ne . . . personne means "no one," as in:

Je n'aime personne.	I like no one; I don't like anyone.

Ne ... pas encore

Ne . . . pas encore means "not yet." Here's an example:

Il n'a pas encore le livre.	He doesn't have the book yet.

Ne . . . que

Ne . . . que means "only," as in the following:

Il n'a que le dictionnaire.	He only has the dictionary.

Ne . . . plus

Ne . . . plus means "no longer," or "not anymore" as in the following:

Je ne suis plus étudiant.	I am no longer a student.

Ne . . . nulle part

This means "nowhere":

Il ne va nulle part.	He is going nowhere.

In this section, you learned how to create common negative expressions. Listen to the CD for the pronunciation of some of the expressions.

TRACK 41

Tu ne parles pas français.	You don't speak French.
Je n'ai pas de lait.	I don't have any milk.
Il ne va jamais à l'opéra.	He never goes to the opera.
Je n'ai rien.	I have nothing; I don't have anything.
Je n'aime personne.	I like no one; I don't like anyone.
Il n'a pas encore le livre.	He doesn't have the book yet.
Il n'a que le dictionnaire.	He only has the dictionary.
Je ne suis plus étudiant.	I am no longer a student.
Il ne va nulle part.	He is going nowhere.

The Negative Construction ne . . . ni . . . ni.

The French construction *ne . . . ni . . . ni* is the equivalent of the English "neither . . . nor" when referring to more than one thing in the negative.

You should expect to see *ni* twice in each sentence. This negative construction can be used with nouns that are acting either as the subject or as the object of the sentence. When used with the object, the negative conjunction follows the same predictable pattern as other negative constructions; the *ni* is simply repeated before each object.

Il n'aime ni le thé ni le café.	He likes neither tea or coffee.

When used with two nouns that are acting as the subject, a *ni* is placed before each subject. The *ne* is placed in front of the verb.

Ni Alain ni Paul ne vient ici.	Neither Alain nor Paul comes here.

You can also use *ne . . . ni . . . ni* with verb actions to indicate that two things are not done. The subject of the sentence appears only one time, because the conjunction serves to join the second verb to the subject:

Il ne sait ni lire ni écrire.	He can neither read nor write.

Negative Pronouns Rien and Personne

Both *rien* and *personne* can be used as a pronoun, in addition to the construction seen above. Negative pronouns operate slightly differently from the negative expressions in the rest of this chapter. The main word is placed at the beginning of the word in the subject position and the *ne* follows it in its regular position after the subject but before the verb.

Personne

Personne (which means "no one" or "nobody") can be used as the subject of the sentence:

Personne ne me voit.	Nobody sees me.

Rien

Use *rien* as the subject of a sentence to say "nothing . . .":

Rien ne m'inquiète. Nothing worries me.

More Negative Adverbs

Many of the negative expressions in this chapter are actually adverbs, used to modify the verb in a negative sense—in fact, *ne . . . pas* is an adverb! Some are used in special situations or to convey certain meanings, so study the subtleties. For practice, use the following negative adverbs to convert sentences to negative expressions—either make up sentences or practice with the examples in this book, turning those into negative expressions using these adverbs.

Ne . . . Aucunement

This expression, which means "not at all" or "not in the least," is an emphatic form compared to *ne . . . pas;* use it when you want to make absolutely sure your listeners appreciate the intensity of your objection.

Ça ne me gêne aucunement. That does not bother me at all.

Ne . . . Guère

This expression, which means "not much," "not very," or "only a little," is the rough equivalent to such French phrases as *pas beaucoup, pas très, peu de, presque pas,* and *à peine.* Whenever those meanings are intended, you can use *ne . . . guère* to achieve the same result.

Il n'a guère d'imagination. He has hardly any imagination.

Ne . . . Nullement

This expression, which means "not at all" or "by no means," is like *ne . . . aucunement*: an emphatic form *of ne . . . pas* that can be used to express an absolute disagreement with a statement or an out-and-out denial of some point made by another speaker.

Il n'est nullement pressé.   He is not at all in a hurry.

Ne . . . Pas du Tout

This expression, which means "not at all," is nearly identically to *ne . . . aucunement* and *ne . . . nullement.* It can also be used as an emphatic form of *ne . . . pas.*

Il n'est pas du tout perturbé.   He is not at all perturbed.

Ne . . . Pas Encore

This expression, which means "not yet," is the opposite of *déjà,* which means "already." This negative adverb is very close in meaning to *ne . . . toujours pas,* covered later in this section.

Il n'est pas encore arrivé.   He hasn't arrived yet.

Ne . . . Pas . . . Non Plus

This construction, which means "no longer," can also be used in response to a negative question posed using *pas.* In that case, it is the opposite of *aussi,* meaning "also" or "too." When used in this sense, the best English equivalent is probably "either," as in "not me, either."

Je ne suis pas pressé non plus. I am not in a hurry either.

Ne . . . Point

Point tends to be an archaic negative adverb, used seldom in modern French. When it is used, however, it is more emphatic than *pas,* even though it means close to the same thing: "no," "not at all," or "none." This tends to be a literary adverb; you may encounter it in written French, especially French from an earlier time period.

Non, Cyrano n'a point d'ennemis.   Indeed, Cyrano has no enemies.

Ne . . . Toujours Pas

While this basically shares the same meaning as *ne . . . pas encore*, it also carries with it a sense of impatience or apprehension: "not yet." It does not carry the same meaning as *pas toujours,* which means "not always," so don't confuse the two expressions.

Le train n'est toujours pas parti.   The train has not yet (still hasn't) left.

In these sections, you learned more negative expressions. Listen to the CD for the pronunciation of some of the expressions you have learned.

TRACK 42

Je ne veux ni le pain ni le lait.	I want neither the bread nor the milk.
Ni Alain ni Paul ne vient ici.	Neither Alain nor Paul come here.
Il ne sait ni lire ni écrire.	He can neither read nor write.
Personne ne me voit.	Nobody sees me.
Rien ne m'inquiète.	Nothing worries me.
Ça ne me gêne aucunement.	That does not bother me at all.
Il n'a guère d'imagination.	He has hardly any imagination.
Il n'est nullement pressé.	He is not at all in a hurry.
Il n'est pas du tout perturbé.	He is not at all perturbed.
Il n'est pas encore arrivé.	He hasn't arrived yet.
Je ne suis pas pressé non plus.	I am not in a hurry either.
Non, Cyrano n'a point d'ennemis.	Indeed, Cyrano has no enemies.
Le train n'est toujours pas parti.	The train has not yet (still hasn't) left.

Use of Articles with Negative Expressions

In general, the partitive *de* is used in most negative expressions.
Est-ce qu'il y a de la farine? Is there any flour?

Il n'y a pas de farine.   There is no flour.

If the negative conjunction *ne . . . ni . . . ni* is used in front of nouns that take an indefinite article or a partitive article when used in the non-negative sense, the articles disappear when cast into a negative construction. (Note that a definite article, however, is maintained.)

As-tu de la farine ou du lait?	Do you have any flour or milk?
Non, je n'ai ni farine ni lait.	No, I have neither flour nor milk
	No, I don't have any flour or milk.

Responding to Negative Questions

Normally, *oui* is the word for "yes." After a negative expression, however, French uses a different word, *si*, to answer in the affirmative. *Non* is used to agree with the negative expression. To refute it, use *si*.

Table 8-1
Responding to Negative Questions

Question	Answer Using *Non*	Answer Using *Si*
Tu n'as pas les clefs?	*Non, je n'ai pas les clefs.*	*Si, j'ai les clefs.*
You don't have the keys?	No, I don't have the keys.	Yes, I have the keys.

Activité 8

Listen to each of the negative sentences and translate each into English.

TRACK 43

1. _____ *(ne . . . pas)*
2. _____ *(ne . . . jamais)*
3. _____ *(ne . . . personne)*
4. _____ *(ne . . . plus)*
5. _____ *(ne . . . nulle part)*

Chapter 9

Objects, Prepositions, and Pronouns

This chapter is a delightful potluck picnic of French grammar: direct and indirect objects, prepositions, and three new types of pronouns: object, demonstrative, and relative. Not sure what any of this means? That's okay. This chapter explains these concepts both in terms of English grammar and your newly acquired French skills.

Direct and Indirect Objects

The subject of the sentence is the person or thing that performs the action indicated by the verb. There is another component to the sentence—the object, or the thing that receives the action of the verb. There are two kinds of objects—direct objects and indirect objects.

Direct Objects

Direct objects receive the action of the verb directly; whatever is being described by the verb is happening to the direct object. To understand how the direct object works, consider the following example:

Il a une voiture.   He has a car.

The verb used in this sentence is *avoir*, or "to have." The subject, as indicated by *il*, is the person who is performing the action of the verb. "The car," placed after the verb, is the thing receiving the action of the verb "to have." It is the thing being affected by the verb. A verb that affects a direct object is called a transitive verb.

QUESTION?

Why can't I directly translate English and French transitive verbs?
The English equivalents of transitive verbs are not always used in the same manner as in French, so be careful. Never try to translate word for word; instead, take apart the meaning of the sentence and translate that.

Table 9-1 gives you some common transitive verbs that take a direct object.

Table 9-1
French Transitive Verbs

Verb	English
aider	to help (someone)
attendre	to wait (for something or someone)

chercher	to look (for something or someone)
écouter	to listen (to something or someone)
entendre	to hear (something or someone)
regarder	to watch (something or someone)
voir	to see (something or someone)

Indirect Objects

The indirect object is usually fairly easy to determine in French. It generally appears with a preposition (see the following section), which will be your major clue:

Il a donné le cadeau à Jean.   He gave the present to Jean.

In French, a preposition is always placed before the indirect object. In this case, the preposition *à* precedes the indirect object, *Jean.* Indirect objects often appear in situations where things—favors, gifts, advice— are given. Indirect objects concern the receiving party.

Table 9-2 contains some verbs that take an indirect object and are indicated with the preposition *à* (see the following section). These verbs may not function in the same way as their English counterparts, so don't translate word for word. In order to help you remember these verbs, the preposition is listed along with the verb.

Table 9-2
French Verbs That Take an Indirect Object

Verb	English
obéir à	to obey (someone)
parler à	to speak (to someone)
plaire à	to please (someone)

ressembler à	to look like, to resemble (someone)
téléphoner à	to telephone (someone)

Prepositions

Prepositions are relational words that are used in front of nouns and articles. English words like "to," "with," "in," and "on" are prepositions. When prepositions are used in a sentence, they take an object. In other words, the preposition must have a noun to complete its meaning.

English grammar tells you never to end a sentence with a preposition, but this rule is often ignored in common usage. In French, a preposition cannot be used without a noun following it, so if you find yourself using a preposition at the end of a sentence, you'd better find a noun to put after it.

In English, many verbs, when used with a preposition, take on a slightly different meaning, such as "to go out." Like English, French has a number of prepositions. This section lists some common ones.

The Preposition À

The preposition *à* is one of the most versatile in the language. It can have a wide variety of meanings, including "at," "to," "in," "of," and "by"; the meaning will usually be associated with the noun, as follows:

à Paris	in Paris
à pied	on foot
à la pharmacie	at the pharmacy

The preposition *à* sometimes contracts when used with a definite article. The following table shows how the various definite articles are used with the preposition.

Table 9-3
Definite Articles Used with À

article	result
le	*au*

la	à la
l'	à l'
les	aux

The following examples illustrate the different functions *à* can perform, including the English equivalents to the constructions.

Location or Destination

Use *à* to indicate a location or destination:

J'habite aux États-Unis.	I live in the United States.
Nous sommes allés au cinéma.	We went to the movies.
Je suis allé à Paris.	I went to Paris.

Distance

À can also be used to indicate a degree of separation in either time or space, as follows:

Il habite à un kilomètre de chez moi.	He lives one kilometer from me.
Je suis à dix minutes de l'école.	I am ten minutes away from the school.

Specific Points in Time

À can be used to refer to specific hours or moments, including calendar dates, as follows:

Il arrivera à dix heures.	He will arrive at ten o'clock.

Characteristics or Manner

À can be used to indicate the fashion in which something is done or the characteristics of something that exists:

J'ai vu le garçon aux cheveux blonds.	I saw the boy with blond hair.
Elle fait la cuisine à la française.	She is cooking in the French way.

Possession

When the preposition *à* is used to indicate possession, it is more emphatic than when a possessive pronoun or the preposition *de* is used to indicate the owner. Use this construction only when you want to make absolutely certain that everyone understands what you mean:

Cette voiture est à moi, pas à lui.	This car is mine, not his.
Non, je lis le roman qui est à Pierre.	No, I am reading Pierre's book.

To Describe How the Action of a Verb Is Performed

Use *à* to describe exactly how verbs are performed:

Elle écrit la lettre à la main.	She writes the letter by hand.

To Describe Weights and Measures

Use *à* for weights and measures:

J'avais acheté la farine au kilo.	I used to buy flour by the kilogram.
Ils boivent la bière au verre.	They drink beer by the glass.

To Describe the Function or Purpose of an Item

Use *à* to describe the function or purpose of an item:

Je porterai mon sac à dos.	I will be wearing my backpack.
Donne-moi une cuillère à soupe.	Give me soup with a soup spoon.

Après

Après means "after," when referring to time, either in a direct or indirect sense, as follows:

après le dîner	after dinner
après 5h00	after 5:00

Après can sometimes be used with verb. The *grave* accent isn't pronounced, but it acts as a reminder not to turn the ending into an "ay" sound.

Avant

Avant means "before," when referring to time.

avant le dîner	before dinner
avant midi	before noon

French often uses what we call military time (24 hour time) to indicate the hour: *Il est dix-sept heures.* (It is 5 p.m.) Note that to abbreviate time, use a small h: *Il est 17h.*

Avec

Avec means "with" and functions very similarly to its English equivalent:

avec un sourire	with a smile

Chez

Chez is a convenient little French word that often takes a number of English words to translate. It is used with names or personal pronouns, and conveys a sense of habitual residence. Possible English translations include "at the home of" and "at the office of." In less formal speech, *chez Pierre* could even be translated as "at Pierre's place."

Dans

Dans means "in." When translating from English to French, however, be careful, because *à* can sometimes be the proper choice. When referring to time, *dans* can also mean "during."

dans la voiture	in the car
dans la journée	during the day

De

De is another versatile French preposition. Normally, it means "of" or "from," as in *de Paris* (from Paris), but it also has other uses, including being used as the partitive article. *De* is used extensively throughout the French language.

Depuis

Depuis is used to indicate a sense of time. It can mean "since" or "for" and is used with events that began at some point in the past but are still occurring, as in the following examples:

depuis cinq ans	for five years
depuis hier	since yesterday

En

En is another versatile preposition. Because it can be used in such a wide variety of situations, it can be difficult to translate. Its meanings include "in," "on," "to," "as," "like," and "by," depending on its usage.

en avion	by plane
en service	in service, working

Pendant

Pendant, which means "during" or "while," can be easily confused with *depuis* or the next preposition in this list, *pour*. *Pendant* refers to duration, whereas *depuis* refers to time elapsed. Finally, *pour* refers to a projected length of time

pendant mes vacances	during my vacation
depuis deux ans	for the last two years
Il part pour deux jours.	He is leaving for two days.

Pour

Pour also means "for" and will be the most common translation for "for" in English.

pour vous	for you
pour la vie	for life

Sans

Like its opposite, *avec, sans*, which means "without," is used much the same as in English, as in the following examples:

sans amour	without love
sans toi	without you

Sur

Sur normally means "on," but can sometimes be translated as "at," "in," or "about," as in the following examples:

sur le bureau	on the desk
deux dentistes sur cinq	two dentists out of five

Vers

Vers can mean "toward" or "around" and can be used in both a physical sense and to convey a sense of time, as in the following examples:

vers New York	toward New York
vers Boston	around Boston
vers midi	around noon

Pronouncing Objects and Prepositions

In these sections, you learned about objects and prepositions. Listen to the CD for the pronunciation of some of the expressions you learned.

TRACK 44

Il a donné le cadeau à Jean.
Il arrivera à dix heures.
avant midi
depuis cinq ans
pendant mes vacances
sans toi

J'habite aux États-Unis.
après le dîner
dans la journée
en avion
pour la vie
sur le bureau
vers Boston

Object Pronouns

Just like subject pronouns are used to represent subjects, you can use object pronouns to represent objects. This way, you don't have to repeat the proper words of nouns over and over in conversation. You can use object pronouns to represent these nouns, in some cases making your sentences considerably shorter.

In English, the most common object pronoun is "it." It is used in a variety of senses, and sometimes you don't even realize it's being used. It represents a noun and in the sentence becomes a shorthand way of referring to that noun so you don't have to keep repeating the same words over and over.

Remember that a pronoun has to link back to a specific noun in some way in order to define it; a pronoun used without this relationship has no meaning at all.

Direct Object Pronouns

When a noun is being used in a sentence as the direct object, the following object pronouns are used.

Table 9-4
French Direct Object Pronouns

Person	Singular	Plural
1st Person	*me*	*nous*
2nd Person	*te*	*vous*
3rd Person Masculine	*le*	*les*
3rd Person Feminine	*la*	*les*

When these pronouns are used to replace a noun in a sentence, they are inserted before the verb. This is much different from English, which tends to maintain the normal word order and places the pronoun after the verb:

Est-ce que tu conduis cette voiture?	Do you drive this car?
Oui, je la conduis.	Yes, I drive it.

When a singular object pronoun appears before a verb that begins with a vowel, it contracts with the verb; simply drop the vowel from the end of the pronoun and add an apostrophe:

Avez-vous vu mon père?	Have you seen my father?
Non, nous ne l'avons pas vu.	No, we have not seen him.

When the object pronoun is used with an infinitive, the pronoun is placed directly before it. Be careful that you don't distort the meaning of sentences by accidentally placing your object pronoun with a conjugated verb instead of with the infinitive where it should be:

Vas-tu finir tes devoirs?	Are you going to finish your homework?
Oui, je vais les finir.	Yes, I am going finish it.

Remember that you can't translate object pronouns directly from one language to the other; the preceding example is a good illustration of one of the reasons it doesn't work.

Some French verbs handle objects differently than English does. Therefore, you have to get to the heart of the true meaning of the sentence before you can start translating any words. You can get away with it when translating a lot of sentences that use actual nouns, but when object pronouns are used, sentences get a little more complicated. As long as you remember to identify which noun is which before you translate, you should have few problems.

Indirect Object Pronouns

In English, we tend to use the same object pronouns for both the direct and indirect object, using prepositions or word order to convey the intended meaning. This is not the case in French. The object pronouns differ slightly and are not interchangeable, but the only actual difference is in the third person formation.

Table 9-5
French Indirect Object Pronouns

Person	Singular	Plural
1st Person	*me*	*nous*
2nd Person	*te*	*vous*
3rd Person (m and f)	*lui*	*leur*

There is really no gender distinction in the third person for indirect object pronouns; the same word suffices for both. In addition, the other forms don't modify to agree with gender, just like the subject pronouns. Don't confuse the object pronouns with possessive adjectives, which must agree in gender and number with their counterpart nouns.

If you try to translate the following sentences word for word, it doesn't work. You have to study the sentence to determine which word is the direct object and which is the indirect object. The word order doesn't help you in French; all object pronouns follow a certain order, no matter what they are being used to represent. The meaning comes from the verb and the context of the sentence.

Normally, the preposition *à* is used to introduce the noun that represents the indirect object in the sentence. When a pronoun is used instead before the conjugated form of the verb, it replaces both the noun and the preposition, so the preposition disappears from the sentence.

Mon copain le donne à mon père.	My friend is giving it to my father.
Mon copain le lui donne.	My friend is giving it to him.

The indirect object pronoun replaces the preposition *à* entirely. With other prepositions, you use the disjunctive pronoun to replace an object referring to a person; in this case, the preposition remains in the same place in the sentence.

Disjunctive Pronouns

Disjunctive pronouns are another set of object pronouns. They are similar to the other object pronouns, but vary in the formation of the third person.

Table 9-6
French Disjunctive Pronouns

Person	Singular	Plural
1st Person	*moi*	*nous*
2nd Person	*toi*	*vous*
3rd Person Masculine	*lui*	*eux*
3rd Person Feminine	*elle*	*elles*

Disjunctive pronouns are used with prepositions placed after the verb, as seen in the following examples:

| *Elle parle de Jean.* | She's talking about Jean. |
| *Elle parle de lui.* | She's talking about him. |

For Emphasis

Inserting the disjunctive pronoun in the sentence can emphasize the subject or the object. When used in this sense, the pronoun doesn't actually replace the subject or object that it modifies; it is used in addition to it.

| *Moi, je n'aime pas regarder la télé.* | Myself, I don't like watching TV. |

THE EVERYTHING LEARNING FRENCH BOOK

Literally, this looks like "Me, I don't like watching TV," but this translation just doesn't make that much sense in English. Rather than translate the words, try to translate the sentiment involved. Perhaps the most appropriate choice in English for the above sentence is "I don't like watching TV, myself."

When used to complement the subject, these pronouns may be placed either at the beginning or the end of the sentence. When used to complement an object, however, the disjunctive pronoun used for emphasis is always placed at the end. The fact that either the subject or the object can appear at the end of the sentence shouldn't cause too much of a problem for you. To tell which is which, simply look at the subject. If the disjunctive pronoun matches it in gender and number, the emphasis is on the subject; if they don't, you'll find they match the object.

Je ne l'ai pas vu, moi.	I didn't see him, myself.
Oui, je l'ai vu, lui.	Yes, I saw him.

To Form Compound Subjects or Objects

The disjunctive pronoun can be used with another noun at the beginning of a sentence. When this happens, the noun is placed first, with the disjunctive pronoun following it. In the first or second person, the subject pronoun is used with the verb, separated from the preceding noun and disjunctive pronoun with a comma. They are joined together using the conjunction *et*:

Jean et moi, nous allons au cinéma.	John and I, we are going to the movies.
Toi et moi, nous avons toujours été de vrais amis	You and I, we have always been true friends.

When used as objects, the noun is placed first with the pronoun placed after it:

Il a téléphoné à Jacques et moi.	He called Jacques and me.

You can also use two disjunctive pronouns to form a compound subject or object; these are joined with the conjunction *et*:

Toi et moi allons aller	You and I are going to go
à Paris avec lui.	to Paris with him.

Alone in Response to a Question

The subject pronoun can never appear without a verb, but a disjunctive pronoun can. For that reason, when responding to a question when you just want the answer to be something like "me" or "him," the disjunctive pronoun is the appropriate choice:

Qui fait ça?	Who is doing that?
Moi.	Me.

In Conjunction with Certain Verb Phrases, When Used to Indicate a Person

The disjunctive pronoun is placed after verbs using the preposition *à*.

être à	to belong to someone
faire attention à	to pay attention to someone
penser à	to think about someone
donner à	to give something to someone
tenir à	to be attached to someone

Here are some examples:

Je n'aime pas le professeur.	I don't like the professor.
Il ne fait jamais attention à moi.	He never pays attention to me.
Je pense souvent à lui.	I often think about him.

The disjunctive pronoun can be used with only the preceding verbs when a person is the object. If the object happens to be a thing, a special pronoun, *y,* is used (covered later in this chapter).

To Make Comparisons Between People

When used in this sense, the disjunctive pronoun is used with the conjunction *que*, which carries the meaning of "than" and is placed at the end of the sentence:

Il est plus intelligent que moi.   He is smarter than I.

To Indicate "Myself" or Its Equivalent

The disjunctive pronoun can be used with *-même* added to the end of it to represent the English usage of words like "myself," "himself," or "themselves." This isn't an exact equivalent; rather, the *-même* ending reinforces and amplifies the disjunctive pronoun, so the most appropriate English translation is usually a variation of "myself":

Il l'a fait lui-même.   He did it himself.

In English, we also use words like "myself" or "yourself" in conjunction with verbs to indicate that an action is being performed by the subject, on the subject; "I am washing myself" is an example. In French, these are known as reflexive verbs.

After the Preposition *De*

When the object of the preposition *de* is a person, the preposition uses the corresponding disjunctive pronoun. The preposition remains in the sentence, retaining its usual location after the verb, and the disjunctive pronoun is placed immediately after it. If the disjunctive pronoun begins with a vowel, *de* contracts to *d'*.

Est-ce que tu as parlé de Sara?   Did you talk about Sara?
Oui, j'ai parlé d'elle.   Yes, I talked about her.

Remember that the disjunctive pronoun can be used only when referring to actual people. If things, locations, ideas, or anything else that isn't a person are used in the sentence, a disjunctive pronoun cannot be used; instead, the object pronoun *en* is used.

The Object Pronoun En

When the preposition *de* is used with an object to indicate a thing, the object pronoun *en* is used to replace the preposition and the noun. *En* is never used in the place of people; only the disjunctive pronouns can be used if the object of the preposition *de* is a person:

Est-ce que tu as beaucoup de stylos?	Do you have a lot of pens?
Oui, j'en ai beaucoup.	Yes, I have many of them.

FACT

If a sentence uses an expression of quantity, as with *assez de* or *beaucoup de,* or even uses a number, *en* replaces the noun. If the preposition *de* is used in the sentence, *en* replaces it, but if a number is used, the number remains in the sentence, in its regular position, without the noun. Here's an example: *Il a écrit deux romans.* (He wrote two novels.) *C'est vrai? Il en a écrit deux?* (Is that right? He wrote two?)

If *de* is being used in the partitive sense, to indicate the English equivalent of "some" or "any," it is not a preposition; instead, it behaves like an article. Don't confuse the preposition *de* with the plural indefinite article *des*, either; if you see *des* being used, you know that it is not the preposition. Note that *liaison* is required after *en* and before a word beginning with a vowel.

The Object Pronoun Y

The direct object pronoun *y* is a versatile French word. For that reason, it can sometimes be confusing, because it can be hard to link back to a noun to give it meaning.

Y is used only when the object it represents is a thing. It can never be used to represent an actual person or even an animate object. If you come across the object pronoun *y* being used in either spoken or written French, you know that it must refer to some inanimate object or place that has already been referred to in the conversation or passage.

The appropriate English translation of *y* is usually either "there" or "it," depending on the particular context of the sentence. The object pronoun *y* is used to replace both the preposition *à* and a noun, much as in the way the indirect object pronouns work for people.

Est-ce que tu es allé au magasin?	Did you go to the store?
Oui, j'y suis allé.	Yes, I went there.
Avez-vous répondu à la lettre?	Did you reply to the letter?
Non, je n'y ai pas répondu.	No, I have not replied to it.

When the object pronoun *y* represents a feminine noun, the past participle agrees if the verb is conjugated using *avoir*; the same holds true when it is used to replace plural nouns. Because *y* is an object pronoun, the past participle must agree both in gender and in number when the pronoun appears before the conjugated auxiliary verb.

The object pronoun *y* doesn't stop there, either. It can also be used to replace other prepositions, such as *dans, sous,* and *devant,* which indicate location. When used in this fashion, it replaces both the preposition and noun, in the same way as with *à*:

Dormirez-vous dans la chambre?	Will you be sleeping in the bedroom?
Oui, nous y dormirons.	Yes, we will be sleeping there.

Object Pronouns and the Imperative

The imperative form of the verb can also be used with object pronouns. When there is only one, it is straightforward; you will have to pay closer attention when more than one is used, however. The pronouns follow a specific order, and each is tacked on to the end of the verb with a hyphen. The pronouns are added in the following order.

1. Direct object: When the imperative form is used with a direct object, the pronoun is placed after the verb and separated with a hyphen. This happens often with reflexive verbs, because the verb requires

an object pronoun to complete its meaning. If the pronoun is *te*, the pronoun *toi* is used instead after the verb:

Dépêchez-vous ! or Dépêche-toi ! Hurry up!

2. Indirect object: When the imperative form is used with an indirect object pronoun, the pronoun is placed after the direct object but still joined to the verb phrase with a hyphen. If the indirect object pronoun is *me*, the pronoun *moi* is used:

Donne-moi le cahier.	Give the notebook to me.
Donne-le-moi.	Give it to me.

3. The pronoun *y*: When the pronoun *y* is used, it is placed after any direct or indirect object pronouns. Note that *liaison* is required when the verb preceding *y* ends with a vowel sound:

Vas-y.	Go there.

4. The pronoun *en*: When the pronoun *en* is used in the imperative construction, it appears last but is still joined to the other words with a hyphen:

Donne-lui-en.	Give some to him.

If the imperative verb is being used with an object pronoun that begins with a vowel, the "s" is kept at the end of the *tu* form. This assists in pronunciation:

Manges-en.	Eat some.

A "t" is sometimes inserted in between an inverted verb and subject; that rule, however, applies only to inverted questions. When the imperative form appears with a pronoun, it will always be an object pronoun, so the rules for inverted questions do not apply.

Negative Imperatives

When the imperative is used with negative expressions, it follows the normal negative construction, despite the absence of a subject pronoun. The *ne* is placed before the verb, and the *pas* or other negative modifier immediately after it.

Ne téléphone pas après minuit.   Do not call after midnight.

Pronouncing Object Pronouns

In these sections, you learned about object pronouns. Listen to the CD for the pronunciation of some of the expressions you learned.

TRACK 45

Oui, je la conduis.
Non, nous ne l'avons pas vu.
Mon copain le lui donne.
Elle parle de lui.
Je ne l'ai pas vu, moi.
Je pense souvent à lui.
Oui, j'en ai beaucoup.
Oui, j'y suis allé.
Dépêchez-vous.
Vas-y.
Manges-en.
Ne lisez pas ce livre-là.
Ne téléphone pas après minuit.

Demonstrative Pronouns

You can use demonstrative adjectives in French to demonstrate the concept of "this" or "that." Instead of having to repeat the noun over and over, French also has demonstrative pronouns you can use to indicate "this one" or "that one." French demonstrative pronouns can never be used on their own; they must be used in a construction with other words. Table 9-7 shows the basic demonstrative pronoun forms. Note their similarities to the object pronouns covered earlier in the chapter.

Table 9-7
French Demonstrative Pronouns

Gender	Singular	Plural
Masculine	*celui*	*ceux*
Feminine	*celle*	*celles*

Demonstrative pronouns are often used with *-ci* and *-là* added to the end to indicate "this one" or "that one."

Veux-tu ce livre-ci ou ce livre-là?	Do you want this book or that book?
Je veux celui-ci, s'il vous plaît.	I would like this one, please.
Je veux celui-là, s'il vous plaît.	I would like that one, please.

Relative Pronouns

A relative pronoun is a pronoun that relates back to something else already mentioned. This sounds a little like all pronouns, except that relative pronouns relate back to something already mentioned within the sentence. Other pronouns are normally used when nouns have been mentioned within the conversation, but not necessarily that sentence.

In English, we encounter relative pronouns all the time, in the form of "that," "who," "whom," "what," and "which." In French, relative pronouns operate differently. Instead of having many separate words, the same ones are used, with the meanings depending on the construction of the sentence.

Relative pronouns are normally used to introduce another thought or idea into the sentence. Consider the following English sentence: "The boy who lives in the red house is my friend." If you strip this sentence to the bare essentials, it boils down to "the boy is my friend." The "who lives in the red house" is included as explanation, expanding the meaning of the sentence and clarifying (in this case) the subject. This part of the sentence is known as a subordinate clause; the word in the sentence that it modifies ("boy") is known as the antecedent.

The subordinate clause is not necessarily integral to the essential meaning of the sentence; it is a separate idea included for more information. When you encounter such sentences, isolate the phrase that can be stripped out: This is your subordinate clause. To translate it into French, you must use the correct French relative pronoun, which may not be obvious from the construction of the English sentence.

Relative pronouns in English are often omitted, so you may have to do a bit of detective work in breaking down the sentence in order to translate it. English is notorious for dropping the word "that" from the sentence, but the presence of its equivalent is a necessity in French.

There are five distinct relative pronouns in French: *que*, *qui*, *lequel*, *dont*, and *où*. The appropriate English translation is based on how the relative pronoun is used in the subordinate clause, depending on whether it is being used as the subject or the object of the clause. This section outlines the combinations that can occur.

Relative Pronoun as the Subject of the Clause

When the relative pronoun is used as the subject of the clause, the pronoun *qui* is used in French to represent both people and things. An easy way to find out whether the English relative pronoun is the subject of the clause is to see if the clause already has a subject and verb inside it. If it does not, *qui* is used as the subject of the clause, with the verb and the rest of the clause immediately following it. The entire clause is then placed after the noun it modifies in the sentence.

C'est l'homme qui m'a fait un cadeau.	He is the man who gave me a present.
Une femme qui avait été ma voisine m'a rendu visite.	A woman who used to be my neighbor came to visit me.

Relative Pronoun as the Object of the Clause

If the subordinate clause has a subject already, there's a good chance that the relative pronoun is going to appear as the object. In this case, use the pronoun *que*. You can also check the clause by seeing whether the person represented by the pronoun is performing the action or receiving it. If the person represented by the pronoun is performing the action, the pronoun *qui* is the subject of the clause. Receiving the action puts the relative pronoun *que* into the object class:

La jeune fille que j'ai rencontrée	The young lady whom I met
à Paris m'a rendu visite.	in Paris visited me.

Relative Pronouns as the Object of a Preposition

When the relative pronoun is used as the object of a preposition, a number of things can occur. If the relative pronoun is being used to represent a person, *qui* or *lequel/laquelle* is the correct form to place after the preposition, which retains its normal place in the sentence.

C'est le copain avec qui j'ai travaillé.   He is the friend with whom I worked.

Note the pronoun *lequel* is simply a combination of a definite article and the word *quel*. When put together, they mean "which" or "that."

Table 9-8
The Relative Pronoun Lequel

Gender	Singular	Plural
Masculine	*lequel*	*lesquels*
Feminine	*laquelle*	*lesquelles*

The pronoun *lequel/laquelle* is always used when a relative pronoun represents a thing. Here's an example:

C'est la chemise pour laquelle	It's the shirt for which I spent a
j'ai dépensé beaucoup d'argent.	lot of money.

If the pronoun *lequel* is being used after the preposition *à*, the following contractions occur, following the same rules used for the contraction of the preposition *à* and the definite article.

Table 9-9
Contractions of Lequel with À

Gender	Singular	Plural
Masculine	*auquel*	*auxquels*
Feminine	*à laquelle*	*auxquelles*

Consider this example:

Céline est la fille à laquelle
    j'ai donné mon cahier.
	Céline is the girl to whom
	    I gave my notebook.

Dont

The preposition *de* is replaced by *dont* when used with relative pronouns that represent things. This looks very much like the English word "don't," but it is not a negative word. It can mean "that" or "which," depending on how it is used in the sentence; because it replaces all forms, it can also mean "who" or "whom." Check out these examples:

Je n'ai pas vu l'homme
    dont tu parlais.
	I did not see the man you were
	    speaking of.

Donnez-moi le livre dont
    j'ai besoin.
	Give me the book that I need;
	    give me the book I need.

Relative Pronouns Without an Antecedent

Sometimes you may want to use a relative pronoun when there is nothing for it to relate back to. When this occurs, simply insert the demonstrative adjective *ce* before the relative pronoun. It is the English equivalent of "that which," which basically just provides a word for the relative pronoun to relate to so it isn't lost on its own,

Achetez ce dont vous avez besoin.	Buy what you need.
Ce dont il a peur reste mystérieux.	What he fears is a mystery.

The Relative Pronoun Où

Whenever the antecedent involves time, the relative pronoun *où* must be used. It will most often be translated as "when."

Je me rappelle du jour
    où je l'ai rencontré.
	I remember the day when I met him;
	    I remember the day I met him.

ALERT!

The relative pronoun *où* looks a lot like the conjunction *ou*, which means "or." Don't confuse the two. In written French, the accent must appear over the *u* when the word is used as a relative pronoun, because they are two different and distinct words. In spoken French, you cannot hear any difference in the pronunciation.

If the relative pronoun represents a location and is being used with a preposition, the relative pronoun *où* replaces the preposition. In English, this can be translated a number of ways; "in which," "where," "at which," and "from which" are examples. If the antecedent is a place where something else occurs, you'll want to use the pronoun *où*:

J'ai vu le magasin où tu
    as acheté ces livres.
	I saw the store at which you bought
	    these books.

Just because the antecedent is a location, however, doesn't always mean that the relative pronoun *où* will be used. When there is no preposition in front of the relative pronoun, you must use the regular *que* or *qui* form, depending on whether it represents the direct object or indirect object of the subordinate clause.

Reported Speech

Sometimes you want to construct a sentence in which you say what someone else said, but without quoting that person directly. This is known as reported speech; you're simply recounting the events rather than using the words that were actually spoken. In English, we do this using the word "that": "He said that he was going to the store."

In French, speech is reported using the relative pronoun *que*. Simply begin the sentence with something that introduces the phrase, like *il m'a dit* for "he told me," and continue with your sentence.

Il dit que je suis leur copain.	He says that I am their friend.
Elle m'a dit que le film commençait à deux heures.	She told me that the film starts at two o'clock.

Pronouncing Demonstrative and Relative Pronouns

In these sections, you learned about demonstrative and relative pronouns. Listen to the CD for the pronunciation.

TRACK 46

Veux-tu ce livre-ci ou ce livre-là?
C'est l'homme qui m'a fait un cadeau.
Une femme qui avait été ma voisine m'a rendu visite.
La jeune fille que j'ai rencontrée à Paris m'a rendu visite.
C'est la chemise pour laquelle j'ai dépensé beaucoup d'argent.
Céline est la fille à laquelle j'ai donné mon cahier.
Donnez-moi le livre dont j'ai besoin.
Je me rappelle du jour où je l'ai rencontré.

Activité 9

Choose the correct word to complete each sentence.

1. _____ est au téléphone? (qui/que)
2. *Je ne veux pas cette chemise . . . je voudrais* _____.
   (celle-là/celui-ci)
3. *Est-ce que tu vois Jean? Non, je ne* _____ *vois pas.* (en/le)
4. *Vous allez à la bibliothèque? Oui, j'*_____ *vais.* (le/y)
5. *C'est le garçon* _____ *j'ai donné un stylo.* (qui/auquel)
6. *C'est le livre* _____ *vous avez besoin?* (de laquelle/dont)

Chapter 10
Using Adjectives

Adjectives are words that are used to modify nouns, describing them and adding depth and meaning. Words like "blue," "big," "bold," and "brilliant" are all examples. The addition of adjectives to your arsenal of French words will allow you to create much more complex—and interesting—sentences. You learned some basic facts about adjectives in Chapter 3; in this chapter, you will learn more complex constructions.

Basic Adjective Use

The endings of adjectives in French are modified to agree with the accompanying noun in number and in gender, so an adjective used with a masculine noun will have a different ending than one used with a feminine noun, and plural nouns will have a special form, too. Some adjectives follow simple patterns for matching the number or gender, but some follow very irregular patterns.

Gender Agreement of Adjectives

As a basic rule, to make an adjective agree with a feminine noun, you simply add an -e to the end of the masculine form.

Note that when the masculine form of an adjective ends in é, another -e is added to make it agree with a feminine noun. To help you remember this, consider the common English practice of referring to a male about to be wed as a *fiancé* and his future wife as his *fiancée*.

Masculine Adjectives Ending in -e

If the masculine form of the adjective already ends in an -e, nothing is added in the feminine; the word is used with the same ending.

Table 10-1
Masculine Adjectives Ending in -e

Masculine	Feminine	English
moderne	*moderne*	modern, up-to-date
riche	*riche*	rich, wealthy, valuable
tranquille	*tranquille*	quiet, calm, tranquil, peaceful
utile	*utile*	useful, beneficial

Pay attention to these types of adjectives; when the other kinds of adjectives are modified to agree with a feminine noun, it makes it easier to determine which noun the adjective is modifying. When the form doesn't change, it can introduce an element of ambiguity, so be careful.

Ma maison est moderne.	My house is modern.
J'ai acheté un livre utile.	I bought a useful book.

Masculine Adjectives Ending in -er

Most masculine adjectives that end in *-er* change their endings to *-ère* to agree in the feminine. This is also a very common form. The *accent grave* that is added to the end of word to form the feminine ensures that the "r" sound is distinctly pronounced, lingering much longer than in the masculine, so you can actually hear the difference and tell by the sound which gender is intended.

Table 10-2
Masculine Adjectives Ending in -er

Masculine	Feminine	English
dernier	*dernière*	last, latest
étranger	*étrangère*	foreign, unknown, strange

Review the following examples:

Nous avons regardé un film étranger.	We watched a foreign film.
Il a mangé le dernier morceau de gâteau.	He ate the last piece of cake.

Masculine Adjectives Ending in -f

Adjectives that end in *-f* change their endings to *-ve* in the feminine; this is very similar to the English pattern of forming plurals, such as turning "wolf" into "wolves." Remember that in French, this change occurs with the gender, not the number. Watch that you don't accidentally change the *-f* to *-ve* when creating a masculine plural.

Table 10-3
Masculine Adjectives Ending in -f

Masculine	Feminine	English
actif	active	active, busy, energetic
bref	brève	short, brief, concise
neuf	neuve	brand-new

Examples are as follows:

L'enfant est actif.	The child is energetic.
C'est une explication brève.	It's a concise explanation.

Watch out for the word *neuf*—it can mean "nine," but when it is used as an adjective to modify another noun, it means "new." If the form *neuve* is used, that's a dead giveaway that the word definitely isn't meant to indicate "nine."

Masculine Adjectives Ending in -eur

Although there are exceptions, many adjectives that end in *-eur* change their endings to *-euse* to agree in the feminine.

Table 10-4
Masculine Adjectives Ending in -eur

Masculine	Feminine	English
flatteur	flatteuse	flattering, complimentary
menteur	menteuse	lying, false, deceitful

The following examples show the *-eur* ending in action:

Elle est très menteuse.	She lies a lot.
Tu portes des vêtements flatteurs.	You are wearing flattering clothes.

Masculine Adjectives Ending in -teur

Many masculine adjectives that end in *-teur* change their endings to *-trice* to agree in the feminine.

Table 10-5
Masculine Adjectives Ending in -teur

Masculine	Feminine	English
conservateur	*conservatrice*	conservative, preserving
créateur	*créatrice*	creative, inventive

The following examples show these endings in action:

C'est un journaliste conservateur.	He is a conservative journalist.
C'est un processus créateur.	It's a creative process.

-eur Adjectives That Change to –eresse in the Feminine

Some relatively rare adjectives that end in *-eur* take the form *-eresse* in the feminine. While these are not all that common, you should still be able to recognize the feminine form when you come across it, such as the following:

J'ai vu une femme enchanteresse.	I saw an enchanting woman.

Table 10-6
Feminine Adjectives Ending in -eur

Masculine	Feminine	English
enchanteur	*enchanteresse*	enchanting
pécheur	*pécheresse*	sinning

Irregular Adjectives Ending in -eur

The following adjectives that end in *-eur* are slightly irregular in that they simply add an *-e* to form agreement in the feminine. Familiarize yourself with these adjectives, as the feminine forms do not use an "s" anywhere in the construction.

Table 10-7
Masculine Adjectives Ending in -eur That Add an -e

Masculine	Feminine	English
antérieur	*antérieure*	anterior, earlier, previous, former
extérieur	*extérieure*	exterior, external
intérieur	*intérieure*	interior, inner, internal
majeur	*majeure*	major, main, chief, greater
mineur	*mineure*	lesser, minor
postérieur	*postérieure*	posterior, later, behind
supérieur	*supérieure*	superior, upper, higher

Note the following examples:

Un kangourou marche sur ses pattes postérieures.	Kangaroos walk on their back feet.
Ce café est de qualité supérieure.	This coffee is of superior quality.

Masculine Adjectives Ending in -et

Masculine adjectives that end in *-et* become *-ète* to agree in the feminine, also changing the "e" before the "t" to an "e" with an *accent grave*. This results in a more distinct pronunciation of the last syllable, so the final "t" sound is easier to hear when the adjective is used to agree in the feminine.

Table 10-8
Masculine Adjectives Ending in -et

Masculine	Feminine	English
concret	*concrète*	concrete, solid
inquiet	*inquiète*	anxious, restless

Take a look at the following examples:

Il a pris un exemple concret.	He took a concrete example.
Je suis inquiet parce que le	I'm worried because the
chat n'est pas là.	cat is not here.

Masculine Adjectives Ending in a Single Consonant

For some masculine adjectives that end in a single consonant, the final consonant is doubled, and an *-e* added to the end to form the feminine.

Table 10-9
Masculine Adjectives Ending in a Single Consonant

Masculine	Feminine	English
actuel	*actuelle*	present, current
cruel	*cruelle*	cruel, merciless
culturel	*culturelle*	cultural
essentiel	*essentielle*	essential
habituel	*habituelle*	habitual
naturel	*naturelle*	natural
traditionnel	*traditionelle*	traditional
universel	*universelle*	universal
usuel	*usuelle*	usual
pareil	*pareille*	similar, equal
canadien	*canadienne*	Canadian
égyptien	*égyptienne*	Egyptian
européen	*européenne*	European
moyen	*moyenne*	middle
parisien	*parisienne*	Parisian
bon	*bonne*	good, kind, favorable

bas	basse	low, inferior
las	lasse	tired, weary, bored

The following gives examples for several different adjective endings:

L'amour est la langue universelle.	Love is the universal language.
Le français est une langue essentielle.	French is an essential language.
Ma mère est européenne.	My mother is European.
David est canadien.	David is Canadian.
J'étais moyen en arithmétique.	I was average in math.

Masculine Adjectives Ending in -eux

Masculine adjectives that end in *-eux* change their endings to *-euse* to agree in the feminine.

Table 10-10
Masculine Adjectives Ending in -eux

Masculine	Feminine	English
amoureux	*amoureuse*	loving, enamored, in love
douloureux	*douloureuse*	painful, hurting, sore
ennuyeux	*ennuyeuse*	boring, tedious, dull, tiresome
jaloux	*jalouse*	jealous, envious

Consider the following examples:

Elle est jalouse.	She is jealous.
Pierre est un homme amoureux.	Pierre is a man in love.

Masculine Adjectives Ending in -gu

When the masculine form of an adjective ends in *-gu*, an *-ë* is added to the end, to form *-guë*.

Table 10-11
Masculine Adjectives Ending in -gu

Masculine	Feminine	English
aigu	aiguë	pointed, sharp, keen, acute
ambigu	ambiguë	ambiguous

The following examples demonstrate this ending:

Elle a une voix aiguë.	She has a sharp voice.
Elle a posé une question ambiguë.	She asked an ambiguous question.

Irregular Adjectives

Some adjectives have completely irregular feminine forms. Although the feminine forms of these adjectives will have to be memorized individually, they tend to be fairly commonly used.

Table 10-12
Irregular Adjectives

Masculine	Feminine	English
blanc	blanche	white, clean, blank
doux	douce	sweet, gentle, calm, fresh
faux	fausse	false, wrong, untrue, fake, forged
favori	favorite	favorite
long	longue	long, slow, tedious, drawn out
public	publique	public
roux	rousse	reddish, red-haired
sec	sèche	dry, arid, plain

Take a look at the following examples:

Elle a porté une blouse blanche.	She wore a white blouse.
J'ai lavé la blouse avec du savon doux.	I washed the blouse with some mild soap.

Plural Agreement of Adjectives

The majority of adjectives in French simply add an "s" at the end to agree with a plural noun, whether masculine or feminine. This is very important in written French, but there is not usually too much of a difference in pronunciation in the plural forms of adjectives. If the adjective is being used to agree with a masculine noun, simply add the "s" to the end of the masculine form. If it is being used to agree with a feminine noun, add the feminine ending, and then add the "s."

Table 10-13
Plural Agreement of Adjectives

Masculine Singular	Masculine Plural	Feminine Singular	Feminine Plural	English
bleu	bleus	bleue	bleues	blue
content	contents	contente	contentes	content, satisfied, pleased, glad
large	larges	large	larges	broad, wide large, extensive
petit	petits	petite	petites	little, small

If a masculine adjective already ends in "s" or "x," there is no change in the masculine plural form. The exact same word is used, whether singular or plural. Because the feminine form will have an "e" at the end, it takes an "s" in the plural, following the regular rules.

Table 10-14
Plural Agreement of Adjectives That End in -s or -x

Masculine Singular	Masculine Plural	Feminine Singular	Feminine Plural	English
dangereux	dangereux	dangereuse	dangereuses	dangerous
frais	frais	fraîche	fraîches	cool, fresh, new

gros	*gros*	*grosse*	*grosses*	big, large, bulky
heureux	*heureux*	*heureuse*	*heureuses*	happy, blissful
malheureux	*malheureux*	*malheureuse*	*malheureuses*	unhappy, unlucky, unfortunate

Check out the following examples:

Je ne pense pas que les avions soient dangereux.
I don't think that planes are dangerous.

Les enfants étaient heureux.
The children were happy.

ALERT!

Remember that if an adjective is used with two feminine nouns, it will take a feminine plural form. If it is used to modify both a masculine and a feminine noun, however, it will take the masculine plural form, as it would if it modified two masculine nouns.

Like conjugating verbs with *ils* and *elles*, the masculine gender kind of trumps the feminine when it comes to agreement of adjectives in the plural. If an adjective appears with two nouns, it must be used in the plural, because it is referring to the two of them together. If both nouns are feminine, the adjective will take the feminine plural form, because it is agreeing with the two nouns collectively. If one is masculine and one is feminine, the masculine plural form is used by convention, as shown in the following example:

Sara et Michel sont amusants.
Sara and Michael are amusing.

Marie et Louise sont amusantes.
Marie and Louise are amusing.

Here's another way of looking at this: An adjective will be used in the feminine plural only when it is used with a plural feminine noun or two singular feminine nouns; but if a masculine noun is present, a masculine plural would be the correct choice, because it breaks that rule.

Pronunciation of Adjectives

In these sections, you learned about adjectives. Listen to the CD for the pronunciation of some of the expressions you learned.

TRACK 47

J'ai acheté un livre utile.
Nous avons regardé un film étranger.
L'enfant est actif.
Tu portes des vêtements flatteurs.
Ce café est de qualité supérieure.
Ma mère est européenne.
Les enfants étaient heureux.
Marie et Louise sont amusantes.

Position of Adjectives

For the most part, place adjectives directly after the nouns they modify. Keep in mind that when you hear adjectives in spoken French, they are usually meant to modify the nouns that precede them. When two adjectives modify a noun, they are joined with a conjunction, such as *et*.

J'ai parlé avec un homme gros et heureux.	I spoke with a large and happy man.
Pierre a un chien dangereux et méchant.	Pierre has a dangerous and bad dog.

A few French adjectives usually appear before the noun, however. The following adjectives, when used to modify a noun, are placed directly before it; if the noun is being used with an article, the adjective is inserted between the article and the noun.

Table 10-15
Adjectives Placed Before Nouns

Masculine Singular	Feminine Singular	Masculine Plural	Feminine Plural	English
beau (bel)	belle	beaux	belles	beautiful, fine, handsome, pretty
court	courte	courts	courtes	short, brief, concise
fou (fol)	folle	fous	folles	crazy
gros	grosse	gros	grosses	big, large, bulky
jeune	jeune	jeunes	jeunes	young, youthful, early
joli	jolie	jolis	jolies	pretty, fine pleasing, neat,
meilleur	meilleure	meilleurs	meilleures	better, preferable
nouveau (nouvel)	nouvelle	nouveaux	nouvelles	new, recent, novel
petit	petite	petits	petites	little, small, short, very young
vieux (vieil)	vieille	vieux	vieilles	old, ancient, aged

Note that some of these adjectives have an alternate masculine form that's used in front of singular masculine nouns that begin with a vowel.

C'était un bel homme.	He was a handsome man.
Mon voisin est un vieil homme.	My neighbor is an old man.

Also note that with the following adjectives, *liaison* is required if the noun following begins with a vowel: *beaux, nouveaux, vieux*.

If two adjectives are used together and are used before the noun, no conjunction is used, so don't insert an *et*. A conjunction is used only when the adjective is in its normal position, immediately following the noun.

Elle a un nouveau petit bébé.   She has a new little baby.

Some adjectives can actually carry different connotations, depending on their position in the sentence. With some adjectives, if they appear before the noun, a figurative meaning is intended and should not be taken literally. When placed after the noun, however, the adjective is meant to be interpreted literally. Placement of an adjective after a noun often lends the statement a more serious tone. Table 10-18 contains many of these idiomatic adjectival constructions.

Table 10-16
Adjectives and Their Meanings

adjective: *ancien / ancienne*	
before the noun	*Un ancien élève travaillera avec moi.*
	A former student will be working with me.
after the noun	*C'est un meuble ancien.*
	It's an antique piece of furniture.
adjective: *bon / bonne*	
before the noun	*J'ai vu un bon film.*
	I saw a good film.
after the noun	*Jacques est un homme bon.*
	Jacques is a kind man.
adjective: *brave*	
before the noun	*C'est un brave homme.*
	He is a decent man.
after the noun	*Ce fut un soldat brave.*
	He was a courageous soldier.
adjective: *certain*	
before the noun	*J'ai une certaine idée.*
	I have a vague idea.
after the noun	*Il a fait des progrès certains.*
	He made definite progress.

adjective: *dernier / dernière*

before the noun	*Demain, il passera le dernier examen.* Tomorrow, he will take the last exam.
after the noun	*Monsieur Allard est venu ici la semaine dernière.* Mr. Allard came here last week.

adjective: *grand / grande*

before the noun	*Edith Piaf était une grande chanteuse.* Edith Piaf was a great singer.
after the noun	*Ce n'est pas une femme grande.* She is not a tall woman.

adjective: *nouveau*

before the noun	*Ce sont des nouveaux riches.* They are recently wealthy.
after the noun	*Le chimiste a trouvé un médicament nouveau.* The chemist found a new medicine.

adjective: *pauvre*

before the noun	*Je connais beaucoup de pauvres gens.* I have known many unfortunate people.
after the noun	*C'est un village très pauvre.* It's a very poor village.

adjective: *prochain / prochaine*

before the noun	*C'est le prochain arrêt.* It's the next stop.
after the noun	*Je ferai mes devoirs à une occasion prochaine.* I'll do my homework some time.

adjective: *propre*

before the noun	*J'aime dormir dans mon propre lit.* I like to sleep in my own bed.
after the noun	*J'aime avoir une chambre propre.* I like to have a clean room.

adjective: *sale*

before the noun	*Il fait un sale temps.* The weather is nasty.
after the noun	*Je dois laver ces vêtements sales.* I have to wash these dirty clothes.

Normally, an adjective is placed after a noun. There are some adjectives that are used before, and some that can be used in either position. These adjectives' positions are not interchangeable. When used before a noun, these adjectives have a figurative meaning, not to be interpreted literally. If the adjective appears after the noun, it should be interpreted literally.

Comparative Sentences

To compare two things or persons in French, use the following construction:

plus (more)
moins (less) + adjective + *que*
aussi (as)

Il est plus gros que toi.	He is fatter than you.
Le film est moins intéressant que le livre.	The film is less interesting than the book.
Vous êtes aussi intelligent que lui.	You are as intelligent as he is.

The adjective always agrees with the noun or pronoun. Remember to use disjunctive pronouns after *que*. To say "better than," note that *bon* has a special form: *meilleur*.

Pronunciation of Adjectives and Comparative Sentences

In these sections, you learned about position of adjectives and comparative sentences. Listen to the CD for the pronunciation of some of the expressions you learned.

TRACK 48

J'ai parlé avec un homme grand et beau.
Mon voisin est un vieil homme.

Il a pris une décision folle et absurde.
Edith Piaf était une grande chanteuse.
Le chimiste a trouvé un médicament nouveau.
C'est le prochain arrêt.
Je dois laver ces vêtements sales.
Le film est moins intéressant que le livre.

Possessive Adjectives

Possessive adjectives, such as "my" or "your" in English, are used to modify the word that follows, indicating possession. Here are examples of possessive adjectives in use:

C'est mon chien devant la maison.   That's my dog in front of my house.
C'est ton cahier?   Is this your notebook?

Possessive adjectives agree with the thing possessed. The following possessive adjectives correspond to *je*, *tu*, and *il* or *elle* respectively. They are used when you wish to indicate that only one person possesses the item in question.

Table 10-17
Possessive Adjectives—One Person

Person	English	Masculine Singular	Feminine Singular	Plural
1st Person	my	*mon*	*ma*	*mes*
2nd Person	your	*ton*	*ta*	*tes*
3rd Person	his or hers	*son*	*sa*	*ses*

The forms that correspond to *nous*, *vous*, and *ils* or *elles* are formed slightly differently. In the singular, the word is the same, whether used with a feminine or masculine noun.

Table 10-18
Possessive Adjectives—More Than One Person

Person	English	Singular	Plural
1st Person	our	*notre*	*nos*
2nd Person	your	*votre*	*vos*
3rd Person	their	*leur*	*leurs*

The following samples show some possessive adjectives in action.

J'ai besoin de votre aide.   I need your help.
Ils habitent dans ma ville.   They live in my city.

Demonstrative Adjectives

Demonstrative adjectives (in English, the words "this," "that," "these," and "those") are used with nouns to indicate specific items. They are known as demonstrative adjectives because they clearly indicate, or demonstrate, exactly what is meant.

Table 10-19
French Demonstrative Adjectives

Gender	Singular	Plural
Masculine	*ce (cet)*	*ces*
Feminine	*cette*	*ces*

In the singular, the meaning will be "this" or "that," depending on the context of the individual sentence. The plural form, *ces*, represents "these" or "those."

When the singular demonstrative adjective *ce* is used in front of a masculine noun that begins with a vowel, no vowel is dropped, and no contraction is formed. Instead, a "t" is added to the end of the adjective, and *cet* is used to separate the vowels. As a result, the linguistic challenge of pronouncing two vowels is addressed with *liaison*, with the final "t" sound running into the beginning of the noun.

In English, the correct choice between "this" and "that" is contextual. The meaning is determined from the circumstances in which the words are used. The French demonstrative adjective covers both meanings. However, when referring to two objects in relation to each other, a slightly different construction is used. In English, we can say "this book or that book" in a single sentence. Because the French adjective *ce* can have either meaning, some modification is needed to show which is which. With the noun you wish to indicate as "this," just put *ci* after the noun, and put a hyphen between them. To indicate "that," use *là* after the noun instead, also with a hyphen:

J'ai acheté ce livre-ci, mais j'ai   I bought this book, but I received
reçu ce livre-là de ma mère.   that book from my mother.

Pronunciation of Possessive Adjectives

In these sections, you learned about possessive and demonstrative adjectives. Listen to the CD for the pronunciation of the expressions..

TRACK 49

C'est ton cahier?
J'ai besoin de votre aide.
Est-ce que tu étudies pour nos examens?
J'ai acheté ce livre-ci, mais j'ai reçu ce livre-là de ma mère.

Activité 10

TRACK 50

Listen to the CD and complete the sentences with the adjective you hear.

1. *C'est un film _____.*
2. *Le café est de qualité _____.*
3. *C'est un _____ homme.*
4. *Il est complètement _____!*
5. *Mon père est _____.*
6. *Je n'ai pas aimé ce livre, qui était _____.*
7. *Qu'est-ce que ce chien est _____!*
8. *Est-ce que les fruits sont _____?*

Chapter 11

Understanding Adverbs

While adjectives are used to modify nouns, adverbs can be used to modify other kinds of words, including verbs, adjectives, or even other adverbs. They are used to describe the manner in which something occurs, or, in other words, how it happens.

Use of Adverbs

Luckily, you get a bit of a break when learning about adverbs, because you don't have to worry about agreement. If you think of adjectives as modifying and describing the physical aspects of a thing, adverbs then describe the style or fashion about how something is done. Adverbs set the circumstances of the sentence.

Forming Adverbs

Most French adverbs are formed by adding -*ment* to the end of the feminine form of an adjective, much the same way as English adds "-ly" to the end of adjectives to turn them into adverbs. Just as the word soft turns into softly, *douce* transforms into *doucement*. Not all adverbs use this ending, however, so be careful not to confuse them with other kinds of words. Also, there are some other ways to form French adverbs; some words make special changes to assist in pronunciation, while others are completely irregular.

Here are the basic rules for forming adverbs:

- Add -*ment* to the feminine form of the adjective: *douce / doucement*
- For adverbs formed from adjectives ending in -*i*, add –*ment* to the masculine form of the adjective: *vrai / vraiment*
- For adverbs formed from adjectives ending in -*u*, add the ending to the masculine form of the adjective: *absolu / absolument*
- For adjectives ending in -*ant*, change to –*amment*: *brillant / brillamment*
- For adjectives ending in -*ent*, change to –*emment*: *patient / patiemment*

Table 11-1
Forming Adverbs from Adjectives

Adjective	Adverb	English
vrai	*vraiment*	truly, in truth, indeed, really
absolu	*absolument*	absolutely

évident	*évidemment*	evidently
fréquent	*fréquemment*	frequently
patient	*patiemment*	patiently

There are also some adverbs that have irregular stems; some change only slightly from the adjectival form, but others change completely.

Table 11-2
Forming Adverbs with Irregular Stems from Adjectives

Adjective	Adverb	English
bref	*brièvement*	briefly, succinctly, in short
bon	*bien*	well, rightly, finely, much, very, entirely
gentil	*gentiment*	prettily, nicely
mauvais	*mal*	wrong, badly
meilleur	*mieux*	better, correctly, more comfortably
petit	*peu*	little, not much, few, not very, not many

In this section, you learned about forming adverbs from adjectives. Listen to the CD for the pronunciation of some of the expressions you learned.

TRACK 51

vrai / vraiment
absolu / absolument
evident / évidemment
fréquent / fréquemment
patient / patiemment
bref / brièvement
bon / bien
gentil / gentiment
mauvais / mal
meilleur / mieux
petit / peu

Memorizing Adverbs

Adverbs in French can be broken out into a number of categories; this may make it easier for you to remember different kinds of adjectives. In addition, if you find yourself forgetting some of the adverbs in the categories, refer back to this section to review these adverbs with similar uses.

Table 11-3
Adverbs Used to Describe Manner

Adverb	English
aisément	easily, readily, freely, comfortably
bien	well, much, very
constamment	steadily, continually, constantly
convenablement	suitably, becomingly, decently
ensemble	together, at the same time
mal	wrong, badly

Table 11-4
Adverbs Used to Describe Time

Adverb	English
aujourd'hui	today
demain	tomorrow
hier	yesterday
longtemps	long, a long while
maintenant	now, at this moment, at present
tard	late
tôt	soon, quickly, early
vite	quick, quickly, fast, rapidly

Table 11-5
Adverbs Used to Describe Frequency

Adverb	English
déjà	already, before, previously
enfin	at last, finally, after all, lastly, in short
jamais	ever; with *ne*, never
quelquefois	sometimes
souvent	often, frequently
toujours	always, ever, forever

Table 11-6
Adverbs Used to Describe Place

Adverb	English
dehors	out, outside, out of doors
derrière	behind, after
devant	in front, ahead
ici	here, in this place, now, this time
là	there
loin	far, distant, at a distance
où	where
près	by, near

Table 11-7
Adverbs Used to Describe an Amount or Quantity

Adverb	English
aussi	also, as, likewise, too, besides
assez	enough
beaucoup	much, many
moins	less, fewer
peu	few, little, not much
tout	all, whole, every

très	very, most, very much
trop	too, too much, too many

FACT

Many of the adverbs you'll encounter can also be used in other ways, such as prepositions. For example, the adverb *aussi* can also be used as a conjunction to join parts of a sentence together; when used in this fashion, the meanings of *aussi* can include "accordingly," "and so," "therefore," and "consequently."

Table 11-8
Other Handy Adverbs to Know

Adverb	English
naturellement	naturally
probablement	probably
peut-être	perhaps, maybe

In this section, you learned about memorizing adverbs. Listen to the CD for the pronunciation of some of the expressions you learned.

TRACK 52

aisément	*vite*	*où*
bien	*déjà*	*près*
constamment	*enfin*	*aussi*
convenablement	*jamais*	*assez*
ensemble	*quelquefois*	*beaucoup*
mal	*souvent*	*moins*
aujourd'hui	*toujours*	*peu*
demain	*dehors*	*tout*
hier	*derrière*	*très*
longtemps	*devant*	*trop*
maintenant	*ici*	*naturellement*
tard	*là*	*probablement*
tôt	*loin*	*peut-être*

Position and Use of Adverbs

In French, the natural position of an adverb is immediately following the verb. Remember that adverbs can't modify a noun, so they must modify something else in the sentence. When the adverb requires a verb to make any sense, the adverb must be placed immediately after the verb. This is especially noticeable with expressions of quantity.

TRACK 53

Il attend patiemment.	He is waiting patiently.
J'ai aussi un chat.	I also have a cat.
Nous avons assez mangé.	We ate enough.

With expressions of frequency, manner, place, and time, you can put the adverb at the beginning, before the subject, or at the absolute end of the sentence. Never, however, place an adverb between the subject and the verb. Watch carefully, because this placement is very common in English. Avoid it at all costs—the sentence won't make sense.

Adverbial Phrases

The following adverbial phrases can be used in sentences to convey a specific meaning. In a sense, these are idiomatic expressions, so don't try to translate them literally, even though some of the literal approximations come close.

TRACK 54

Table 11-9
Adverbial Phrases

French	English
en attendant	in the meantime
à peu près	nearly, about
à propos	by the way, at the right time
en même temps	at the same time
quelque part	somewhere

par hasard	by accident, by chance
bien sûr	of course
tout de suite	immediately
sans doute	probably
à moitié	half

Activité 11

Listen to each of the following adjectives and write the corresponding adverb in the space provided.

TRACK 55

1. *vrai* _____
2. *évident* _____
3. *fréquent* _____
4. *bref* _____
5. *bon* _____
6. *gentil* _____
7. *mauvais* _____
8. *meilleur* _____

Chapter 12

Forming Past-Tense Verbs

Most of what you have seen prior to this chapter has been limited to the present tense, referring to events that occur *now*. In this chapter, you find out how to use verbs in the past tense. The past tense is very different from the present-tense conjugated verb forms, but with a little practice and patience, you'll learn the concepts with ease.

Past-Tense Constructions

The *passé composé* is used to indicate a specific event that was begun in the past and is now completely finished.

Il a fait ses devoirs.	He did his homework.
Je suis allé au magasin.	I went to the store

Sometimes, you want to refer to past events that don't have a concrete beginning or ending or something that was ongoing over a period of time. This tense is often known as the *imparfait*, or the "imperfect" tense, because the event can't be isolated at any one particular point in time. In this book, we use the term "imperfect" to describe this tense.

À l'époque, je travaillais à la bibliothèque.	At that time, I worked at the library.
L'été, j'aimais faire des promenades.	In the summer, I liked to take walks.

The *plus-que-parfait* is used to describe an event that occurred before another past event. It is often used in conjunction with the *passé composé* to indicate events that took place before, but the construction can appear alone. When it does, a more recent past event is implied. The *plus-que-parfait* must have another point of reference in the past to give it meaning.

The distant past tense works as follows:

J'avais quitté le restaurant.	I had left the restaurant.

To keep these tenses straight in your mind, think of the old story of the son who received a letter from his mother; he opened and read it, and at the end of the letter, it said, "I tried to send you some money with this letter, but I had already sealed the envelope."

This is completely absurd, of course, because of the events described by the tenses. "I had already sealed the envelope" is a *plus-que-parfait* construction, indicating that it occurred before the other event—the mother's attempt at sending the money with the letter. If she had already sealed the letter, though, how did she write that line?

The Simple Past Tense: Le Passé Composé

French uses auxiliary verbs (either *avoir* or *être*) to form the *passé composé* (or simple past). Most verbs use *avoir* to form the past tense, but a few use *être*. The present tense conjugation of *avoir* or *être* is then followed by the past participle (in English, the "-ed" form of the verb). Note that the *passé composé* in French covers a variety of meanings in English, as seen in the following example.

J'ai parlé.   I spoke./ I have spoken. / I did speak.

> The *passé composé* is always a compound tense, meaning that it's made up of two elements: the conjugated form of *avoir* or *être* and the past participle, which is formed by dropping the infinitive endings (see the following sections for more on past participles).

Passé Composé *with* Avoir

The formation of the past participle for most regular verbs tends to follow a predictable pattern, depending on the ending of the verb.

-er Verbs

To form the past participle, simply drop the *-er* ending and replace it with *é*. Table 12-1 shows the verb *parler* conjugated in the *passé composé*.

Table 12-1
Parler Conjugated in the Passé Composé

Person	Singular	Plural
1st Person	*j'ai parlé*	*nous avons parlé*

2nd Person	*tu as parlé*	*vous avez parlé*	
3rd Person	*il/elle a parlé*	*ils/elles ont parlé*	

Take a look at the following examples:

Les Dumont ont acheté une maison.	The Dumont family bought a house.
Je n'ai pas téléphoné.	I did not call.
Ils n'ont pas changé de chaîne.	They did not change the channel.

FACT

You'll recall that some *-er* verbs change stems in present-tense conjugations. When creating the past participle, however, the regular *-er* verb rules for the formation of the past participle apply. Don't change the stem; simply add *é* after dropping the *-er*.

-re Verbs

To form the past participle, simply drop the *-re* ending and replace it with *u*.

Table 12-2
Perdre Conjugated in the Passé Composé

Person	Singular	Plural
1st Person	*j'ai perdu*	*nous avons perdu*
2nd Person	*tu as perdu*	*vous avez perdu*
3rd Person	*il/elle a perdu*	*ils/elles ont perdu*

Here are some examples:

Nous n'avons pas répondu au téléphone.	We didn't answer the telephone.
Avez-vous perdu le livre?	Have you lost the book??

-ir Verbs

To form the past participle with most *-ir* verbs, simply drop the *r* from the end, so the verb ends in an *i*.

Table 12-3
Finir Conjugated in the Passé Composé

Person	Singular	Plural
1st Person	*j'ai fini*	*nous avons fini*
2nd Person	*tu as fini*	*vous avez fini*
3rd Person	*il/elle a fini*	*ils/elles ont fini*

Take a look at this example:

Il n'a rien choisi.	He did not choose anything.

Irregular Past Participles

Just as there are a number of verbs with irregular conjugations in the present indicative tense, there are a number of exceptions with the past participle, too. The verbs that use these irregular past participles don't have any easy rules, so they will have to be memorized.

Because many of the past participles of some verbs use the same ending, it may be helpful to memorize these verbs in groups.

Table 12-4
Irregular Verbs

Verb	Past Participle
avoir	*eu*
être	*été*
faire	*fait*

The following examples show irregular verbs in sentences:

J'ai eu de la chance.	I had some luck.
Il a eu un accident.	He had an accident.

Elle a été renvoyée.	She was fired.
Ils ont été surpris de ma réponse.	They were surprised by my response.
Elles ont fait leurs devoirs.	They did their homework.

Table 12-5
Past Participles Ending in -ert

Verb	Past Participle	English
découvrir	*découvert*	discovered, did discover, have discovered
offrir	*offert*	offered, did offer, have offered
ouvrir	*ouvert*	opened, did open, have opened
souffrir	*souffert*	suffered, did suffer, have suffered

Consider the following examples:

Nous avons souffert.	We have suffered.
J'ai offert de l'argent.	I offered some money.

Table 12-6
Past Participles Ending in -i

Verb	Past Participle	English
sourire	*souri*	smiled, did smile, have smiled
suivre	*suivi*	followed, did follow, have followed

Note the following examples:

Il a suivi le guide.	He followed the guide.
J'ai souri.	I smiled.

Table 12-7
Past Participles Ending in -is

Verb	Past Participle	English
apprendre	*appris*	learned, did learn, have learned

comprendre	*compris*	understood, did understand, have understood
mettre	*mis*	placed, did place, have placed
prendre	*pris*	took, did take, have taken

The following examples demonstrate this ending:

Il a appris le français.	He learned French.
Nous avons pris les clefs.	We took the keys.

Table 12-8
Past Participles Ending in -it

Verb	Past Participle	English
conduire	*conduit*	drove, did drive, have driven
dire	*dit*	said, did say, have said
écrire	*écrit*	wrote, did write, have written

Take a look at the following examples:

J'ai dit «Oui.»	I said, "Yes."
Il a conduit un camion.	He drove a truck.

Table 12-9
Past Participles Ending in -u

Verb	Past Participle	English
boire	*bu*	drank, did drink, have drunk
connaître	*connu*	knew, did know
devoir	*dû*	had to, needed to
falloir	*fallu*	was necessary
lire	*lu*	read, did read, have read
plaire	*plu*	pleased, did please, have pleased
pleuvoir	*plu*	rained, did rain, has rained
pouvoir	*pu*	was able to, could

recevoir	*reçu*	received, did receive, have received
savoir	*su*	knew, did know, have known
voir	*vu*	saw, did see, have seen
vouloir	*voulu*	wanted, did want, have wanted

Here are some examples:

J'ai bu du lait.	I drank some milk.
As-tu lu le livre?	Did you read the book?
Avez-vous pu aller au cinéma?	Were you able to go to the movies?
Je connais son père.	I know his father.
Il connaît ce musée.	He knows this museum.

The verb *savoir* is used to refer to knowing how to do something.

Je sais jouer de la guitare.	I know how to play the guitar.

The Negative and the Passé Composé

In general, place the negatives *ne . . . pas (jamais, guère,* etc.) around the auxiliary verb to form the negative:

Je n'ai pas vu ce film I didn't see this film.

For *personne,* place the word after the participle:

Je n'ai vu personne.	I saw no one.

Ne . . . ni . . . ni . . . are placed before the words modified.

Je n'ai vu ni le film ni la pièce.	I saw neither the film nor the play.

Object Pronouns and Past Participles

Note that when a direct object pronoun appears before the conjugated verb, the past participle conjugated with *avoir* must agree with the object, both in gender and in number. It is not merely the presence of an object pronoun that makes the past participle agree; it is the fact that the pronoun appears before the verb that kicks the past participle into gear. When this happens, an *e* is added to the end of the past participle to make it agree in the feminine, and an *s* is added to make it agree in the plural, much like the formation of adjectives.

Avez-vous vu la voiture?	Have you seen the car?
Oui, nous l'avons vue.	Yes, we have seen it.
Est-ce que vous avez regardé les films?	Have you watched the films?
Oui, nous les avons regardés.	Yes, we have watched them.

In these sections, you learned about forming the *passé composé* with *avoir*. Listen to the CD for the pronunciation of the expressions you learned.

TRACK 56

Les Dumont ont acheté une maison.
Je n'ai pas téléphoné.
Ils n'ont pas changé de chaîne.
Nous n'avons pas répondu au téléphone.
Elle a écouté de la musique.
Avez-vous perdu le livre?
Elles ont fini l'examen.
Elles ont fait leurs devoirs.
Nous avons souffert.
Il a suivi le guide.
Il a appris le français.
Il a conduit un camion.
Avez-vous pu aller au cinéma?

Verbs That Use Être as the Auxiliary

Instead of using *avoir*, some verbs use *être* instead as the auxiliary verb to conjugate in tenses other than the present. These are often verbs of motion, as you will see.

Here is a list of common verbs that use *être*. Many of the verbs follow regular rules for the formation of the past participle, but note that there are some exceptions, such as *mourir* and *naître*. The more you practice French, the more adept you will become at using these verbs.

Table 12-10
Verbs That Use Être as the Auxiliary Verb

Verb	Past Participle	English
aller	*allé*	went, did go, have gone
arriver	*arrivé*	arrived, did arrive, have arrived
descendre	*descendu*	descended, did descend, went downstairs
entrer	*entré*	entered, did enter, have entered, came in
partir	*parti*	left, did leave, has left
rester	*resté*	stayed, did stay, have stayed
retourner	*retourné*	returned, did return, has returned
sortir	*sorti*	went out, did go out, has gone out
tomber	*tombé*	fell, did fall, has fallen
venir	*venu*	came, did come, has come

Agreement of the Past Participle with *Être*

The past participle, when used with the verb *être*, agrees with the subject of the sentence, both in gender and in number.

If you get into the habit now, these endings will come naturally with some practice. Save yourself some time later and learn the proper endings from the beginning. Some people benefit from visualizing the past participle written out on an imaginary blackboard with the proper ending attached. Try it with spoken French and see if it helps you!

Fortunately, agreement of past participles conjugated with *être* is fairly straightforward. If the subject is feminine, simply add an *e* to the end of the past participle. If the subject is plural, add an *s*. If the subject is both feminine and plural, add *-es* to the end of the word.

Here are some examples of sentences using *être* as the auxiliary verb in the past tense. Listen to the CD for their pronunciation:

TRACK 57

Nous ne sommes pas allés à la plage.	We did not go to the beach.
Ils sont rentrés hier.	They came back yesterday.
Nous sommes partis à six heures.	We left at six o'clock.
Je suis passé chez Henri.	I stopped by at Henri's.
Êtes-vous tombé?	Did you fall?
Elles sont allées à la piscine.	They went to the pool.

The following verbs are derived from shorter French verbs; many of them are modified with a prefix and use the same past participle as the shorter verb. Study the following table and note how prefixes can change the meaning of verbs. That way, if you come across new verbs that have prefixes, you will be more likely to be able to decipher the meaning without having to reach for your dictionary. In the beginning, though, remember that it's a good exercise to guess first, and then check to see whether you're right.

Table 12-11
Derivative Verbs

Verb	Past Participle	English
devenir	*devenu*	became, did become, have become
parvenir	*parvenu*	attained, did attain, has succeeded
redescendre	*redescendu*	came down again, has come down again
remonter	*remonté*	went up again, did go up again
renaître	*rené*	was born again, has been revived
rentrer	*rentré*	returned, came in again, did return
repartir	*reparti*	went out again, has gone away again
ressortir	*ressorti*	came out again, has come out again
retomber	*retombé*	fell again, has fallen again
revenir	*revenu*	came back, did come back, has returned

You may have noticed that some of the verbs that use *être* as the auxiliary are the complete opposite to other verbs that also use *être* as the auxiliary. You can use this to your advantage in memorizing which verbs use *être* as the auxiliary verb; remember them in pairs, and each will be easier to recall.

- *arriver* and *partir*: The first means "to arrive"; the second means "to leave."
- *entrer* and *sortir*: The first means "to enter"; the second means "to go out."
- *monter* and *descendre*: The first means "to go up"; the second means "to go down."
- *naître* and *mourir*: The first means "to be born"; the second means "to die."

Using Infinitives with Après

The preposition *après*, meaning "after," is used in French in a construction known as the past infinitive. To form the past infinitive in French, simply use the infinitive of *avoir* or *être* and follow it with the French past participle.

Après avoir écouté son message,	After having listening to her message,
j'ai téléphoné à ma mère.	I called my mother.
Après être rentré, je me suis couché.	After having come back home,
	I went to bed.

When the auxiliary verb is *être*, even though it may appear before the subject of the sentence, the past participle still must agree in gender and number with the subject:

Après être rentrées, elles se sont	After having come back home, they
couchées.	went to bed.

Uses of the Passé Composé

Like the present indicative tense in French, the *passé composé* can carry a number of meanings: *J'ai parlé* means "I spoke," "I did speak," and "I have spoken."

ALERT!

Remember that English and French don't always treat verbs the same when referring to events in the past tense. When translating sentences using the *passé composé*, be careful not to translate the verbs literally. Recognize that a past construction is being used, and then choose the appropriate auxiliary verb to use with the past participle.

The *passé composé* is used to indicate specific events that occurred in the past. In order to be referred to with the *passé composé*, the event must have occurred in the past, usually within a specified time period. If the time period is indefinite, the *imparfait* is probably the better choice.

You will often see the *passé composé* used in the following cases. It can also be used in conjunction with the other past tenses in French to establish the chronology of events, telling you exactly when each event happened in relation to the others.

Simple Completed Actions

The *passé composé* is used to describe an event that occurred at some concrete point in the past, whose action is now completed. The *passé composé* is also used when a physical or emotional state changes as a result of an event that can be fixed in a specific point.

Je suis né à l'hôpital.	I was born in the hospital.
Il a gagné le jeu.	He won the game.

Actions with a Specified Time Period

When referring to a specific time in the past, the *passé composé* is used.

Le film a commencé à six heures.	The film started at six o'clock.
J'ai lu le livre pendant une heure.	I read the book for an hour.

A Series of Actions

You use the *passé composé* when referring to a series of events, each of which occurred in the past:

> *Il a écrit une lettre, a mis la lettre*   He wrote a letter, put the letter in an
>   *dans une enveloppe, et puis*   envelope, and then mailed it.
>   *a mis la lettre à la poste.*

In these sections, you learned about uses of the *passé composé.* Listen to the CD for the pronunciation of the expressions you learned.

TRACK 58

> *Je suis né à l'hôpital.*
> *Il a gagné le jeu.*
> *Le film a commencé à six heures.*
> *J'ai lu le livre pendant une heure.*
> *Il a écrit une lettre, a mis la lettre dans une enveloppe, et puis a mis la lettre*
>   *à la poste.*

The Imperfect Past Tense: L'Imparfait

The imperfect past, or *imparfait*, is less definite than the *passé composé.* It refers to events without a specific duration. It is relatively easy to understand and remember because it follows very simple formation rules. The *imparfait* is an important tense in French and can be used in a variety of ways, including the formation of other tenses.

Uses of the Imparfait

One of the most common uses of the *imparfait* in French is to indicate actions or events that occurred habitually in the past. Because one cannot place these events within a specific time period, the *imparfait* is used to place these actions or events in an indefinite period. English equivalents include using words like "would" or "used to" to indicate the events that occurred over time in the past. Here are some examples:

> *J'écoutais la radio chaque matin.*   I used to listen to the radio every
>   morning.
> *Nous mangions à la maison.*   We used to eat at the house.

You will often encounter the *imparfait* in written French to set tone or setting, describing the general conditions that existed, as follows:

Quand j'étais jeune, j'étais heureux.	When I was young, I was happy.
Il pleuvait.	It was raining.
Il n'aimait pas les cerises.	He didn't like cherries.

You can also use the *imparfait* to describe the existence of past states or conditions:

Je voulais y aller.	I wanted to go.
J'avais peur.	I used to be afraid.

The following verbs, which are used to describe circumstances or states, are often seen in the *imparfait*.

avoir	to have, to hold
désirer	to want, to desire
être	to be
préférer	to prefer
penser	to think
détester	to hate
espérer	to hope, to wish
trouver	to find
songer	to dream, to imagine
pouvoir	to be able
savoir	to know
vouloir	to want

The *imparfait* is also used with *depuis* to indicate something that occurred for a period of time before another event occurred:

J'attendais depuis deux heures	I had been waiting for two hours
quand il est arrivé.	when he arrived.

Nous habitions à Paris depuis un an quand nous avons acheté le magasin.	We had been living in Paris for a year when we bought the store.

Verbs with Special Meanings in the Imparfait

The *imparfait* is often used in specific circumstances to convey certain subtleties of time in past events. Because the tense is used to indicate an ongoing period in the past, some verbs take on a unique meaning when cast in the hazy time period indicated with the *imparfait*.

Être

When used in the imperfect, *être* takes on the meaning of "was," because it indicates an ongoing event. When used in the *passé composé*, the verb carries the sense of "became," because it indicates a specific time when the event occurred.

Savoir

Because knowledge is assumed to be something held over a long period of time, the imperfect carries the sense of the English word "knew." When used in the *passé composé*, *savoir* tends to indicate that you "found out" something, as we would say in English, to convey the sense of coming upon the knowledge at some particular point in time.

Devoir

In the present tense, *devoir* means "to have to" do something. In the *passé composé*, the correct translation would be "had to." In the *imparfait*, however, it carries a slightly different sense, instead carrying the sense of "was/were supposed to." This actually makes sense, because the *imparfait* is used to indicate events that you cannot pinpoint in time. Because the action or event was something that had to be done, as indicated by the verb *devoir*, putting it in the *imparfait* indicates that it didn't happen at a certain time. Therefore, it carries the sense that the obligation was something that occurred over a period of time in the past; "we were supposed to" is the best English approximation.

Vouloir

When *vouloir* is used to indicate a past state of mind, such as "wanted to write," the *imparfait* is the appropriate choice in French. The *passé composé* is used when you wish to show that the actual act of wanting occurred at a specific point in time, as in "I wanted to write this morning" versus a general state of mind.

Venir de

When *venir de* is used in the present, it conveys the sense of having just done something. It is used in the *imparfait* to convey the sense of "had just done something." This usage is rather idiomatic, so remember to choose the *imparfait* to avoid confusion.

Pouvoir

When used in the *imparfait*, *pouvoir* is much like saying "could have." In the *imparfait*, it tends to indicate that it was a possible state of events, but no attempt was ever actually made to achieve the objective. Using *pouvoir* in the *passé composé* indicates that an attempt was actually made, because it can be tied to a specific point in time.

Formation of the Imparfait

Instead of using an auxiliary verb, the *imparfait* is indicated by a special verb ending, so you don't need to watch for extra words. The *imparfait* is based on the present tense conjugation of the verb; to form the imperfect, instead of using the verb stem, you use the first person plural present-tense conjugation—the form of the verb used with *nous*. Simply drop the *-ons* ending and add the correct *imparfait* ending.

Table 12-12
Imparfait Verb Endings

Person	Singular	Plural
1st Person	*-ais*	*-ions*
2nd Person	*-ais*	*-iez*
3rd Person	*-ait*	*-aient*

The good news is that all French verbs follow this conjugation pattern to form the imperfect tense, with the exception of *être*, making the imparfait one of the easiest forms to learn. Because it is based on the present-tense *nous* form, it also has a unique sound from present-tense conjugations, so you will quickly learn to recognize it.

Table 12-13
Regarder Conjugated in the Imparfait

Person	Singular	Plural
1st Person	*je regardais*	*nous regardions*
2nd Person	*tu regardais*	*vous regardiez*
3rd Person	*il/elle regardait*	*ils/elles regardaient*

Sometimes, when forming the *imparfait*, you will end up with a stem that ends in -*i*. The *nous* and *vous* endings begin with an "i," so you end up with two. Don't accidentally drop the second "i" in written French.

Table 12-14
Étudier Conjugated in the Imparfait

Person	Singular	Plural
1st Person	*j'étudiais*	*nous étudiions*
2nd Person	*tu étudiais*	*vous étudiiez*
3rd Person	*il/elle étudiait*	*ils/elles étudiaient*

Être follows a different conjugation pattern in the imperfect. Instead of using the *nous* form *sommes*, which doesn't have an -*ons* ending to drop anyway, it uses *ét-* at the beginning as the stem, with the same endings as the other verbs tacked on at the end.

Table 12-15
Être Conjugated in the Imparfait

Person	Singular	Plural
1st Person	*j'étais*	*nous étions*

2nd Person	*tu étais*	*vous étiez*
3rd Person	*il/elle était*	*ils/elles étaient*

In these sections, you learned about the *imparfait*. Listen to the CD for the pronunciation of some of the expressions you learned.

TRACK 59

J'écoutais la radio chaque matin.
Nous mangions à la maison.
Quand j'étais jeune, j'étais heureux.
Il pleuvait.
Il n'aimait pas les cerises.
Je voulais y aller.
J'avais peur.
J'attendais depuis deux heures quand il est arrivé.
Nous habitions à Paris depuis un an quand nous avons acheté le magasin.

The Pluperfect Tense: Le Plus-Que-Parfait

The *plus-que-parfait* is used in French to go back in time as far as possible from the present. It is more distant than both the *passé composé* and the *imparfait*; in a sense, you can think of it as French's "oldest" tense. In English, this tense is usually achieved by using "had" as the auxiliary word in front of the verb.

Now that you have learned the *passé composé* and the *imparfait*, the *plus-que-parfait* should be relatively easy for you. In a sense, its formation is a combination of both the other tenses. It uses the same past participle as is used to construct the *passé composé*, but instead of using the present-tense conjugation of the auxiliary verb *avoir* or *être*, it uses the *imparfait*. As for the choice of auxiliary verb (*avoir* or *être*), verbs conjugated in the *plus-que-parfait* will use the same auxiliary verb as if it had been conjugated in the *passé composé*.

For these reasons, the *plus-que-parfait* is fairly easy to construct after you have mastered the other past tenses. Note the following examples.

TRACK 60

J'avais déjà vu le film   I had already seen the film before
    avant d'aller en France.   going to France.

Il avait dîné quand je suis arrivé.	He had had dinner by the time I arrived.
Ils étaient déjà nés quand leur père est arrivé à l'hôpital.	They had already been born when their father arrived at the hospital.
Elle avait fini l'article quand il a appelé.	She had finished the article when he called.

As a rule, the *plus-que-parfait* is used to indicate a time relationship, so you almost never find it used on its own. When you do come across it, it will usually be used to show chronology: that some event took place before another, more recent event, whether it was a continuous state as indicated by the *imparfait* or a specific action or event that took place at a discernible moment in time, as indicated by the *passé composé*.

Choosing the Appropriate Past Tense

As long as you keep the following points in mind, you should be well on your way to keeping the past tense choices straight.

- *Passé composé:* The *passé composé* is used to indicate events that have a concrete beginning and ending at some point in the past.
- *Imparfait*: The *imparfait* is used for actions or events that don't have a definite beginning or end, but happened over a course of time in the past.
- *Plus-que-parfait*: The *plus-que-parfait* is used in relation with other tenses to show that something occurred at an even earlier point in time, further back in the past.

Literary Tenses

In written French, there are special tenses known as literary tenses. These appear mainly in written texts and in literature, as a rule, although you never know when you'll run across them. Even though you may not ever actually use them, you should at least be able to recognize them.

Le Passé Simple

The *passé simple*, or simple past tense, is used like the *passé composé* to refer to events that occurred in the past. There is a major difference, however; while the *passé composé* uses either *avoir* or *être* as an auxiliary verb, the *passé simple* does not take any auxiliary; instead, the following endings are added to the stem of verbs ending in *-er*.

Table 12-16
Passé Simple with -er Verb Endings

Person	Singular	Plural
1st Person	*-ai*	*-âmes*
2nd Person	*-as*	*-âtes*
3rd Person	*-a*	*-èrent*

Table 12-17
Conjugation of Parler in the Passé Simple

Singular	Plural
je parlai	*nous parlâmes*
tu parlas	*vous parlâtes*
il/elle parla	*ils/elles parlèrent*

With verbs ending in *-ir* and *-re*, the *passé simple* is formed a little differently, adding the endings in Table 12-25, instead. Unlike the endings of *-er* verbs, only the *nous* and *vous* forms have accents in the conjugated verb endings.

Table 12-18
Passé Simple -re and -ir Verb Endings

Person	Singular	Plural
1st Person	*-is*	*-îmes*
2nd Person	*-is*	*-îtes*
3rd Person	*-it*	*-irent*

Table 12-19
Conjugation of Partir in the Passé Simple

Singular	Plural
je partis	nous partîmes
tu partis	vous partîtes
il partit	ils partirent

Table 12-20
Conjugation of Rire in the Passé Simple

Singular	Plural
je ris	nous rîmes
tu ris	vous rîtes
il/elle rit	ils rirent
ils/elles rit	elles rirent

You will need to be careful that you don't confuse *-ir* and *-re* verbs conjugated in the *passé simple* with the conditional or future forms of the words. Normally, the presence of an "r" is a great pointer to the tense. Fortunately, you won't have to worry about hearing these verbs conjugated in this tense; however, you may encounter them in books, magazines, or even on commemorative plaques. Best to be prepared.

The following irregular verbs have completely irregular formations in the *passé simple,* as they do in most other tenses, too. *Avoir* and *être* are used in the construction of another literary tense, called the *passé antérieur,* which is covered in the following section.

Table 12-21
Conjugation of Avoir in the Passé Simple

Singular	Plural
j'eus	nous eûmes
tu eus	vous eûtes
il/elle eut	ils eurent

Table 12-22
Conjugation of Être in the Passé Simple

Singular	Plural
je fus	nous fûmes
tu fus	vous fûtes
il/elle fut	ils/elles furent

The following verbs, *tenir* and *venir*, also have irregular conjugations in the *passé simple*. The verbs are not readily recognizable from the conjugation; as a matter of fact, you may find yourself confusing them with a number of words, so familiarize yourself with the forms.

Table 12-23
Conjugation of Tenir in the Passé Simple

Singular	Plural
je tins	nous tînmes
tu tins	vous tîntes
il/elle tint	ils/elles tinrent

Table 12-24
Conjugation of Venir in the Passé Simple

Singular	Plural
je vins	nous vînmes
tu vins	vous vîntes
il vint	ils vinrent

Le Passé Antérieur

If the *passé simple* is similar in use to the *passé composé*, then the *passé antérieur* is similar to the *plus-que-parfait*. It is used to refer to events that happened before the action described using the *passé simple*. However, in formation, it is very much like the *passé composé*. It uses *avoir* or *être* conjugated in the *passé simple* as the auxiliary verb, along with the past participle. As usual, the past participle will agree with any necessary preceding object pronouns. Refer to earlier in this chapter for information on agreement with verbs conjugated with *être* as the auxiliary verb and for agreement with verbs using *avoir* as the auxiliary. Here is an example:

J'avais entendu arriver la voiture.	*Peu après il en descendit un homme.*
I (had) heard the car arrive.	A bit later, a man got out of it.

Idiomatic Expressions—the Recent Past

In English, we often use constructions like "I just got back from the store." While technically this refers to a past event, we don't really put this in the past tense; instead, we use the recent past construction, using the word "just." This is an English idiomatic expression.

In French, you can do the exact same thing with the verb *venir*, following it with the preposition *de*. When used in the present indicative, the verb has the exact same meaning as the English "just" construction, being conjugated in the present tense:

Je viens de rentrer de l'école.	I just got back from school; I just returned from school.

Activité 12

Complete each sentence with the *passé composé* of the verb in parentheses.

1. *Elle* _____ *de la musique. (écouter)*
2. *Elles* _____ *leur devoir. (faire)*
3. _____-*vous* _____ *le livre? (perdre)*
4. *Je* (m) _____ *à l'hôpital. (naître)*

Complete each sentence with the *imparfait* of the verb in parentheses.

5. *Il* _____. *(pleuvoir)*
6. *J* _____ *depuis deux heures quand il est arrivé. (attendre)*
7. *Nous* _____ *à la maison. (manger)*
8. *Il n'*_____ *pas les cerises.   (aimer)*

Chapter 13

Using Reflexive Verbs

Reflexive verbs generally indicate an action that the subject performs on his or her own self. In English, the words "himself" or "herself" point back to the subject. In French, this is done with a reflexive pronoun. The reflexive pronoun shows that the action goes back to the subject; this is important, because the verb will usually have another meaning if it appears without the reflexive pronoun.

Understanding Reflexive Verbs

The reflexive pronouns found in reflexive verbs bear great similarity to the pronouns discussed in Chapter 9. The only difference is in the third person, where there is no gender distinction and, thus, the same word is used for both masculine and feminine subjects.

Table 13-1
French Reflexive Pronouns

Person	Singular	Plural
1st Person	me (m')	nous
2nd Person	te (t')	vous
3rd Person	se (s')	se (s')

Fortunately, reflexive pronouns are pretty easy to keep straight because they always match the subject of the sentence. Whenever the object of the verb, or reflexive pronoun, (for example, *te* or "you") is the same as the subject (for example, *tu* or "you"), the action is being performed reflexively. When you use a reflexive verb, all you have to do is match the object pronoun with the subject and use it with the appropriate verb.

Je me lève à six heures.	I get up at 6 a.m.
Il se brosse les dents.	He is brushing his teeth.

These reflexive verbs describe actions that occur around the house.

TRACK 61

Table 13-2

Reflexive Verb	English
s'appeler	to be named; to be called
se réveiller	to wake up
se lever	to get up
s'endormir	to fall asleep
se laver	to wash (oneself)

se sécher	to dry (oneself)
se raser	to shave (oneself)
s'habiller	to get dressed
se coiffer	to comb one's hair
se brosser	to brush
se maquiller	to put on makeup
se reposer	to rest
se déshabiller	to undress (oneself)

In theory, all of these verbs can be used with other pronouns as the direct object, but then the verbs are not being used reflexively. Only when the direct object matches the subject is the verb being used in a reflexive construction.

English also tends to handle many of these verbs idiomatically. Just because a reflexive pronoun appears in French, it doesn't mean that a corresponding English word is required; "to wash up," "to wake up," and "to fall asleep" are all examples of English verbs that use a completely different construction from French. Treat them all as idiomatic expressions that require a little bit of extra care in translation. Treat reflexive pronouns as a signpost that tells you that the action is reverting back to the subject, and then choose the most appropriate English equivalent based on that.

Je m'appelle David.	My name is David.
Il s'habille dans sa chambre.	He is getting dressed in his bedroom.

Other verbs that are not usually reflexive can be used reflexively. When they are, their meaning changes, as seen in the following chart:

Table 13-3
Verbs Used Reflexively

Verb	English
s'en aller	to go away
s'amuser	to have a good time

se débrouiller	to get by, to manage
se demander	to wonder
se dépêcher	to hurry
s'ennuyer	to get bored
s'entendre	to get along
s'habituer à	to get used to
se rendre compte de	to realize
se tromper	to be wrong, to make a mistake

Forming Negatives with Reflexive Verbs

To form a negative, place the *ne* before the pronoun and the negative expression (*pas, guère,* etc.) after it.

Vous ne vous trompez pas souvent.　　You are not often mistaken.

Asking Questions with Reflexive Verbs

When asking questions with inversion, the pronoun retains its position in front of the verb. As a result, the reflexive pronoun tends to appear as the subject, especially when the *nous* or *vous* form is used. In actuality, the subject is situated after the verb, due to the inversion:

Vous êtes-vous amusés au　　Did you have fun at the movies
　cinéma hier soir?　　　　　last night?

Reflexive Verbs in the Past

Reflexive verbs always take *être* as their auxiliary verb.

Je me suis réveillé à huit heures.　　I woke up at 8 a.m.
Nous nous sommes amusés au parc.　　We had fun at the park.

In general, the ending of the past participle agrees with the subject. With *venir de*, place the conjugated expression before the pronoun + infinitive of the reflexive verb:

Je viens de me lever.   I just got up.

In these sections, you learned about reflexive verbs. Listen to the CD for the pronunciation of some of the expressions you learned.

TRACK 62

Je m'appelle David.
Il s'habille dans sa chambre.
Vous ne vous trompez pas souvent.
Vous êtes-vous amusés au cinéma hier soir?
Je me suis réveillé à huit heures.
Nous nous sommes amusés au parc.
Je viens de me lever.

Reciprocal Verbs

Reciprocal verbs take the same construction as reflexive verbs, but are used when two or more persons are involved. Because of the nature of reciprocal verbs, you encounter them only in the plural; it is not possible to have a singular construction occur because it requires more than one person.

When considering reciprocal verbs, the object of the sentence and how it is used is important. When the object and the subject are different, the verb is reciprocal.

Reciprocal verbs don't always translate into English very easily. There is no direct equivalent translation, and the appropriate choice can vary. For the most part, "each other" will suffice to complete the meaning. Listen to the CD for the pronunciation of the following sentences.

TRACK 63

Vous vous parlez.   You are speaking to each other.
Nous nous regardons.   We are looking at each other.
Ils se téléphonent tous les jours.   They call each other every day.

Verbs That Are Always Pronominal

The following verbs must be used in either reflexive or reciprocal constructions, because the verbs are always pronominal: In other words, they do not have a nonreflexive meaning. In this case, their usage can be seen as idiomatic; their reflexive nature does NOT indicate an action being done to someone. In addition to using the pronoun in front of the verb, some also take the preposition "*de*" after the verb. If the word immediately following *de* begins with a vowel, *de* is contracted to *d'*.

Table 13-4
Verbs That Are Always Pronominal

Verb	English
s'empresser de	to hasten
s'enfuir	to flee
s'envoler	to fly away
s'évanouir	to faint
se moquer de	to make fun of
se soucier de	to mind
se souvenir de	to remember
se suicider	to kill oneself

 **Activité 13**

TRACK 64

Listen to the sentences on your CD and write each one in the space provided here.

1. _____
2. _____
3. _____
4. _____
5. _____
6. _____

Chapter 14

Forming the Future Tense

The future tense adds another dimension to your growing French vocabulary. By understanding this tense, you can talk about what is going to happen in the near future and the distant future and also talk about a future action that will be completed before another action or event, such as "Will you have finished this chapter by noon tomorrow?"

English Future-Tense Constructions

To refer to events that will occur in the future, English uses the word "will."

I will go to the store.
We'll do it later.

There is another future tense in English that's used to indicate events that will be completed at some point in the future. In English, it is known as the future perfect because it is an event that will be completely finished, or perfected. Here are some examples:

By six o'clock, I will have gone to the store.
When the dessert has finished baking, we will have finished supper.

In French you have three forms of the future tense: *le futur proche, le futur simple*, and *le futur antérieur*.

Le Futur Proche

In English, we can use the verb "to go" to indicate something that is going to happen in the immediate future, such as "I am going to sing in the choir." The verb *aller* can be used the same way in French to indicate something that will happen in the near future. This is known as the *futur proche* (near future) and is very simple. Listen to the CD for the pronunciation of the following sentences:

TRACK 65

Je vais chanter à la chorale.	I am going to sing in the choir.
Je vais acheter un billet.	I am going to buy a ticket.
Je vais vendre le livre.	I am going to sell the book.

Le Futur Simple

There are more formal ways of speaking of future events, and the *futur simple* is the most commonly used. In some ways, it is one of the more interesting tenses, because it follows a unique conjugation pattern. Like the others, it uses special verb endings, but instead of chopping off parts of the infinitive, it uses the infinitive itself.

To form the future tense with most verbs, simply add the following endings to the infinitive form.

Table 14-1
Futur Simple Verb Endings

Person	Singular	Plural
1st Person	-ai	-ons
2nd Person	-as	-ez
3rd Person	-a	-ont

Here is an example of an *-er* verb conjugated in the *futur simple:*

Table 14-2
Regarder Conjugated in the Futur Simple

Person	Singular	Plural
1st Person	je regarderai	nous regarderons
2nd Person	tu regarderas	vous regarderez
3rd Person	il/elle regardera	ils/elles regarderont

When conjugating verbs that end in *-re* in the future tense, simply drop the "e" from the ending, but keep the "r," as shown in Table 14-3.

Table 14-3
Prendre Conjugated in the Futur Simple

Person	Singular	Plural
1st Person	je prendrai	nous prendrons

| 2nd Person | *tu prendras* | *vous prendrez* |
| 3rd Person | *il/elle prendra* | *ils/elles prendront* |

As you can see, the verb takes on a unique appearance with the presence of the "*r*." The "*r*" is distinctly pronounced in spoken French, so when you hear it, you know that someone is referring to something in the future tense.

TRACK 66

Je prendrai un café.	I will have a coffee.
Nous voyagerons.	We will travel.
	We are going to travel.
Nous ne regarderons pas le film.	We will not see the film.
	We won't watch the film.

Naturally, there are exceptions with irregular formations that you will have to watch for—a number of verbs have an irregular stem when used in the future tense—but you will get used to them with practice, because they tend to be fairly commonly used. Not all irregular verbs have irregular future stems, so you'll need to memorize these individually.

Table 14-4
Irregular Stems in the Futur Simple

Verb	Future Stem	Verb	Future Stem
avoir	*aur-*	*pouvoir*	*pourr-*
être	*ser-*	*recevoir*	*recevr-*
aller	*ir-*	*savoir*	*saur-*
devoir	*devr-*	*valoir*	*vaudr-*
envoyer	*enverr-*	*venir*	*viendr-*
faire	*fer-*	*voir*	*verr-*
falloir	*faudr-*	*vouloir*	*voudr-*
pleuvoir	*pleuvr-*		

Use of Future with **Si** and **Quand**

With sentences beginning with *si* (if) to refer to future events, the verb in the subordinate clause (the part following *si*) is in the present, and the main clause (which expresses the result) is in the future:

Si j'ai le temps, j'irai au cinéma.   If I have the time, I will go to the movies.

When sentences beginning with *quand* refer to future events, the verbs in both the subordinate and the main clause are in the future:

*Quand j'irai à Paris, je verrai   When I go to Paris, I will
   la tour Eiffel.*   see the Eiffel Tower.

Note that this is different from English, which expresses the same idea using the present tense in the subordinate clause. Instead of saying, "When I will go to Paris," English speakers say, "When I go to Paris." English relies on the word "when" and the present tense "go" in order to imply the event will take place in the future.

Le Futur Antérieur

There is another tense you can use to refer to events in the future, known as the *futur antérieur*. It is similar to the *plus-que-parfait*, in that it compares the time relationship between two events; it just operates in the other direction.

TRACK 67

*Est-ce que vous serez partis   Will you have left by 5 o'clock
   à cinq heures demain?*   tomorrow?
*Nous aurons étudié le livre   We will have studied the book
   quand nous passerons l'examen.*   when we take the test.

Also like the *plus-que-parfait*, it is relatively easy to form, combining other tenses to refer to events in the future. You can conjugate any verb

THE EVERYTHING LEARNING FRENCH BOOK

in the *futur antérieur* by using its past participle with its auxiliary verb conjugated in the *futur simple*.

Table 14-5
Aller Conjugated in the futur antérieur

Person	Singular	Plural
1st Person	je serai allé(e)	nous serons allé(e)s
2nd Person	tu seras allé(e)	vous serez allé(e)s
3rd Person	il/elle sera allé(e)	ils/elles seront allé(e)s

Because the future perfect is formed with the past participle (see Chapter 12), you won't have to worry about the irregular endings some verbs use in the future, because you'll only be conjugating *avoir* or *être* in the future. You will, however, have to make sure that the past participle agrees with the subject when the verb is conjugated with *être* as the auxiliary.

Activité 14

Listen to the sentences on your CD and write each one in the space provided here.

TRACK 68

1. _____
2. _____
3. _____
4. _____
5. _____
6. _____

Chapter 15

Forming the Conditional Tense

In English, you sometimes refer to events that haven't yet happened or that may not happen at all. These are known as conditional statements. They usually imply something that could happen, but whose outcome depends on some other event. We often construct these phrases in English using the word "would."

Uses of the Conditional Tense

In some ways, the conditional tense is like an imaginary tense. It doesn't refer to concrete events in the past, present, or future. It refers to things that could happen or may happen, but there is no guarantee as to the actual outcome, as in "I would go to the store if it weren't raining." The conditional tense is used to refer to potential situations. The expression may contain an element of doubt or uncertainty about the statement. It is a rather abstract tense in both English and French because it does not refer to the here and now but rather to an uncertain state of events, such as in the following example:

J'achèterais un billet si j'avais   I would buy a ticket if I had money.
de l'argent.

There is nothing certain about the outcome of any of this event; it is a mere statement of intention.

The word *si* is often used with the conditional tense (as seen in the example above) to describe uncertain events. If the *si* clause is in the imperfect (see Chapter 12), the main clause will be in the conditional:

Je parlerais à l'homme si   I would speak to the
je le connaissais.   man if I knew him.

TRACK 69

As you are learning the language, pay special attention to the conditional tense to make sure that you don't confuse it with the future. You will also have to remember how to balance each conditional tense, using the appropriate past tense to complement it. For more information on the future tense, see Chapter 14.

Using the Conditional Tense to Be Polite

With certain verbs, the conditional tense lends the statement a very polite tone. As a result, these verbs are often used in the conditional, especially when making requests. It is considered more formal and less demanding.

You will often encounter the verbs *aimer, pouvoir,* and *vouloir* used in the conditional tense. This is actually very similar to the English way of asking questions politely. *Aimer* transforms into "would like," *pouvoir* into "could," and *vouloir* into "would like."

When ordering a meal in a restaurant, the exchange with your waiter will almost always occur using the conditional tense. Here is a typical conversation in a restaurant:

Waiter:	*Voudriez-vous quelque chose, madame?*
	Would you like something, Madam?
Diner:	*Oui. Je voudrais un filet mignon.*
	Yes. I would like a filet mignon.
Waiter:	*Et qu'est-ce que vous voudriez aimeriez boire?*
	And what would you like to drink?
Diner:	*Du thé, s'il vous plaît.*
	Some tea, please.
Waiter:	*C'est tout?*
	That's all?
Diner:	*Oui. Merci.*
	Yes. Thank you.

The waiter is being very polite, using the conditional tense in addition to referring to the diner using the formal *vous* form. Responding in the conditional allows you to politely order the food you desire. Phrasing such a request in the present tense indicative conjugation would be more abrupt and less polite. This level of respect is evident in English, too; it's very similar to the phrase "I'll have . . ." you often use when ordering. Remember to be polite to your waiter, thank him or her, and refer to him as *monsieur* or to her as *madame* or *mademoiselle.*

Forming the Conditional Tense

In French, the conditional tense has its own verb form, so you will always be able to recognize it. You have to be careful, however, not to confuse it with the future tense. To form the conditional tense in French, you use the future stem of the verb, but you conjugate it with the *imparfait* verb endings. Here is a reminder of those endings:

Table 15-1
Imparfait Verb Endings

Person	Singular	Plural
1st Person	-ais	-ions
2nd Person	-ais	-iez
3rd Person	-ait	-aient

As a result, the construction of the conditional tense is relatively straightforward. Just use the same stem of the verb you would use to create the future tense and tack on the imperfect ending. The conditional tense conjugation of the regular verbs is illustrated in the following sections.

-er and -ir Verbs

For -*er* and -*ir* verbs, simply use the infinitive form of the verb as the stem:

Table 15-2
Conditionnel Conjugation of Parler

Singular	Plural
je parlerais	nous parlerions
tu parlerais	vous parleriez
il/elle parlerait	ils/elles parleraient

Table 15-3
Conditionnel Conjugation of Finir

Singular	Plural
je finirais	nous finirions
tu finirais	vous finiriez
il/elle finirait	ils/elles finiraient

-re Verbs

To form the conditional stem of *-re* verbs, simply drop the "e" from the end, as with *prendre*.

Table 15-4
Conditionnel Conjugation of Prendre

Singular	Plural
je prendrais	nous prendrions
tu prendrais	vous prendriez
il/elle prendrait	ils/elles prendraient

Like the *imparfait*, the unique pronunciation of the endings should help you to discern quite easily between the future and the conditional. The only ones that are pronounced the same are the *je* forms, so pay close attention to them.

Verbs that have an irregular stem in the future tense also use that same irregular stem to form the conditional. The following list of verbs with irregular future stems is included for your convenience; for more information, consult Chapter 14, where the future tense is discussed in detail.

Table 15-5
Irregular Future Stems

Verb	Future Stem	Verb	Future Stem
avoir	aur-	pouvoir	pourr-
être	ser-	recevoir	recevr-
aller	ir-	savoir	saur-
devoir	devr-	valoir	vaudr-
envoyer	enverr-	venir	viendr-
faire	fer-	voir	verr-
falloir	faudr-	vouloir	voudr-
pleuvoir	pleuvr-		

The Past Conditional Tense

The past conditional tense is used to refer to the same kinds of events as the conditional, but simply in the past. Don't let its construction fool you. Despite the fact that it looks complex with its auxiliary construction, it is a simple reference to past events in French. In English, this is often accomplished by saying "would have," for example:

Nous aurions voulu aller au théâtre.   We would have liked to go to the theater.

Keep in mind that the past conditional tense is a past tense; don't fall into the trap of thinking it's in the future because the formation of the auxiliary verb reminds you of the future. Learn to recognize when *avoir* or *être* is being conjugated in the conditional; the distinct sounds of the conjugated verb endings should help (see the following section). Then let the past participle remind you that this is occurring in the conditional past and doesn't have anything to do with the future tense.

Note that when the main clause is used in the past conditional, the subordinate clause must be conjugated using the *plus-que-parfait* (see Chapter 12). If used with any other tenses, the statements just wouldn't make sense:

J'aurais été riche si j'avais acheté   I would have been rich if I had
   cette propriété.   bought this property.

Forming the Past Conditional Tense

The similarities between the conditional and future tenses extend to the past, too. Like the construction of the future perfect, the past conditional tense uses the present conditional conjugation of the auxiliary verb, whether it is *avoir* or *être*. The appropriate past participle is then added, and any necessary agreements are made. For more information on the agreement of past participles, refer to Chapter 12.

Avoir

Remember that past participles used with *avoir* must agree in gender and number with any preceding direct object pronouns. Refer to Chapter 12 for more information.

Table 15-6
Conditionnel Conjugation of Avoir

Singular	Plural
j'aurais	nous aurions
tu aurais	vous auriez
il/elle aurait	ils/elles auraient

Être

Remember that past participles used with *être* must agree with the preceding subject pronoun; object pronouns do not modify the past participle when used with *être* as the auxiliary verb.

Table 15-7
Conditionnel Conjugation of Être

Singular	Plural
je serais	nous serions
tu serais	vous seriez
il/elle serait	ils/elles seraient

Here are some examples. Listen to the CD for their pronunciation:

TRACK 70

Tu serais venu.	You would have come.
Elle serait allée.	She would have gone.
Ils seraient nés.	They would have already been born.

The Verb Devoir in the Conditional Tense

The verb *devoir* takes on a unique meaning when used in the conditional tense. It is the equivalent of the English construction "should" or "ought to," as in "I should go to the store."

Je devrais lui passer un coup de fil.	I should call him.
Il devrait travailler plus.	He should work more.

When placed in the conditional, therefore, *devoir* implies that there is some doubt as to whether the event will actually occur. It imports an obligation of an almost moral nature; quite often, there will be an unspoken "but," implying that the event may, in fact, never take place at all. In some grammatical circles, using *devoir* in the conditional is known as the "tense of regret" for that very reason.

Devoir has an irregular future stem, so it uses *devr-* as the stem in the conditional. Remember not to confuse the conditional conjugation of *devoir* with the imperfect conjugation, because they each have completely different meanings. In the imperfect tense, *devoir* means "used to have to." It still implies the obligation. Only when the statement is cast in the conditional does the necessary doubt enter the picture to trigger the same response as a "should" construction does in English.

Activité 15

Listen to the waiter's questions on the CD and fill in your part of the conversation below.

TRACK 71

Waiter: *Bonjour.*
You: _____

Waiter: *Qu'est-ce que vous voudriez?*
You: _____

Waiter: *Et qu'est-ce que vous voudriez boire?*
You: _____

Waiter: *C'est tout?*
You: _____

Chapter 16

Understanding the Subjunctive Mood

The subjunctive mood is used to convey statements of opinion or things that aren't based in complete fact. It carries a degree of subjectivity or personal desire. In French, the subjunctive mood is widely used in certain constructions, and you will encounter it often.

Understanding the French Subjunctive

Most of what you have learned so far is in the indicative mood, used to express factual, certain information. The subjunctive mood expresses emotional, subjective information. English makes limited use of the subjunctive, but it can be heard in sentences such as "I wish it were not raining," and "It is necessary that you be on time." To help keep it straight in your head, think of the subjunctive as an emotive expression. It is quite often used with phrases like "wish," "hope," and "doubt," to express desires, opinions, or uncertainties.

The subjunctive construction consists in general of a main clause that expresses doubt, desire, or opinion, and a subordinate clause with a verb in the subjunctive form, preceded by *que* (see Chapter 9):

Il doute que nous soyons à l'heure.	He doubts that we will be on time.
Il veut que tu sois heureux.	He wants you to be happy.

The subjunctive itself does not necessarily carry any specific meaning; it simply points out an element of subjectivity or doubt. In the subordinate clause, the fact that the subjunctive is used tells you that the statement is not factual. It is based on the main clause, which is an expression of the desire, doubt, or opinion of the subject.

The subjunctive mood is very much an advanced construction, and mastering it will put you well on the way to full fluency. Even if you're not comfortable using it, you should at least be able to recognize when other people are using it.

The subjunctive mood is used only when the main clause has a different subject from the subordinate clause. If the two clauses use the same subject, the subjunctive clause is grafted onto the main clause using infinitives, much like we tend to do in English.

Il veut que je finisse mes devoirs.	He wants me to finish my homework.
Je veux finir mes devoirs.	I want to finish my homework.

If the sentence does not have an element of doubt or subjectivity, the subjunctive is not used; the sentence is cast in the regular indicative mood, relating a fact.

Il sait que nous finirons à temps.   He knows that we will finish in time.

Forming the Subjunctive Mood

Fortunately, the subjunctive is rather unique in its formation, so you should usually be able to tell when it's being used. To form the present subjunctive with regular verbs, you must first obtain the subjunctive stem. This is based on the present indicative conjugation of the verb in the third person plural. Simply drop the *-ent* ending, and you have your stem. Because of this construction, most irregular verbs end up following a regular formation pattern in the subjunctive. The following endings are then added to the end of the subjunctive stem.

Table 16-1
Subjunctive Verb Endings

Person	Singular	Plural
1st Person	*-e*	*-ions*
2nd Person	*-es*	*-iez*
3rd Person	*-e*	*-ent*

You'll note that the third person plural endings are actually the same in the subjunctive and the indicative. When the third person plural is used in the subjunctive, you'll have to know from the sentence construction that it is being used in the construction, because nothing about the verb actually tells you.

This section demonstrates the present-tense conjugation of the three kinds of regular verb endings and the forms of irregular verbs. Pay attention to the *nous* and *vous* forms; these endings sound very much like the imperfect endings but are, in fact, present subjunctive. You need to rely on the construction to know that these are being used in the subjunctive.

-er Verbs

All -er verbs follow the pattern seen in Table 16-2.

Table 16-2
Subjunctive Conjugation of Parler

Singular	Plural
je parle	nous parlions
tu parles	vous parliez
il/elle parle	ils/elles parlent

-ir Verbs

All -ir verbs follow the pattern seen in Table 16-3.

Table 16-3
Subjunctive Conjugation of Finir

Singular	Plural
je finisse	nous finissions
tu finisses	vous finissiez
il/elle finisse	ils/elles finissent

-re Verbs

All -re verbs follow the pattern seen in Table 16-4.

Table 16-4
Subjunctive Conjugation of Répondre

Singular	Plural
je réponde	nous répondions
tu répondes	vous répondiez
il/elle réponde	ils/elles répondent

Irregular Verbs in the Subjunctive

The following irregular verbs also have irregular formations in the subjunctive, following no real consistent pattern.

Table 16-5
Subjunctive Conjugation of Aller

Singular	Plural
j'aille	nous allions
tu ailles	vous alliez
il/elle aille	ils/elles aillent

Table 16-6
Subjunctive Conjugation of Avoir

Singular	Plural
j'aie	nous ayons
tu aies	vous ayez
il/elle aie	ils/elles aient

Table 16-7
Subjunctive Conjugation of Être

Singular	Plural
je sois	nous soyons
tu sois	vous soyez
il/elle soit	ils/elles soient

Table 16-8
Subjunctive Conjugation of Faire

Singular	Plural
je fasse	nous fassions
tu fasses	vous fassiez
il/elle fasse	ils/elles fassent

Table 16-9
Subjunctive Conjugation of Pouvoir

Singular	Plural
je puisse	nous puissions
tu puisses	vous puissiez
il/elle puisse	ils/elles puissent

Table 16-10
Subjunctive Conjugation of Savoir

Singular	Plural
je sache	nous sachions
tu saches	vous sachiez
il/elle sache	ils/elles sachent

Table 16-11
Subjunctive Conjugation of Vouloir

Singular	Plural
je veuille	nous voulions
tu veuilles	vous vouliez
il/elle veuille	ils/elles veuillent

Common Irregular Subjunctive Verbs

The following tables contain a number of common verbs that have slightly irregular constructions in the subjunctive. The only difference is in the *nous* and *vous* forms, which change to assist in the pronunciation.

Table 16-12
Subjunctive Conjugation of Boire

Singular	Plural
je boive	nous buvions
tu boives	vous buviez

il/elle boive	ils/elles boivent

Table 16-13
Subjunctive Conjugation of Croire

Singular	Plural
je croie	nous croyions
tu croies	vous croyiez
il/elle croie	ils/elles croient

Table 16-14
Subjunctive Conjugation of Devoir

Singular	Plural
je doive	nous devions
tu doives	vous deviez
il/elle doive	ils/elles doivent

Table 16-15
Subjunctive Conjugation of Prendre

Singular	Plural
je prenne	nous prenions
tu prennes	vous preniez
il/elle prenne	ils/elles prennent

Table 16-16
Subjunctive Conjugation of Tenir

Singular	Plural
je tienne	nous tenions
tu tiennes	vous teniez
il/elle tienne	ils/elles tiennent

Table 16-17
Subjunctive Conjugation of Venir

Singular	Plural
je vienne	*nous venions*
tu viennes	*vous veniez*
il/elle vienne	*ils/elles viennent*

Table 16-18
Subjunctive Conjugation of Voir

Singular	Plural
je voie	*nous voyions*
tu voies	*vous voyiez*
il/elle voie	*ils/elles voient*

Listen to the CD for the pronunciation of the expressions you learned.

TRACK 72

Il doute que nous soyons à l'heure.
Il veut que tu sois heureux.
Il veut que je finisse mes devoirs.

Specific Uses of the Subjunctive

This section outlines a number of specific uses of the subjunctive mood. The subjunctive generally follows the following format: There is a main clause, which expresses doubt, desire, emotion, or opinion, followed by a subordinate clause, beginning with *que*.

Je doute que tu viennes.	I doubt you are coming.
Elle veut que tu sois heureux.	She wants you to be happy.
Tu es content qu'elle réussisse.	You are happy that she is succeeding.

For the subjunctive to be required, the subject of the main clause and the subordinate clause must be different. If the subject is the same, use the infinitive form of the verb instead.

Je veux réussir mes examens.	I want to succeed at my exams.

If the main clause implies factual, certain information, then the subjunctive is not called for, and the indicative is used.

Il est certain que tu vas réussir tes examens	It is certain that you will succeed at your exams.

Expressions of Emotion Using the Subjunctive

Emotive statements are inherently subjective; they describe something that the subject of the main clause is feeling. The element of doubt or subjectivity is present, because an emotion isn't considered fact.

Here are a number of expressions that can be used to convey emotion. When they are used with a subordinate clause that has a different subject from the main clause, the subjunctive is used.

être content que	to be pleased that
être désolé que	to be sorry that

The subjunctive is not used when the two clauses share the same subject. If there is no change in subject between the main and subordinate clauses, an infinitive is used after the preposition *de*, as follows:

Il est content de finir le livre.	He is pleased to finish the book.
Est-ce que tu es fâché de ne pas réussir à cet examen?	Are you angry at not passing this test?

Expressions of Opinion Using the Subjunctive

Opinions are not, as a rule, subjective. They usually indicate the thoughts or beliefs of the subject of the main clause, which is a statement of fact, thus removing the element of subjectivity. But when opinions are used in the negative or in interrogative statements to ask a question, an element of doubt or subjectivity is introduced; therefore, the subjunctive is used in these constructions.

Remember that when a sentence is used interrogatively, the subjectivity of the statement is determined from the perspective of the subject of the main clause. This is why these expressions call for the subjunctive when used negatively or interrogatively; when you're asking these types of questions, you're introducing a subjective element, asking for another person's opinion. Watch for the following verbs, because whenever they are used in an interrogative or a negative construction, the subordinate clause uses the subjunctive mood: *croire* (to believe), *penser* (to think), and *espérer* (to hope). Note the following examples:

Je ne pense pas que tu aies raison.	I do not think that you are correct.
Crois-tu que le guichet soit ouvert?	Do you believe that the ticket office is open?
Espères-tu qu'il gagne à la loterie?	Are you hoping he will win the lottery?

When constructions of thought or opinion are used affirmatively, these sentences may still use the word *que*. While *que* is necessary in most subjunctive constructions, its presence doesn't automatically tell you that the subjunctive is present or required.

If the sentence is being used affirmatively, there is no doubt; it is simply a statement of belief. While it is indeed a statement of subjective belief, the subjective belief itself is a fact and is therefore conjugated in the indicative mood instead of the subjunctive:

Je crois que tu partiras demain.	I believe that you will leave tomorrow.

Note that when either of the following expressions are used in the negative or as a question, they take the subjunctive. When used affirmatively, they take the indicative.

être certain(e)(s	to be certain
être sûr(e)(s)	to be sure

Expressions of Doubt Using the Subjunctive

When either of the expressions *douter* (to doubt) or *être douteux* (to be doubtful) are used and the phrase is affirmative or a question, the subjunctive is used in the subordinate clause, as follows:

Je doute que vous parliez à ma mère. I doubt that you will talk to my mother.

Il est douteux que nous finissions. He is doubtful that we will finish.

If the doubt is expressed negatively, the indicative mood is used:

Je ne doute pas que tu es intelligent. I don't doubt that you are intelligent.

Expressions of Desire Using the Subjunctive

Expressions of desire can also be termed as expressions of will. They illustrate the wants or desires of the subject of the main clause, so if the subordinate clause has a different subject, the subjunctive mood is used. These verbs are commonly used in this construction: *désirer* (to desire), *préférer* (to prefer), *souhaiter* (to wish), and *vouloir* (to want).

Il veut que tu ailles avec lui. He wants you to go with him.
Je préfère que nous parlions avec lui. I prefer that we speak with him.
Est-ce que vous voulez que je le fasse? Do you want me to do it?

With certain verbs that involve granting permission or issuing an order, even though they express will, the subjunctive is not used. The following verbs are the ones to watch out for: *conseiller* (to advise), *demander* (to ask for), *dire* (to say, to tell), *permettre* (to permit; to allow). When these verbs are used, they generally appear with two prepositions. The preposition *à* is used to indicate the other person involved, as the direct object, while the preposition *de* is used to indicate the thing that the person is being asked to do, as in the following examples:

Je demande à Jean d'aller au magasin. I am asking John to go to the store.
Il a dit à son fils de faire les achats. He told his son to do the shopping.

This construction can seem a little backward to us, because we very seldom have the direct object used with a preposition in English.

The Subjunctive Used after Impersonal Expressions

There are certain impersonal expressions in French that always take the subjunctive. A few of the common ones are listed here:

il faut que	it is necessary that
il vaut mieux que	it is better that
il semble que	it seems that
il est dommage que	it's too bad that

In this section, you learned about uses of the subjunctive. Listen to the CD for the pronunciation of some of the expressions you learned.

TRACK 73

Je doute que tu viennes.
Elle veut que tu sois heureux.
Tu es content qu'elle réussisse.
Je ne pense pas que tu aies raison.
Crois-tu que le guichet soit ouvert?
Espères-tu qu'il gagne à la loterie?
Je doute que vous parliez à ma mère.
Il est douteux que nous finissions.
Il veut que tu ailles avec lui.
Je préfère que nous parlions avec lui.
Est-ce que vous voulez que je le fasse?

The Past Subjunctive

The past subjunctive is formed much like the simple past tense, the *passé composé*. Simply conjugate the auxiliary verb in the subjunctive and use the past participle, making sure that the past participle makes any necessary pronoun agreements.

The past subjunctive is used to indicate events that took place before the action described by the verb in the main sentence. If the event in the subordinate clause took place later or actually did not take place at all, the subjunctive is not used. Remember, too, that the subjunctive is used only with two different subjects; if the subject of the subordinate clause is the same, use an infinitive instead.

TRACK 74

Il a été heureux qu'elle soit venue à la fête.	He was happy that she came to the reception.
J'ai douté qu'il ait réussi.	I doubted that he had succeeded.

Activité 16

Transform each of the following sentences into a sentence with the subjunctive, substituting the underlined phrase with the phrase found in parentheses.

1. *Je sais que tu viendras. (douter que)*

   _____

2. *Elle est certaine que tu es heureux. (vouloir que)*

   _____

3. *Tu es sûr qu'elle réussira. (être content que)*

   _____

4. *Je pense que tu as raison. (ne penser pas que)*

   _____

5. *Il est certain que nous finirons. (il est douteux que)*

   _____

6. *Il sait que tu iras avec lui. (vouloir que)*

   _____

Chapter 17

Traveling in French-Speaking Countries

Pack up your carry-on; it's time to travel with your French skills. Whether you're traveling in French-speaking regions of North America or in one of the French-speaking countries in Europe or Africa, you'll need to build your travel vocabulary. This chapter shows you how.

Modes of Transportation

You need a way to get around, even if it's only *à pied*. The following vocabulary list includes a number of French words associated with travel and methods of transportation. Quiz yourself on these words by making yourself say the French names whenever you see a car, bus, train, or anything else.

TRACK 75

Table 17-1
Types of Transportation

French	English
le transport	transportation
la voiture	car
le taxi	taxi
le camion	truck
un autobus	bus
le bus	bus
le métro	subway
un avion	plane
le vélo	bicycle
la bicyclette	bicycle

Table 17-2
At the Airport

French	English
un aéroport	airport
la piste	runway
la tour de contrôle	control tower
la compagnie aérienne	airline
une information	information
un enregistrement	baggage check-in

les bagages (m)	bags
les bagages à main (m)	handbags, carry-on luggage
un embarquement (m)	boarding
la salle d'embarquement	departure lounge
la carte d'embarquement	boarding pass
la porte	gate
la livraison des bagages	baggage claim area
le terminal	terminal
un ascenseur	elevator
faire la queue	to wait in line

Table 17-3
Customs

French	English
le passeport	passport
une ambassade	embassy
la douane	customs
le visa	visa

Table 17-4
On the Plane

TRACK 76

French	English
un avion supersonique	supersonic plane
le jet	jet
le jumbo-jet	jumbo jet
le charter	charter flight
une aile	wing
une hélice	propeller
le hublot	window
la ceinture	seat belt

une issue de secours	emergency exit
la sortie de secours	emergency exit
la place	seat
le vol	flight
le vol direct	direct flight
le vol intérieur	domestic flight
le vol international	international flight
l'altitude (f)	altitude
la vitesse	speed
le départ	departure
le décollage	take-off
l'arrivée (f)	arrival
l'atterrissage (m)	landing
l'atterrissage forcé (m)	emergency landing
une escale	stopover
le retard	delay
en retard	delayed
annulé	canceled
le pilote	pilot
le steward	steward, flight attendant
l'hôtesse de l'air (f)	stewardess, flight attendant
le passager	male passenger
la passagère	female passenger
fumeur	smoking
non-fumeur	nonsmoking

Table 17-5
Trains, Buses, and Subways

French	English
l'arrière (m)	the back
l'avant (m)	the front
la gare routière	bus station
la gare d'autobus	bus station
l'arrêt d'autobus (m)	bus stop
le guichet	ticket office
la salle d'attente	waiting room
le métro	subway
la gare	train/subway station
la station de métro	subway station
le train	train
le quai	platform

Travel Destinations

This section helps you navigate your hotel and other common destinations. It also provides translations for directions.

TRACK 77

Table 17-6
In the Hotel

French	English
un hôtel	hotel
complet	no vacancies
fermé	closed
confortable	comfortable
compris	included
le prix par jour	price per day

la note	bill
le pourboire	tip
le service	service
la réclamation	complaint
la réservation	booking, reservation
le bar	bar
le parking	parking lot
un ascenseur (m)	elevator
le directeur	manager
le réceptionniste	male receptionist
la réceptionniste	female receptionist
le gardien de nuit	night guard, porter
la femme de chambre	maid, chambermaid
l'eau chaude (f)	hot water
la chambre pour une personne	single room
la chambre pour deux personnes	double room
la chambre à deux lits	twin room
le grand lit	double bed

ALERT!

When asking for directions and information, use the formal *vous*, and say "please" and "thank you." In general, rather than trying to formulate a complete sentence, you can just abbreviate with the essential, as in "La gare, s'il vous plait . . .?" or "Les toilettes, s'il vous plait . . .?" using intonation to indicate a question.

TRACK 78

Table 17-7

Directions

French	English
à gauche	left
à droite	right
tout droit	straight ahead
à côté de	next to
devant	in front of
derrière	in back of
en haut	up
en bas	down
près	near
près de	near to
loin	far
loin de	far from

Table 17-8

Places

French	English
Londres (f)	London
Genève (f)	Geneva
l'Angleterre (f)	England
l'Allemagne (f)	Germany
les États-Unis (m)	United States
le Canada	Canada
l'Europe (f)	Europe
l'Asie (f)	Asia
l'Amérique du Nord (f)	North America

l'Amérique du Sud (f)	South America
l'Afrique (f)	Africa
un Français	a Frenchman
une Française	a Frenchwoman

ALERT!

To describe a person's nationality, French sometimes uses the name of a language. When used in this fashion, it is capitalized. If the same word, such as *le français*, is used to indicate a language, the word is not capitalized.

Money

Because money is always an issue when traveling, the following vocabulary list includes some common French terms related to money and banking.

Table 17-9
Money

French	English
l'argent (m)	money
l'argent de poche (m)	pocket money
l'argent liquide (m)	cash
l'euro (m)	euro
le billet de banque	bill, bank note
le porte-monnaie	purse
le portefeuille	wallet
le paiement	payment
les économies (f)	savings
la banque	bank
le bureau de change	currency exchange outlet
le taux de change	exchange rate

le distributeur automatique	cash machine
le compte d'épargne	savings account
le retrait	withdrawal
le virement	transfer
la carte de crédit	credit card
la carte d'identité bancaire	bank card
le chéquier	check book
le carnet de chèques	check book
le chèque	check
le chèque de voyage	traveler's check

In a Restaurant

The following vocabulary list includes a number of French words you may come across in a restaurant. Don't forget to peruse the beverage section later in this chapter.

Table 17-10

Basic Restaurant Terms

TRACK 79

French	English
le restaurant	restaurant
le serveur	waiter
la serveuse	waitress
le chef	cook
le menu	menu
commander	to order
l'addition (f)	check, bill
le pourboire	tip
service compris	tip included
service non compris	tip not included
prix fixe	fixed price

Table 17-11
Placing Your Order

French	English
pané	breaded
farci	stuffed
bouilli	boiled
rôti	roasted
au gratin	with melted cheese
saignant	rare
à point	medium rare
bien cuit	well done
trop cuit	overdone
les hors-d'œuvre (m)	appetizers
la soupe	soup
le potage	soup
le plat principal	main course
la salade	salad
à la carte	side order
bon appétit	enjoy your meal
prix fixe	fixed price

FACT

You may have noticed there are two different words for soup. Traditionally, *la soupe* described broth-based soups, while *le potage* was used for thicker, creamier stews. Today many restaurants use the words interchangeably.

Beverages

The following list contains a number of French terms for things you can drink—memorize your favorites.

Table 17-12
Hot Beverages

French	English
le café	coffee
le café au lait	coffee with milk
la camomille	chamomile tea
le chocolat chaud	hot chocolate

Table 17-13
Cold Beverages

French	English
l'eau (f)	water
le lait	milk
le jus de pomme	apple juice
le jus d'orange	orange juice
la boisson	drink, beverage

Table 17-14
Alcohol and Spirits

French	English
l'alcool (m)	alcohol
la bière	beer
le vin rouge	red wine
le vin blanc	white wine

What's the difference between brandy and cognac?
The French pride themselves on both their brandy and cognac. Cognacs are a form of brandy, noted for their higher quality. Brandy and cognac are made by distilling wine, but don't mistake either of them for wine—they are much stronger and have a completely different taste.

Shopping Terms

The following vocabulary list contains a number of French verbs and expressions related to shopping.

TRACK 80

Table 17-15

Shopping Vocabulary

French	English
acheter	to buy
choisir	to choose
coûter	to cost
dépenser	to spend
échanger	to exchange
payer	to pay
vendre	to sell
faire les courses	to do the shopping
faire du shopping	to go shopping
faire des achats	to go shopping
bon marché	cheap
cher / chère	expensive
gratuit	free
en solde	on sale
d'occasion	secondhand

la caisse	cash register
le client	male customer
la cliente	female customer
le prix	price
le reçu	receipt
le vendeur	male clerk, cashier
la vendeuse	female clerk, cashier
les provisions	supplies, groceries
la taille	size
la pointure	shoe (and glove) size

Stores, Shops, and Markets

The following vocabulary list contains a number of French terms for different kinds of stores. If you get stuck when asking for a particular kind of store, you can always try asking for *le magasin de . . .* whatever it is you're trying to find; if that doesn't work, try describing the kinds of things you buy there. As a last resort, you can always try the English word and hope that it conveys the message.

Table 17-16
Shopping Vocabulary

French	English
une épicerie	grocery store
une agence de voyages	travel agency
le lavomatic	laundromat
la boulangerie	bakery
la pâtisserie	pastry shop
la librairie	bookstore
le grand magasin	department store
la pharmacie	pharmacy

le coiffeur	hairdresser
la quincaillerie	hardware store
le marchand de vins	wine merchant

Books, Newspapers, and Magazines

Spoken French is one thing to master, but it doesn't hurt to brush up on your written French, too. Signs, newspapers, books, and letters are all forms of written French you may encounter, so get used to reading it.

Reading these materials can help you hone your French skills, too. Here is a list of words that are commonly used when referring to media that contain written French.

TRACK 81

Table 17-17

Media Vocabulary

French	English
un livre	book
un roman	novel
un écrivain	writer
une librairie	bookstore
un journal	newspaper
un journaliste	male journalist
une journaliste	female journalist
un article	article
un magazine	magazine
une revue	magazine
les petites annonces	classified ads
une photo	photograph
la photographie	photography
la poésie	poetry
un poème	poem

une bande dessinée	comic strip
écrire	to write
lire	to read

TV, Radio, and the Internet

Depending on where you live, you may be able to access some French TV shows or radio broadcasts. Many television shows are available via satellite transmission, while others are broadcast on local special-interest stations, and many French radio stations are available via shortwave radio transmissions. Check your local listings for details. You can also find a good number of broadcasts on the Internet, in addition to other French resources available on the Web.

The Internet has made an impact on the entire world, bringing it much closer together. There is an incredible variety of French Web sites available, including sites that will help you with your pronunciation by providing you with sound clips to listen to. Don't forget about this wonderful free resource while you're learning the French language. .

Table 17-18
Television Vocabulary

French	English
la télévision	television
le petit écran	television (literally "the small screen")
regarder	to watch
allumer	to turn on
une chaîne	channel
en direct	live
diffuser	to broadcast
passer à la télé	to appear on tv

un documentaire	documentary
un épisode	episode
une publicité	commercial

Table 17-19
Internet Vocabulary

French	English
la toile d'araignée mondiale (TAM)	World Wide Web
la toile	Web
un logiciel de navigation	Web browser
un navigateur	Web browser
l'Internet (m)	Internet
une adresse universelle (f)	Uniform Resource Locator; URL
l'hypertexte (m)	hypertext
un domaine	domain
un forum	newsgroup
un signet	bookmark
une liste de signets	bookmark file, bookmark list

Activité 17

Listen to the CD and write each sentence that you hear in the space provided below.

TRACK 82

1. _____
2. _____
3. _____
4. _____
5. _____
6. _____

Chapter 18

Studying and Working in French-Speaking Countries

If you have the opportunity to study or work in a French-speaking region, take it! The experience will allow you to immerse yourself in the French language, which is an ideal way to learn—and learn quickly! This chapter helps you master some of the French terminology that goes along with studying and working.

18

School Terms

The following vocabulary list includes some of the more common terms associated with going to school.

Table 18-1
School Terms

French	English
le livre	book
le dictionnaire	dictionary
le professeur	teacher
la bibliothèque	library
le cahier	notebook
une école	school
un étudiant	student
une étudiante	student (f)
le stylo	pen
le crayon	pencil
la gomme	eraser
les devoirs (m)	homework
un examen	test
la salle de classe	classroom
le classeur	binder
le papier	paper
le cours	course

In French, the word *professeur* is always masculine, even if the teacher is female. Other words, such as *étudiant* and *étudiante*, can change to reflect the sex of the person to whom the word refers. You can learn more about these kinds of words in Chapter 5.

Technology

Technology has become increasingly important in our lives, to the point where it has become difficult to avoid a computer, if you were so inclined.

Table 18-2
Computer Terms

TRACK 83

French	English
le lecteur de disquettes	disk drive
la messagerie électronique	e-mail
un e-mail	e-mail
un courriel	e-mail
une erreur	error
une icône	icon
le fichier	file
le clavier	keyboard
la mémoire	memory
la souris	mouse
le mot de passe	password
une imprimante	printer
un écran	screen
le logiciel	software
le virus	virus

The Working World

The following vocabulary lists contain a number of French words that are often used to describe various aspects of the working world. In order to make it easier for you to remember, the categories are broken out between verbs, adjectives, and nouns.

Table 18-3
Verbs Commonly Associated with Work

French	English
travailler	to work
avoir l'intention de	to intend to
devenir	to become
s'intéresser à	to be interested in
avoir de l'ambition	to be ambitious
avoir de l'expérience	to have experience
manquer d'expérience	to lack experience
être sans emploi	to be unemployed
chercher un emploi	to look for work; to look for a job
refuser	to reject
accepter	to accept
trouver un emploi	to find a job
trouver du travail	to find work
réussir	to be successful
gagner	to earn
gagner sa vie	to earn a living
payer	to pay
prendre des vacances	to take a vacation
prendre un jour de congé	to take a day off
licencier	to lay off, to fire

démissionner	to resign
quitter	to leave
prendre sa retraite	to retire

Table 18-4
Adjectives Commonly Associated with Work

French	English
difficile	difficult
facile	easy
intéressant	interesting
passionnant	exciting
ennuyeux	boring
dangereux	dangerous
important	important

TRACK 84

Table 18-5
Nouns Commonly Associated with Work

French	English
le contrat	contract
le contrat de travail	employment contract
la demande d'emploi	job application
une annonce	advertisement, announcement
une offre d'emploi	job offer
la paye	wages
le salaire	salary, wages
la semaine de trente-cinq heures	thirty-five-hour week
les impôts	taxes
une augmentation	pay raise
un voyage d'affaires	business trip
un voyage d'agrément	leisure trip

Professions and Jobs

The vocabulary in this section includes a number of French terms for different types of occupations. Many of them have an alternate masculine and feminine form, depending on the sex of the person the word is being used to represent. With some of the words, only the article changes, while others undergo more of a transformation.

Table 18-6
List of Professions

TRACK 85

French	English
un agriculteur	farmer
un artiste	artist
une artiste	female artist
un assistant social	male social worker
une assistante sociale	female social worker
un astronaute	male astronaut
une astronaute	female astronaut
un avocat	male lawyer
une avocate	female lawyer
le bijoutier	male jeweler
la bijoutière	female jeweler
le boucher	male butcher
la bouchère	female butcher
le douanier	male customs officer
la douanière	female customs officer
le facteur	male letter carrier
la factrice	female letter carrier
le fleuriste	male florist
la fleuriste	female florist

le gendarme	police officer
un infirmier	male nurse
une infirmière	female nurse
un ingénieur	engineer
le journaliste	male journalist
la journaliste	female journalist
le pasteur	minister
le prêtre	priest
la religieuse	nun
le secrétaire	male secretary
la secrétaire	female secretary
le traducteur	male translator
la traductrice	female translator

The following professions don't differentiate gender when it comes to the sex of the person the word is being used to represent. *Un mannequin*, for example, can be used to describe both male and female models, but there is no feminine form of the word. It is always used in the masculine. Review the following words and remember not to use them with another gender.

Table 18-7
Professions That Do Not Differentiate Gender

French	English
le mannequin	model
un écrivain	writer
le docteur	doctor
le médecin	doctor
le savant	scholar, scientist

Activité 18

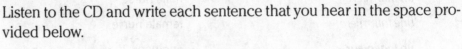

Listen to the CD and write each sentence that you hear in the space provided below.

TRACK 86

1. _____
2. _____
3. _____
4. _____
5. _____
6. _____

Chapter 19

Family, Friends, and You

Even if your family and friends aren't remotely French and have no desire to speak the language, you can practice your French skills by thinking of (and referring to) to your family, friends, pets, body parts, and clothing by their French terms. Your loved ones—including, perhaps, Rover—may tire of your game, but you'll benefit by rapidly improving your vocabulary.

Family

The following vocabulary list includes French terms for common familial relationships. These words are all nouns, can appear as the subject or object of the sentence, and follow the same rules as the nouns in Chapter 5.

TRACK 87

Table 19-1
Your Family

French	English
la famille	family
le mari	husband
la femme	wife
les parents (m)	parents
le père	father
la mère	mother
le fils	son
la fille	daughter
le frère	brother
la sœur	sister
les grand-parents (m)	grandparents
le grand-père	grandfather
la grand-mère	grandmother
les petits-enfants	grandchildren
le petit-fils	grandson
la petite-fille	granddaughter
un oncle	uncle
la tante	aunt
le neveu	nephew

la nièce	niece
le cousin	male cousin
la cousine	female cousin
le beau-père	stepfather / father-in-law
la belle-mère	stepmother / mother-in-law
le demi-frère	half-brother
la demi-sœur	half-sister

Holidays and Occasions

The following vocabulary list includes some special occasions and holidays that you probably spend celebrating with friends or family members. These expressions can stand on their own as simple expressions, or you can use them as part of other sentences.

Table 19-2
Holiday Greetings

French	English
Bon anniversaire !	Happy birthday!
Bonne année !	Happy New Year!
félicitations	congratulations
Joyeux Noël	Merry Christmas
Joyeuses Pâques	Happy Easter
meilleurs vœux	best wishes

Friends

The following vocabulary list includes some common French terms for friends.

Table 19-3
Your Friends

French	English
un ami	male friend
une amie	female friend
le copain (m)	male friend, pal, mate
la copine (f)	female friend, pal, mate
le petit ami	boyfriend
la petite amie	girlfriend
le voisin	male neighbor
la voisine	female neighbor

FACT

There is a subtle difference in meaning between the terms *un ami* and *un copain* in French. In French, *un ami* is a very endearing term; it is used only for the closest of friends. In English, we sometimes assign a broad meaning to the term "friends," so the words are not really interchangeable. A person can go through life having many *copains*, but he or she will have a select few true *amis*.

Pets

To many people, pets can be like members of the family, so what better place to learn some words for different kinds of pets? The following list includes some common household pets. If you have a pet, be sure to memorize the word for him or her in French!

Table 19-4
Pets

French	English
un animal de compagnie	pet
un chat	cat
un chien	dog
une souris	mouse
un cheval	horse
un poisson	fish
un hamster	hamster
un oiseau	bird
un lapin	rabbit
un serpent	snake
une tortue	tortoise

Parts of the Body

The following vocabulary list contains some French terms for parts of the body. To help yourself remember these, touch each part of the body as you say the French word out loud.

TRACK 89

Table 19-5
Parts of the Body

French	English
les cheveux (m)	hair
le corps	body
la tête	head
le visage	face

un œil	eye
les yeux (m)	eyes
le nez	nose
une joue	cheek
la bouche	mouth
les dents	teeth
une oreille	ear
le cou	neck
la poitrine	chest
l'estomac	stomach
un bras	arm
une épaule	shoulder
le coude	elbow
le poignet	wrist
la main	hand
le doigt	finger
un ongle	fingernail
le pouce	thumb
le dos	back
une jambe	leg
un genou	knee
une cheville	ankle
un pied	foot
un orteil	toe

When referring to parts of the body in French, you don't use a possessive adjective like you do in English. While we say things like "my hand" or "my arm," in French, a reflexive verb is generally used instead (see Chapter 13):

Je me brosse les dents.	I am brushing my teeth.
Je me lave les mains.	I am washing my hands.
Je me coiffe les cheveux.	I am doing my hair.

Clothing

The following vocabulary list contains a number of French terms for clothing and other things you can buy in a shop. For your convenience, a separate section is broken out for men's and women's clothes.

TRACK 90

Table 19-6
General Clothing Items: Les Vêtements

French	English
le manteau	coat
le pardessus	overcoat
un imperméable	raincoat
la veste	jacket
le blouson	jacket
le costume	suit
le maillot de bain	bathing suit
un uniforme	uniform
le pantalon	pants, trousers
le blue-jean	blue jeans
le jean	jeans
le pyjama	pajamas
la chemise	shirt
les chaussettes (f)	socks

Table 19-7
Women's Clothing: Les Vêtements de Femme

French	English
le bikini	bikini
la chemise de nuit	nightgown
le chemisier	blouse
le collant	pantyhose, tights
un ensemble	woman's suit
la jupe	skirt
la minijupe	miniskirt
la robe	dress
la robe de chambre	robe, nightgown
le slip	panties
le soutien-gorge	bra
le tailleur	woman's suit

Table 19-8
Men's Clothing: Les Vêtements d'Homme

French	English
la ceinture	belt
la chemise	shirt
le costume	suit
la cravate	tie
le maillot de corps	undershirt
le nœud papillon	bow tie
le smoking	tuxedo
la veste sport	sport jacket

Table 19-9
Accessories: Les Accessoires

French	English
une alliance (f)	wedding ring
la bague	ring
la bague de fiançailles	engagement ring
le béret	beret
la bijouterie	jewelry
la boucle d'oreille	earring
le bouton de manchette	cufflink
le bracelet	bracelet
la broche	brooch
le châle	shawl
le chapeau	hat
les chaussures (f)	shoes
les chaussures à talons hauts (f)	high-heeled shoes
le collier	necklace
le foulard	scarf
les gants (m)	gloves
les lunettes (f)	glasses
les lunettes de soleil (f)	sunglasses
la montre	watch
le mouchoir	handkerchief
le pendentif	pendant
le parapluie	umbrella
le ruban	ribbon
le sac à dos	backpack
le sac à main	purse, handbag

Colors

The following vocabulary list contains a number of French adjectives for colors. As adjectives, when they are used with a noun, they must agree in number and in gender. The masculine form of the adjective can also be used with an article to represent the color as a noun; for the most part, however, you will most often use these colors as adjectives to modify and describe nouns. See Chapter 10 for more on adjectives.

TRACK 91

Table 19-10
Colors

Masculine	Feminine	English
noir	*noire*	black
bleu	*bleue*	blue
marron	*marron*	brown
vert	*verte*	green
gris	*grise*	grey
orange	*orange*	orange
rose	*rose*	pink
violet	*violette*	purple
rouge	*rouge*	red
blanc	*blanche*	white
jaune	*jaune*	yellow

To form the plural for most of these adjectives, simply add an "s" to the end of the word, with the following exceptions:

- *Marron* and *orange* do not change in the plural; simply use the singular form of the word.
- The masculine plural form of grey still uses the word *gris*; because it already ends in an "s," so you don't add one.

Activité 19

Listen to the CD and write each sentence that you hear in the space provided below.

TRACK 92

1. _____
2. _____
3. _____
4. _____
5. _____
6. _____

Chapter 20

Your House or Apartment

This chapter provides you with a number of French words commonly used to describe your daily routine and your home. To assist your memory, visualize each room and the things inside it and use the French words to describe them. You may also want to walk around the room and name things as you touch them.

Your Daily Routine

The following vocabulary list includes a number of French terms for activities you find yourself doing throughout the day. For convenience, the list is broken out into morning, afternoon, and evening routines.

Table 20-1
Morning Routine

French	English
le matin	morning
allumer la radio	to turn on the radio
bâiller	to yawn
faire sa toilette	to have a wash, to wash up
aller aux toilettes	to go to the bathroom
mettre ses verres de contact	to put one's contact lenses
faire son lit	to make one's bed
prendre son petit déjeuner	to have breakfast
aller travailler	to go to work
verrouiller la porte	to lock the door
tous les matins	every morning

Table 20-2
Afternoon Routine

French	English
l'après-midi (m)	afternoon
allumer la télévision	to turn on the television
arroser les plantes	to water the plants
éteindre la radio	to turn off the radio
rentrer à la maison	to come home, to go home
rentrer de l'école	to come back from school
rentrer du travail	to come back from work

Table 20-3
Evening Routine

French	English
le soir	evening
éteindre la télévision	to turn off the television
se reposer	to have a rest
faire la sieste	to have a nap
se déshabiller	to get undressed
fermer la porte	to close the door
fermer les rideaux	to close the curtains
mettre son réveil	to set the alarm clock

A Tour of Your Home

To continue to build your vocabulary, take a tour of your home, noting the following items.

TRACK 93

Table 20-4

French	English
la fenêtre	window
la moquette	wall-to-wall carpeting
les meubles	furniture
le mur	wall
le plafond	ceiling
la porte	door
le rideau	curtain
le sol	floor
le tapis	rug
le divan	divan
le piano	piano

la table basse	coffee table
le canapé	sofa
le fauteuil	armchair
le fauteuil à bascule	rocking chair
le bureau	desk, office
la chaise	chair
une imprimante	printer
la lampe	lamp
le téléphone	telephone
le buffet	sideboard
la table	table
la pendule	grandfather clock
une étagère	shelf
une cheminée	fireplace
la baignoire	bathtub
le bain	bath
la douche	shower
le lavabo	sink
une armoire de toilette	medicine cabinet
la balance	bathroom scale
le savon	soap
la serviette de toilette	towel
le drap de bain	bath towel
une éponge	sponge
la brosse	brush
le peigne	comb
la brosse à dents	toothbrush
la dentifrice	toothpaste
le shampooing	shampoo

le bain moussant	bubble bath
les sels de bain (m)	bath salts
le déodorant	deodorant
le papier hygiénique	toilet paper
le sèche-cheveux	hair dryer
une affiche	poster
une armoire	wardrobe, closet
la commode	chest of drawers
la couverture	blanket
le couvre-lit	bedspread
le drap	sheet
une couette	down quilt, comforter
la lampe	lamp
le lit	bed
le matelas	mattress
le miroir	mirror
un oreiller	pillow
le réveil	alarm clock

Rooms in a House

In this vocabulary list, you'll learn words for parts of the house and various rooms.

Table 20-5
Rooms

French	English
le balcon	balcony
la buanderie	laundry room
le bureau	study

la cave	cellar
la chambre	bedroom
le couloir	hall
la cuisine	kitchen
un étage	floor, story
les escaliers (m)	stairs
le garage	garage
le grenier	attic
le jardin	garden
la marche	step
la porte	door
le sous-sol	basement
la salle à manger	dining room
la salle de séjour	living room
le salon	living room
le toit	roof
dedans	inside
dehors	outside
en haut	upstairs
en bas	downstairs

Want an easy and fun way to practice the French words for rooms of the house? Why not play the Parker Brothers game *Clue* in French? Not too many people have conservatories or ballrooms in the house, or even a library or study, for that matter, but it's still good practice. Simply use the rooms from the vocabulary list in Table 20-5 and rename the rooms to whatever you like. Following is a list of translations for the weapons and some rooms, should you decide to play.

le couteau	knife
le chandelier	candlestick
le revolver	revolver
la corde	rope
la clé anglaise	wrench
le tuyau de plomb	lead pipe
le conservatoire	conservatory
le petit salon	lounge
la salle de bal	ballroom
la salle de billard	billiard room

Apartments

The following vocabulary list includes some French terms associated with renting an apartment.

Table 20-6
Apartment Vocabulary

French	English
habiter	to live
le loyer	rent
louer	to rent
le locataire	tenant
un appartement	apartment
un immeuble	apartment building
le propriétaire	male owner
la propriétaire	female owner
le concierge	male buliding manager
la concierge	female building manager

Housework

The following vocabulary list includes a number of French terms associated with cleaning up and other actions that are performed around the house.

TRACK 94

Table 20-7
Housework

French	English
jeter	to throw out
épousseter	to dust
laver	to wash
rincer	to rinse
essuyer	to wipe, to dry
sécher	to dry
faire les lits	to make the beds
repasser	to iron
s'occuper de	to look after
utiliser	to use
aider	to help
donner un coup de main	to give a hand
la ménagère	housewife
la femme de ménage	maid, cleaning lady
une aide ménagère	help, home care
lave la vaisselle	to wash the dishes
le lave-vaisselle	dishwasher
le micro-onde	microwave

In the Kitchen and at the Market

This vocabulary list includes a number of French terms associated with the kitchen and cooking. Later in this chapter, you'll even get to follow a recipe for authentic French bread!

Table 20-8
Kitchen and Market Terms

French	English
la chaise	chair
la cuisine	kitchen
la table	table
un évier	kitchen sink
un four à micro-ondes	microwave oven
le frigo	fridge
le réfrigérateur	refrigerator
le congélateur	freezer
la nourriture	food
le lave-vaisselle	dishwasher
le four	oven
la cuisinière	stove top
la cuisinière électrique	electric stovetop
la cuisinière à gaz	gas stovetop
le gaz	gas
l'électricité (f)	electricity
le grille-pain	toaster
la bouilloire électrique	electric kettle
avoir faim	to be hungry

manger	to eat
avoir soif	to be thirsty
boire	to drink
le repas	meal
le petit déjeuner	breakfast
le déjeuner	lunch
le dîner	dinner
le goûter	snack
le pique-nique	picnic
faire la cuisine	to cook
faire à manger	to prepare a meal
faire la vaisselle	to do the dishes
nettoyer	to clean
préparer	to prepare
couper	to cut
râper	to grate
éplucher	to peel
bouillir	to boil
frire	to fry
griller	to grill; to toast
rôtir	to roast
mettre la table	to set the table
débarrasser la table	to clear the table

Your Grocery List

The following vocabulary lists contain a number of French words for food and grocery items. They are broken out into sections to make it easier for you to memorize.

TRACK 95

Table 20-9
Vegetables

French	English
le légume	vegetable
la pomme de terre	potato
les petits pois (m)	green peas
un haricot	bean
les frites (f)	French fries
le chou	cabbage
le chou-fleur	cauliflower
les choux de Bruxelles (m)	brussels sprouts
la laitue	lettuce
les épinards (m)	spinach
les brocolis (m)	broccoli
le maïs	corn
la tomate	tomato
le concombre	cucumber

Table 20-10
Fruit

French	English
le fruit	fruit, a piece of fruit
la pomme	apple
la poire	pear
un abricot	apricot
la pêche	peach
la prune	plum

la nectarine	nectarine
le melon	melon
un ananas	pineapple
la banane	banana
une orange	orange
le pamplemousse	grapefruit
le citron	lemon
la fraise	strawberry
la framboise	raspberry
la cerise	cherry

TRACK 96

Table 20-11
Staples

French	English
le pain	bread
la baguette	French bread
la tartine	bread and butter
le pain grillé	toast
le croissant	croissant, crescent roll
le beurre	butter
la margarine	margarine
la confiture	jam
le miel	honey
le sucre	sugar
le sal	salt
le poivre	pepper

Table 20-12
Meat, Poultry, Seafood, and Eggs

French	English
la viande	meat
le porc	pork
le jambon	ham
le veau	veal
le boeuf	beef
un agneau	lamb
le mouton	mutton
le poulet	chicken
la dinde	turkey
le canard	duck
la volaille	poultry
le biftek	steak
les escargots (m)	snails
les cuisses de grenouille (f)	frogs' legs
la morue	cod
la sardine	sardine
la sole	sole
le thon	tuna fish
la truite	trout
le saumon	salmon
le saumon fumé	smoked salmon
les fruits de mer (m)	seafood
le homard	lobster

l'huître	oyster
la crevette	shrimp
la moule	mussel
un oeuf	egg
un œuf à la coque	soft-boiled egg
un œuf sur le plat	fried egg
les œufs au jambon (m)	ham and eggs
les œufs brouillés (m)	scrambled eggs
une omelette	omelet

ALERT!

There are a number of ways you can increase your French food vocabulary. Try calling familiar foods by their French names. Write the French word on a label, and stick it to the package. When you're cooking, make a conscious effort to think about the names of the items in French. Working with them actively helps to entrench the words in your memory.

If you have friends who are learning the language, you can have great fun by having a French party. Have each friend bring a French dish and set up little signs with the French name on it next to each container. Have the guests quiz each other on the names of the food items.

Activité 20

Listen to the CD and write each sentence that you hear in the space provided below.

TRACK 97

1. _____
2. _____
3. _____
4. _____
5. _____
6. _____

Answer Key

Activité 3

1. *grande*
2. *courte*
3. *courtoise*
4. *fermée*
5. *intelligente*
6. *vraie*
7. *française*
8. *amusante*

Activité 4

1. *Le professeur est en classe.*
2. *La viande n'est pas bonne.*
3. *Je déteste le café.*
4. *As-tu du lait?*
5. *Non, je n'ai pas de farine.*

Activité 5

1. *les fils*
2. *les repas*
3. *les prix*
4. *les détails*
5. *les baux*
6. *les couteaux*
7. *les animaux*
8. *les yeux*

Activité 6

1. *J'ai soif.*
2. *Vous courez très vite !*
3. *Nous sommes très heureux.*
4. *Ils finissent leur devoir.*
5. *Vous devez travailler plus.*
6. *Est-ce que tu étudies la littérature anglaise?*
7. *Je te présente mon cousin André.*
8. *Vous parlez français?*

Activité 7

1. *Qu'est-ce que tu fais?*
2. *Est-ce que vous voulez un café?*

3. *Lisez le journal.*
4. *Parlez-vous anglais?*

Activité 8

1. *I do not go to the library.*
2. *You never go downtown.*
3. *We do not love anybody.*
4. *They are not at the university anymore.*
5. *It does not go anywhere.*

Activité 9

1. *Qui est au téléphone?*
2. *Je ne veux pas cette chemise . . . je voudrais celle-là.*
3. *Est-ce que tu vois Jean? Non, je ne le vois pas.*
4. *Vous allez à la bibliothèque? Oui, j'y vais.*
5. *C'est le garçon auquel j'ai donné un stylo.*
6. *C'est le livre dont vous avez besoin?*

Activité 10

1. *C'est un film étranger.*
2. *Le café est de qualité supérieure.*
3. *C'est un vieil homme.*
4. *Il est complètement fou !*
5. *Mon père est français.*
6. *Je n'ai pas aimé ce livre, qui était ennuyeux.*
7. *Qu'est-ce que ce chien est gros !*
8. *Est-ce que les fruits sont frais?*

Activité 11

1. *vraiment*
2. *évidemment*
3. *fréquemment*

4. *brièvement*
5. *bien*
6. *gentiment*
7. *mal*
8. *mieux*

Activité 12

1. *Elle a écouté de la musique.*
2. *Elles ont fait leur devoir.*
3. *Avez-vous perdu le livre?*
4. *Je suis né à l'hôpital.*
5. *Il pleuvait.*
6. *J'attendais depuis deux heures quand il est arrivé.*
7. *Nous mangions à la maison.*
8. *Il n'aimait pas les cerises.*

Activité 13

1. *Je m'appelle David.*
2. *Il s'habille dans sa chambre.*
3. *Vous ne vous trompez pas souvent.*
4. *Vous êtes-vous amusés au cinéma hier soir?*
5. *Je me suis réveillé à huit heures.*
6. *Nous nous sommes amusés au parc.*

Activité 14

1. *Je vais chanter à la chorale.*
2. *Je vais acheter un billet.*
3. *Je prendrai un café.*
4. *Nous voyagerons.*
5. *Nous ne regarderons pas le film.*
6. *Est-ce que vous serez parti(e)s à cinq heures demain?*

Activité 15

Answers will vary. Responses shown below are examples.

Bonjour, Monsieur.

Je voudrais un filet mignon.

Je prendrais du thé, s'il vous plaît.

Oui. Merci.

Activité 16

1. *Je doute que tu viennes.*
2. *Elle veut que tu sois heureux.*
3. *Tu es content qu'elle réussisse.*
4. *Je ne pense pas que tu aies raison.*
5. *Il est douteux que nous finissions.*
6. *Il veut que tu ailles avec lui.*

Activité 17

1. *Pour circuler dans Paris, prenez le métro.*
2. *Votre carte d'embarquement, s'il vous plaît?*
3. *Ce vol est un vol non-fumeur.*
4. *Est-ce que vous voulez un billet simple ou un billet aller-retour?*
5. *Est-ce que le service est compris dans l'addition?*
6. *Bonjour. Je voudrais une chambre pour une personne, s'il vous plaît.*

Activité 18

1. *Je t'ai envoyé un e-mail. Tu ne l'as pas reçu?!*
2. *Quel est votre mot de passe?*
3. *Je cherche un emploi depuis trois mois.*
4. *J'étudie l'histoire à l'université. J'aimerais être avocat.*
5. *Mon père est journaliste.*
6. *Ma mère fait un voyage d'affaires cette semaine.*

Activité 19

1. *Est-ce que tu as un petit ami?*
2. *À la maison, nous avons un chat et deux chiens.*
3. *Je me lave le visage.*
4. *Je cherche un nouveau maillot de bain.*
5. *Où est-ce que tu as acheté cette jolie jupe?*
6. *Il porte un costume.*

Activité 20

1. *Aline, est-ce que tu as fait ton lit?*
2. *Je suis rentré de l'école à 6 heures.*
3. *Dans le salon, il y a un canapé, deux fauteuils, et une table basse.*
4. *Je loue un appartement en ville.*
5. *Est-ce que vous avez un four à micro-ondes?*
6. *Je vais chez le marchand de primeurs pour acheter des fraises.*

French-to-English Glossary

à (prep)
at, to, in, of, by

à bientôt
see you soon

à côté de
next to

à demain
see you tomorrow

à droite
right

à gauche
left

à la carte
side order

à la longue
in the long run

à moitié
half

à peu près
nearly, about

à point
medium rare

à propos
by the way, at the right time

à quelle heure
when, at what time

à tout à l'heure
see you later

à vos souhaits
bless you (after someone sneezes)

abribus (n m)
bus shelter

abricot (n m)
apricot

absolu (a)
absolute

absolument (a)
absolutely

accent (n m)
accent

accepter (v)
to accept

accessoire (n m)
accessory

accident (n m)
accident

accomplir (v)
to accomplish

accourir (v)
to hasten

accueillir (v)
to welcome

achat (n m)
purchase

acheter (v)
to buy

acteur (n m)
actor

actif, active (a)
active, busy, energetic

actrice (n f)
actress

actuel, actuelle (a)
present, current

addition (n f)
check, bill

adieu (n m)
farewell

admirateur, admiratrice (a)
admirer

adresse universelle (n f)
Uniform Resource Locator (URL)

aéroport (n m)
airport

affiche (n f)
poster

Afrique (n f)
Africa

agacer (v)
to irritate

agence de voyages (n f)
travel agency

agir (v)
to act

agneau (n m)
lamb

agriculteur (n m)
farmer

aide ménagère (n f)
help, home care

aider (v)
to help

aigu
acute (accent)

aigu, aiguë (a)
pointed, sharp, keen, acute

aile (n f)
wing

aimer (v)
to like, to love

aisément (adv)
easily, readily, freely, comfortably

alcool (n m)
alcohol

Allemagne (n f)
Germany

Allemand (n m)
German

aller (v irr)
to go; (past p.) allé

aller aux toilettes
to go to the restroom

aller travailler
to go to work

alliance (n f)
wedding ring

allumer la radio
to turn on the radio

allumer la télévision
to turn on the television

allumer (v)
to turn on

alphabet (n m)
alphabet

altitude (n f)
altitude

ambassade (n f)
embassy

ambigu, ambiguë (a)
ambiguous

Amérique du Nord (n f)
North America

Amérique du Sud (n f)
South America

ami (n m)
friend

amie (n f)
female friend

amitié (n f)
friendship

amoureux, amoureuse (a)
loving, enamored, in love

amusant, amusante, (a)
amusing, entertaining

ananas (n m)
pineapple

ancien, ancienne
before the noun former; after the noun old, ancient, antique

anglais (n m)
English

Anglais (n m)
an Englishman

Anglaise (n f)
an Englishwoman

Angleterre (n f)
England

animal (n m)
animal

annonce (n f)
advertisement, announcement

annoncer (v)
to announce

annulé (a)
canceled

antérieur, antérieure, (a)
anterior, earlier, previous, former

août
August

appartement (m)
apartment

appeler (v)
to call; (se) to be named; to be called

applaudir (v)
to applaud

appuyer (v)
to support, to press on

après (prep)
after

après-midi (n m)
afternoon

architecte (n m) (m only)
architect

argent (n m)
money

argent de poche (n m)
pocket money

armoire (n f)
wardrobe, closet

armoire de toilette (n f)
medicine cabinet

arrêt d'autobus (n m)
bus stop

arrière (n m)
the back

arrivée (n f)
arrival

arriver (v)
to arrive; (past p.) arrivé

arroser les plantes
to water the plants

article (n m)
article

artiste (n f)
female artist

artiste (n m)
male artist

ascenseur (n m)
elevator

Asie (n f)
Asia

assez (adv)
enough

assistance (n f)
assistance

assistant social (n m)
social worker

assistante sociale (n f)
female social worker

astronaute (n m et f)
astronaut

attendre (v)
to wait

atterrissage forcé (n m)
emergency landing

atterrissage (n m)
landing

au gratin
with melted cheese

au revoir
goodbye

ne ... aucun
no one, not one

augmentation (n f)
pay raise

aujourd'hui (adv)
today

aussi (conj)
also, as, likewise, too, besides

Australie (n f)
Australia

auto (n f)
car

autobus (n m)
bus

automne (n m)
autumn

autre (a)
other, another, different

avant (prep)
before

avant (n m)
the front

avant-bras (n m)
forearm

avec (conj)
with

aventure (n f)
adventure

avion (n m)
plane

avion supersonique (n m)
supersonic plane

avocat (n m)
male lawyer

avocate (n f)
female lawyer

avoir (v)
to have, to hold; (past p.) eu

avoir ... ans
to be an age

avoir besoin de
to need

avoir chaud
to be hot, to feel hot

avoir de l'ambition
to be ambitious

avoir de l'expérience
to have experience

avoir de la chance
to be lucky

avoir envie de
to feel like

avoir faim
to be hungry

avoir froid
to be cold, to feel cold

avoir honte de
to be ashamed of

avoir l'air
to seem

avoir l'intention de
to intend to

avoir l'occasion de
to have the opportunity

avoir lieu
to take place

avoir mal
to have an ache

avoir peur de
to be afraid

avoir raison
to be right

avoir soif
to be thirsty

avoir sommeil
to be sleepy

avoir tort
to be wrong

avril (n m)
April

bagages à main (m pl.)
handbags, carry-on luggage

bague de fiançailles (n f)
engagement ring

bague (n f)
ring

baguette (n f)
French bread

baignoire (n f)
bath

bail (n m)
lease; (pl.) baux

bâiller (v)
to yawn

bain (n m)
bath

bain moussant (n m)
bubble bath

balance (n f)
scale

balayer (v)
to sweep

balcon (n m)
balcony

banane (n f)
banana

bande dessinée (n f)
comic strip

banque (n f)
bank

bar (n m)
bar

bas, basse (a)
low, inferior

bateau (n m)
boat

bâtir (v)
to construct, build

beau, belle (a)
beautiful, fine, handsome, pretty

beaucoup (adv)
much, many

beau-père (n m)
stepfather

beauté (n f)
beauty

bégayer (v)
to stammer

bel
see beau

belle-mère (n f)
stepmother

béret (n m)
beret

beurre (n m)
butter

bibliothèque (n f)
library

bidet (n m)
bidet

bien (adv)
well, rightly, finely, much, very,
entirely, completely

bien cuit
well done

bien sûr
of course

bière (n f)
beer

biftek (n m)
steak

bijou (n m)
jewel

bijouterie (n f)
jewelry store

bijoutier (n m)
male jeweler

bijoutière (n f)
female jeweler

bikini (n m)
bikini

billet (n m)
ticket

billet aller-retour (n m)
round trip ticket

billet de banque (n m)
bill, bank note

billet simple (n m)
one-way ticket

blanc, blanche (a)
white, clean, blank

blé (n m)
wheat

bleu, bleue (a)
blue

blouson (n m)
jacket

blue-jean (n m)
blue jeans

boeuf (n m)
beef

boire (v)
to drink; (past p.) bu

boire (n m)
drink, beverage

boisson (n f)
drink

bon, bonne
before the noun: enjoyable; after
the noun: good, kind, favorable

bon appétit
enjoy your meal

bon marché
cheap

bonjour
hello, good morning, good
afternoon

bonne (n f)
maid

bonne chance !
good luck!

bonne nuit
good night, sleep well

bonsoir
good evening

bouche (n f)
mouth

boucher (n m)
male butcher

bouchère (n f)
female butcher

boucherie (n f)
butcher store

boucle d'oreille (n f)
earring

bouilli (a)
boiled

bouillir (v)
to boil

bouilloire électrique (n f)
electric kettle

boulangerie (n f)
bakery

boutique (n f)
small shop

bouton de manchette (n m)
cufflink

bracelet (n m)
bracelet

bras (n m)
arm

brave (a)
before the noun: nice; after the
noun: courageous

bravo
well done

bref, brève (a)
short, brief, concise

brièvement (adv)
briefly, succinctly, in short

brillamment (adv)
brilliantly, in a brilliant manner

broche (n f)
brooch

brocoli (n m)
broccoli

brosse (n f)
brush

brosse à dents (n f)
toothbrush

brosser (v se)
to brush

bruit (m)
noise

buanderie (n f)
laundry room

buffet (n m)
sideboard

bureau (n m)
study, office, desk

bureau de change (n m)
currency exchange outlet

bus (n m)
bus

cadeau (n m)
gift

café (n m)
coffee

café au lait (n m)
coffee with milk

cahier (n m)
notebook

caisse (n f)
cash register

calme (a)
tranquil, quiet, serene, calm

camion (n m)
truck

camomille (n f)
chamomile tea

Canada (n m)
Canada

canadien, canadienne (a)
Canadian

canal (n m)
canal

canapé (n m)
sofa

canard (n m)
duck

carnaval (n m)
carnival

carnet de chèques (n m)
checkbook

carte (n f)
menu

carte d'embarquement (n f)
boarding pass

carte bancaire (n f)
bank card

carte de crédit (n f)
credit card

casse-croûte (n m)
snack

cave (n f)
cellar

ce, cet
this

cédille
cedilla (accent)

ceinture (n f)
belt, seat belt

célébrer (v)
to celebrate

cerise (n f)
cherry

certain, certaine (a)
before the noun: unique; after the noun: guaranteed

ces (adj pl.)
these

cette (adj f)
this

chaîne (n f)
a channel, chain

chaise (n f)
chair

châle (n m)
shawl

chambre (n f)
bedroom

chambre à deux lits (n f)
twin room

chambre pour deux personnes (n f)
double room

chambre pour une personne (n f)
single room

chance (n f)
chance, luck

chandelier (n m)
candlestick

changer (v)
to change

chanson (n f)
song

chapeau (n m)
hat

chaque (adj)
each, every

charger (v)
to charge

charter (n m)
charter flight

chaussettes (f pl.)
socks

chat (n m)
cat

chaud (a)
hot

chaussures (f pl.)
shoes

chaussures à talons hauts (f pl.)
high-heeled shoes

chef (n m and f)
cook

cheminée (n f)
fireplace

chemise (n f)
shirt

chemise de nuit (n f)
nightgown

chemisier (n m)
blouse

chèque (n m)
check

chèque de voyage (n m)
traveler's check

chéquier (n m)
checkbook

cher, chère (a)
before the noun: dear; after the
noun: dear, precious, expensive

chercher (v)
to look

chercher un emploi
to look for work; to look for a job

cheval (n m)
horse

cheveux (n m pl.)
hair

cheville (n f)
ankle

chez (prep)
at the home of, at the office of

chien (n m)
dog

Chinois (n m)
Chinese

chocolat chaud (n m)
hot chocolate

choisir (v)
to choose

choix (n m)
choice

chou (n m)
cabbage

chou-fleur (n m)
cauliflower

choux de Bruxelles (m pl.)
Brussels sprouts

cinéma (n m)
movie theater; cinema

cinquième (a)
fifth

circonflexe (a)
circumflex (accent)

cité (n f)
city

citron (n m)
lemon

classeur (n m)
binder

clavier (n m)
keyboard

clé anglaise (n f)
wrench

client (n m)
male customer

cliente (n f)
female customer

coiffeur (n m)
hairdresser, barber

coin (n m)
corner

collant (n m)
pantyhose, tights

collier (n m)
necklace

combien (adv)
how much

combien de
how many

comédie (n f)
comedy

commande (n f)
order, commission

commander (v)
to order

commencer (v)
to begin

comment (adv)
how

commissariat (n m)
police station

commode (n f)
chest of drawers

compagnie aérienne (n f)
airline

complet
no vacancies

costume (n m)
suit

complet, complète (a)
complete, whole

comprendre (v)
to understand; (past p.) compris

compris
included

compte d'épargne (n m)
savings account

compte sur livret (n m)
deposit account

concierge
caretaker

concombre (n.m)
cucumber

concret, concrète (a)
concrete, solid

conduire (v)
to drive (past p.) conduit

confiture (n f)
jam

confortable (a)
comfortable

congélateur (n m)
freezer

conseiller (v)
to advise

conservateur, conservatrice (a)
conservative, preserving

constamment (adv)
steadily, continually, constantly

content, contente (a)
content, satisfied, pleased, glad

contigu, contiguë (a)
adjoining, contiguous

contrat (n m)
contract

contrat de travail (n m)
employment contract

contribution (n f)
posting, contribution

convenablement (adv)
suitably, becomingly, decently

copain (n m)
friend, pal, mate

copine (n f)
female friend; (f) of copain

corail (n m)
coral

corde (n f)
rope

corps (n m)
body

corriger (v)
to correct

corrompre (v)
to corrupt

costume (n m)
suit

côté (n m)
side

cou (n m)
neck

coude (n m)
elbow

couette (n f)
comforter

couloir (n m)
hall

couper (v)
to cut

couper en tranches
to slice

courir (v irr)
to run

courriel
e-mail

cours (n m)
course, class

court, courte (a)
short, brief, concise, limited

courtois, courtoise (a)
courteous, polite

cousin (n m)
male cousin

cousine (n f)
female cousin

couteau (n m)
knife

coûter (v)
to cost

couverture (n f)
blanket

couvre-lit (n m)
bedspread

cravate (n f)
tie

crayon (n m)
pencil

créateur, créatrice (a)
creative, inventive

crémerie (n f)
dairy

crevette (n f)
shrimp

croire (v)
to believe

croissant (n m)
croissant, crescent roll

cruel, cruelle (a)
cruel, merciless

cuisine (n f)
kitchen

cuisinière à gaz (n f)
gas stovetop

cuisinière électrique (n f)
electric stovetop

cuisinière (n f)
stovetop, female cook

cuisses de grenouille (n f pl.)
frogs' legs

cuit (a)
cooked

culture (n f)
culture

culturel, culturelle (a)
cultural

d'occasion
secondhand

dangereux, dangereuse (a)
dangerous

dans (prep)
in, during

de (prep)
of, from

débarrasser (v)
to clear the table

décembre (n m)
December

décollage (n m)
take-off

découvrir (v)
to discover; (past p.) découvert

dedans (adv)
inside

défendre (v)
to defend, to protect

dehors (adv, n m)
out, outside, out of doors

déjà (adv)
already, before, previously

déjeuner (n m)
lunch

demain (adv)
tomorrow

demande (n f)
request

demande d'emploi (n f)
job application

demander (v)
to ask for, (se) to wonder

demi-frère (n m)
half-brother

demi-sœur (n f)
half-sister

démissionner (v)
to resign

dentifrice (n m)
toothpaste

dentiste (n m and f)
dentist

déodorant (n m)
deodorant

départ (n m)
departure

dépêcher (v se)
to hurry

dépense (n f)
expense

dépenser (v)
to spend

depuis (prep and adv)
since, for

dernier, dernière (a)
last, latest

derrière (prep)
behind, after

des (art)
some, any

descendre (v)
to go down, to get off; (past p.) descendu

déshabiller (v se)
to undress (oneself)

désirer (v)
to want, to desire

dessert (n m)
dessert

dessin animé (n m)
cartoon

détail (n m)
detail

détester (v)
to hate

deuxième (a)
second

devant (prep)
in front, ahead

devenir (v irr)
to become; (past p.) devenu

devoir (v irr)
to have to; to owe; (past p.) dû

devoirs (n m)
homework

dictionnaire (n m)
dictionary

différence (n f)
difference

différent, différente
before the noun: diverse; after the noun: different, other

difficile (a)
difficult

diffuser (v)
to broadcast

dimanche (n m)
Sunday

dinde (n f)
turkey

dîner (n m)
dinner

dire (v)
to say, to tell; (past p.) dit

directeur (n m)
manager

discret, discrète (a)
discreet, cautious, shy

disquaire (n m)
music shop

disque dur (n m)
hard disk

disquette (n f)
floppy disk

distributeur automatique des billets de banque (n m)
cash machine

distributeur de tickets (n m)
ticket-dispensing machine

divan (n m)
divan

dixième (a)
tenth

docteur (n m) (m only)
doctor

documentaire (n m)
documentary

doigt (n m)
finger

domaine (n m)
domain

donc (conj)
so, then, therefore

donner un coup de main (v)
to give a hand

dormir (v irr)
to sleep

dos (n m)
back

douane (n f)
customs

douanier (n m)
male customs officer

douanière (n f)
female customs officer

douche (n f)
shower

douloureux, douloureuse (a)
painful, hurting, sore

doux, douce (a)
sweet, gentle, calm, fresh

drap (n m)
sheet

drap de bain (n m)
bath towel

drôle (a)
before the noun: bizarre; after the noun: funny

eau (n f)
water

eau chaude (n f)
hot water

eau minérale (n f)
mineral water

échanger (v)
to exchange

école (n f)
school

économies (f pl.)
savings

écouter (v)
to listen

écran (n m)
screen

écrire (v)
to write; (se) to exclaim; (past p.) écrit

écrivain, écrivaine (n)
writer

effacer (v)
to erase

effrayer (v)
to frighten

église (n f)
church

égyptien, égyptienne (a)
Egyptian

électricité (n f)
electricity

elle (pron f)
she

elles (pron f pl)
they

émail (n m)
enamel

embarquement (n m)
boarding

employé (n m)
male employee

employer (v)
to employ

en (prep)
in, on, to, as, like, by

en aller (v se)
to go away

en arrière de (adv)
in back of

en attendant
in the meantime

en avant de
in front of

en bas (adv)
down, downstairs

en direct
live

en haut (adv)
up, upstairs

en même temps
at the same time

en retard
delayed

en solde
on sale

enchanté (m)
pleased to meet you

enchanté(e) (m, f)
pleased to meet you

enchanteur, enchanteresse (a)
enchanting

encore (adv)
again

enfant (n m)
child

enfin (adv)
at last, finally, after all, lastly, in short

ennuyer (v)
to bore, to annoy (se) to get bored, annoyed

ennuyeux, ennuyeuse (a)
boring, tedious, dull, tiresome

enrayer (v)
to check

ensemble (adv)
together, at the same time

ensemble (n m)
woman's suit

ensuite (adv)
next

entendre (v)
to hear. (se) to get along

entrer (v)
to enter, to come in; (past p.) entré

enveloppe (n f)
envelope

envoyer (v)
to send

épais, épaisse (a)
thick, dense

épandre (v)
to scatter, to strew

épaule (n f)
shoulder

épicé (a)
spicy

épicer (v)
to spice

épicerie (n f)
grocery store

épinards (n m pl.)
spinach

épingle (n f)
pin

épisode (n m)
episode

éplucher (v)
to peel

éponge (n f)
sponge

épousseter (v)
to dust

erreur (n f)
error

escale (n f)
stopover

escalier (n m)
stairs

escargots (m pl.)
snails

espagnol (n m)
Spanish

espérer (v)
to expect, to hope, to wish

espoir (n m)
hope

essayer (v)
to try

essence (n f)
gasoline

essentiel, essentielle (a)
essential

essuyer (v)
to wipe, to dry

est (n m)
east

est-ce que (int)
is it that

estomac (n m)
stomach

et (conj)
and

étage (n m)
floor, story

étagère (n f)
shelf

États-Unis (n m pl.)
United States

été (n m)
summer

éteindre (v)
to turn off

éteindre la radio
to turn off the radio

éteindre la télévision
to turn off the television

étirer (v se)
to stretch

étranger, étrangère (a)
foreign, unknown, strange

être (v irr)
to be; (past p.) été

être à
to belong to someone

être content
to be pleased

être désolé
to be sorry

être fâché
to be angry

être heureux
to be happy

être sans emploi
to be unemployed

être surpris
to be surprised

étude (n f)
study

étudiant (n m)
student

étudiante (n f)
female student

étudier (v)
to study

Europe (n f)
Europe

européen, européenne (a)
European

s'évanouir (v se)
to faint

éventail (m)
fan

évidemment (adv)
evidently

évier (n m)
kitchen sink

évocateur, évocatrice (a)
evocative

examen (n m)
test

excellence (n f)
excellence

excusez-moi
excuse me

extérieur, extérieure (a)
exterior, external

facile (a)
easy

façon (n f)
manner

facteur (n m)
letter carrier

facture (n f)
invoice, bill

faillir (v)
to fail

faim (n f)
hunger

faire (v)
to do, to make; (past p.) fait

faire à manger
to prepare a meal

faire attention à
to pay attention to someone

faire des achats
to go shopping

faire du shopping
to go shopping

faire la cuisine
to cook

faire la queue
to wait in line

faire la sieste
to have a nap

faire la vaisselle
to do the dishes

faire les courses
to do the shopping

faire les lits
to make the beds

faire sa toilette
to have a wash, to wash up

faire son lit
to make one's bed

falloir (v)
to be necessary

famille (n f)
family

farci (a)
stuffed

farine (n f)
flour

fauteuil (n m)
armchair

fauteuil à bascule (n m)
rocking chair

faux, fausse (a)
false, wrong, untrue, fake, forged

favori, favorite (a)
favorite

femme (n f)
wife, woman

femme de chambre (n f)
maid, chambermaid

femme de ménage (n f)
maid, cleaning woman

fendre (v)
to split, to crack, to cut open

fenêtre (n f)
window

fermé, fermée (a)
closed

fermer (v)
to close

fermer la porte
to close the door

fermer les rideaux
to close the curtains

festival (n m)
festival

feu (n m)
fire

février (n m)
February

fichier (n m)
file

fille (n f)
daughter, girl

film d'horreur (n m)
horror film

film de science-fiction (n m)
science fiction film

film documentaire (n m)
documentary

film en noir et blanc (n m)
black and white film

film historique (n m)
historical film

film (n m)
film

fils (n m)
son

finir (v)
to finish

flatteur, flatteuse (a)
flattering, complimentary

fleurir (v)
to blossom, to bloom

fleuriste (n f)
female florist

fleuriste (n m)
male florist

fol (a)
see fou

fondre (v)
to melt, to dissolve

forêt (n f)
forest

forum (n m)
newsgroup

fou, folle (a)
mad, wild, foolish

foulard (n m)
scarf

four à micro-ondes (n m)
microwave oven

four (n m)
oven

fournir (v)
to furnish

frais (n f pl.)
expenses

frais, fraîche
cool, fresh, new, youthful

fraise (n f)
strawberry

framboise (n f)
raspberry

franc (n m)
franc (monetary unit)

franc suisse (n m)
Swiss franc

Français (n m)
a Frenchman

français, française (a)
French

Française (n f)
a Frenchwoman

France (n f)
France

fréquemment (adv)
frequently

frère (n m)
brother

frigo (n m)
fridge

frire (v)
to fry

frit, frite (a)
fried

frites (f pl.)
French fries

froid, froide (a)
cold

fruit (n m)
fruit, a piece of fruit

fruits de mer (n m)
seafood

fumeur (n m)
smoker

gagner (v)
to earn, to win

gagner sa vie
to earn a living

gants (m pl.)
gloves

garage (n m)
garage

garantir (v)
to guarantee

garçon (n m)
boy

gardien de nuit (n m)
night guard, porter

gare (v)
station, train station

gare d'autobus (n f)
bus station

gare routière (n f)
bus station

gâteau (n m)
cake

gaz (n m)
gas

gendarme (n m)
police officer

Genève (f)
Geneva

genou (n m)
knee

gens (n m pl.)
people

gentil, gentille (a)
noble, gentle, pretty, nice, kind

gentiment (adv)
prettily, gracefully

gomme (n f)
eraser

goûter (n m)
snack

grammaire (n f)
grammar

grand, grande (a)
large, big; before the noun: great;
after the noun: tall

grand lit (n m)
double bed

grand magasin (n m)
supermarket

grand-mère (n f)
grandmother

grand-parents (n m)
grandparents

grand-père (n m)
grandfather

gras, grasse (a)
fat, greasy, rich

gratuit (a)
free

grave (a)
accent (grave)

grec, grecque (a)
Greek, Grecian

grenier (n m)
attic

grille-pain (n m)
toaster

griller (v)
to grill, to toast

gris, grise (a)
gray

gros, grosse (a)
big, large, bulky

guichet (n m)
ticket office

habiter (v)
to live

habitude (n f)
habit

habituel, habituelle (a)
habitual

s'habituer à (v se)
to get used to

hamster (a)
hamster

haricot (n m)
bean

haut, haute (a)
high, tall, upper

hélice (n f)
propeller

heure (n f)
hour

heureux, heureuse (a)
happy, blissful

hibou (n m)
owl

hier (adv)
yesterday

hiver (n m)
winter

homard (n m)
lobster

hôpital (n m)
hospital

hors-d'oeuvre (n m pl.)
appetizer

hôtel (n m)
hotel

hôtesse de l'air (n f)
stewardess, flight attendant

hublot (n m)
window (plane, boat)

huitième (a)
eighth

huître (n f)
oyster

hypertexte (n m)
hypertext

ici (adv)
here, in this place, now, this time

icône (n f)
icon

il (pron m)
he

il y a
there is, there are

ils (pron m pl.)
they

immeuble (n m)
apartment building

imperméable (n m)
rain coat

important, importante (a)
important

inférieur, inférieure (a)
inferior, lower

infirmier (n m)
male nurse

infirmière (n f)
female nurse

informations (n f pl.)
information

ingénieur (n m)
engineer

inquiet, inquiète (a)
anxious

insérer (v)
to insert

insulter, injurier (v)
to insult

intelligent, intelligente (a)
intelligent, smart

intéressant (a)
interesting

intéresser à (v se)
to be interested in

intérieur, intérieure (a)
interior, inner, internal

Internet (n m)
Internet

interrompre (v)
to interrupt

Irlande (n f)
Ireland

israélien, israélienne (a)
Israeli

issue de secours (n f)
emergency exit

italien, italienne (a)
Italian

jaloux, jalouse (a)
jealous, envious

jamais (adv)
ever; with ne, never

jambe (n f)
leg

jambon (n m)
ham

janvier (n m)
January

japonais (a)
Japanese

jardin (n m)
garden

jaune (a)
yellow

je (pron)
I

jean (n m)
jeans

jet (n m)
jet

jeter (v)
to throw, to throw out

jeu (n m)
game

jeudi (n m)
Thursday

joli, jolie (a)
pretty, pleasing, neat, fine, nice

joue (n f)
cheek

journal (n m)
newspaper

journaliste (n f)
female journalist

journaliste (n m)
male journalist

juillet (n m)
July

juin (n m)
June

jupe (n f)
skirt

jus d'orange (n m)
orange juice

jus de fruit (n m)
fruit juice

jus de pomme (n m)
apple juice

là (pron)
there

lait (n m)
milk

lait écrémé (n m)
skim milk

laitue (n f)
lettuce

lampe (n f)
lamp

lapin (n m)
rabbit

laquelle (pron)
which, that

large (a)
broad, wide, large, extensive

las, lasse (a)
tired, weary, bored

lavabo (n m)
sink

laver (v)
to wash; (se) to wash (oneself)

lave-vaisselle (n m)
dishwasher

lavomatic (n m)
laundromat

leçon (n f)
lesson

lecteur de disquettes (n m)
disk drive

légume (n m)
vegetable

lequel (pron)
which, that

lesquelles (pron. f. pl.)
which, that

lesquels (pron. m. pl.)
which, that

lettre (n f)
letter

leur (pron)
their

liberté (n f)
liberty

librairie (n f)
bookstore

licencier (v)
to lay off

limonade (n f)
lemonade

lire (v)
to read; (past p.) lu

liste de signets (n f)
bookmark file, bookmark list

lit (n m)
bed

livre (n f)
pound

livre (n m)
book

locataire (m)
tenant

logiciel (n m)
software

logiciel de navigation (n m)
Web browser

loin (adv)
far, distant, at a distance

loin de (adv)
far from

Londres
London

long, longue (a)
long, slow, tedious, drawn out

longtemps (adv)
long, a long while

louer (v)
to rent

loyer (n m)
rent

lundi (n m)
Monday

lunettes (f pl.)
glasses

lunettes de soleil (f pl.)
sunglasses

madame, mesdames (pl.)
Mrs.

**mademoiselle, mes-
demoiselles (pl.)**
Miss

magasin (n m)
shop

**magasin de vins et spi-
ritueux (n m)**
liquor store

magazine (n m)
magazine

magicien (n m)
magician

mai (n m)
May

maillot de corps (n m)
undershirt

maillot de bain (n m)
bathing suit

main (n f)
hand

maintenant
now, at this moment, at present

mais (conj)
but

maïs (n m)
corn

maison (n f)
house

majeur, majeure (a)
major, main, chief, greater

mal (adv)
wrong, badly

malheureux, malheureuse (a)
unhappy, unfortunate, unlucky

malin, maligne (a)
malicious, mischievous, malignant

manche (n f)
sleeve

manche (n m)
handle

manger (v)
to eat

mannequin (n m)
model

manquer d'expérience
to lack experience

manteau (n m)
coat

marchand de légumes (n m)
vegetable merchant

marchand de vin (n m)
wine merchant

marche (n f)
step

marché (n m)
market

mardi (n m)
Tuesday

margarine (n f)
margarine

mari (n m)
husband

marron, marron (a)
brown

mars (n m)
March

matelas (n m)
mattress

mathématiques (pl.)
mathematics

matin (n m)
morning

mauvais, mauvaise (a)
bad poor, faulty

me (pron)
me

médecin (n m) (m only)
doctor

meilleur, meilleure (a)
better, preferable, correctly, more comfortably

mélanger (v)
to mix

melon (n m)
melon

même (a)
before the noun: same; after the noun: exact

mémoire (n f)
memory

ménagère (n f)
housewife

menteur, menteuse (a)
lying, false, deceitful

menu (n m)
set-price meal

merci (n m)
thank you

merci beaucoup
thank you very much

mercredi (n m)
Wednesday

mère (n f)
mother

messagerie électronique (n f)
e-mail

métro (n m)
subway

mettre (v)
to put, to place; (past p.) mis

metteur en scène (n m)
director

mettre la table
to set the table

mettre ses verres de contact
to put in one's contact lenses

mettre son dentier
to put in one's false teeth

mettre son réveil
to set the alarm clock

meuble (n m)
furniture

miel (n m)
honey

mineur, mineure (a)
lesser, minor

minijupe (n f)
miniskirt

miroir (n m)
mirror

mode (n f)
fashion, manner, way, custom

mode (n m)
mode

moderne, moderne (a)
modern, up to date

moins (adv)
less, fewer

moitié (n f)
half

mol (a)
see mou

monsieur, messieurs (pl.)
Mr.

monter (v)
to climb; (past p.) monté

montre (n f)
watch

moquette (n f)
carpet

morceler (v)
to break up, to parcel

mordre (v)
to bite

morue (n f)
cod

Moscou
Moscow

mot de passe (n m)
password

mou, molle (a)
soft, limp, flabby, weak

mouchoir (n m)
handkerchief

moufles (f pl.)
mittens

moule (n f)
mussel

mourir (v)
to die; (past p.) mort

moutarde (n f)
mustard

moyen, moyenne (a)
middle, average

muet (a)
silent

mur (n m)
wall

musée (n m)
museum

musicien (n m)
male musician

nager (v)
to swim

naissance (n f)
birth

naître (v)
to be born; (past p.) né

nationalité (n f)
nationality

naturel, naturelle (a)
natural

naturellement (adv)
naturally

navigateur (n m)
Web browser

ne . . . aucunement (adv)
not at all, not in the least

ne . . . guère (adv)
not much, not very, only a little

ne . . . jamais (adv)
never (adv)

ne . . . nul (n m)
no one, nobody, not one

ne . . . nulle part (adv)
nowhere

ne . . . nullement
not at all, by no means

ne . . . pas
not

ne . . . pas . . . non plus (adv)
no longer

ne . . . pas du tout (adv)
not at all

ne . . . pas encore (adv)
not yet

ne . . . pas un (a)
not one, not even one

ne . . . personne (pron)
no one, nobody

ne . . . plus
no longer

ne . . . point
no, not at all, none

ne . . . que
only

ne . . . rien
nothing, not anything

ne . . . toujours pas
not yet

nettoyage à sec (n m)
dry cleaning

nettoyer (v)
to clean

neuf, neuve (a)
new, brand-new

neuvième (a)
ninth

neveu (n m)
nephew

nez (n m)
nose

ni (conj)
neither, nor

nièce (n f)
niece

nœud papillon (n m)
bow tie

noir, noire (a)
black

nombreux, nombreuse (a)
numerous

non
no

non fumeur
non smoking

nord (n m)
north

note (n f)
bill

nourriture (n f)
food

nous (pron)
we, us

nouveau, nouvel, nouvelle (a)
before the noun: additional; after
the noun: new, recent, novel

novembre (n m)
November

noyer (v)
to drown

obéir à (v)
to obey

objet (n m)
object

obtenir (v irr)
to obtain

octobre (n m)
October

œil (n m)
eye

œuf (n m)
egg

œuf à la coque (n m)
soft-boiled egg

œuf sur le plat (n m)
fried egg

œufs au jambon (n m pl.)
ham and eggs

œufs brouillés (n m pl.)
scrambled eggs

offre d'emploi (n f)
job offer

offrir (v irr)
to offer; (past p.) offert

oiseau (n m)
bird

omelette (n f)
omelet

oncle (n m)
uncle

ongle (n m)
fingernail

optimisme (n m)
optimism

orange (n f)
orange

ordinateur (n m)
computer

oreille (n f)
ear

oreiller (n m)
pillow

orteil (n m)
toe

ou (conj)
or

où (prep)
when, in which, where, at which,
from which

ouest (n m)
west

oui
yes

ouvrir (v irr)
to open; (past p.) ouvert

paiement (n m)
payment

pain (n m)
bread

pain grillé (n m)
toast

pamplemousse (n m)
grapefruit

pané (a)
breaded

pantalon (n m)
pants, trousers

papier (n m)
paper

papier hygiénique (n m)
toilet paper

par hasard
by accident, by chance

parade (n f)
parade

parapluie (n m)
umbrella

parc (n m)
park

pardessus (n m)
overcoat

pardon?
pardon me?

pareil, pareille (a)
similar, equal

parent (n m)
parent

Paris (n m)
Paris

parisien, parisienne (a)
Parisian

parking (n m)
parking lot

parler (v)
to speak

parler à
to speak to someone

partir (v irr)
to leave; (past p.) parti

parvenir (v)
to attain, to succeed; (past p.)
parvenu

passager (n m)
passenger

passagère (n f)
female passenger

passeport (n m)
passport

passer à la télé
to appear on TV

passionnant (a)
exciting

pasteur (n m)
minister

patiemment (adv)
patiently

pâtisserie (n f)
cake shop

pauvre (a)
before the noun: unfortunate;
after the noun: penniless

pavé (n m)
pavement

paye (n f)
pay, wages

payer (v)
to pay

pêche (n f)
peach

pécheur, pécheresse (a)
sinning

peigne (n m)
comb

pendant (prep)
during, while

pendentif (n m)
pendant

pendre (v)
to hang, to hang up, to suspend

pendule (n f)
grandfather clock

penser (v)
to think

penser à
to think about someone

perdre (v)
to lose, to waste

père (n m)
father

permettre (v)
to permit, to allow

personne (n f)
person

pèse-personne (n m)
bathroom scale

pessimisme (n m)
pessimism

petit (a)
little, small, short, very young

petit ami (n m)
boyfriend

petit écran (n m)
television

petit peu
little, not much, few, not very, not
many

petit déjeuner (n m)
breakfast

petite amie (n f)
girlfriend

petites annonces (n f)
classified ads

petits pois (m pl.)
peas

peu (a)
few, little, not much

peut-être
perhaps, maybe

pharmacie (n f)
pharmacy

pharmacien (n m)
male pharmacist

photo (n f)
photograph

photographie (n f)
photography

piano (n m)
piano

pièce (n f)
coin

pied (n m)
foot

pilote (n m)
pilot

pique-nique (n m)
picnic

piste (n f)
runway

pitié (n f)
pity

place (n f)
seat, place

placer (v)
to place, to put

plafond (n m)
ceiling

plaire (v)
to please; (past p.) plu

plaire à
to please (someone)

plat principal (n m)
main course

pleuvoir (v)
to rain; (past p.) plu

poème (n m)
a poem

poésie (n f)
poetry

poignet (n m)
wrist

pointure (n f)
shoe size

poire (n f)
pear

poisson (n m)
fish

poitrine (n f)
chest

pomme (n f)
apple

pomme de terre (n f)
potato

pondre (v)
to lay (as in eggs)

porc (n m)
pork

porte (n f)
door, gate

portefeuille (n m)
wallet

porte-monnaie (n m)
purse

porter (v)
to wear, to carry

portugais (n m)
Portuguese

poste (n f)
mail, post office, postal service

poste (n m)
position

postérieur, postérieure (a)
posterior, later, behind

potage (n m)
soup

pouce (n m)
thumb

poulet (n m)
chicken

pour (prep)
for

pourboire (n m)
tip

pourquoi (int)
why

pouvoir (v irr)
to be able; (past p.) pu

préférer (v)
to prefer

premier, première (a)
first

prendre (v)
to take; (past p.) pris

prendre des vacances
to take a vacation

prendre sa retraite
to retire

prendre son petit déjeuner
to have breakfast

prendre un jour de congé
to take a day off

préparer (v)
to prepare

près de
near to

près (prep)
near, by

prêtre (n m)
priest

printemps (n m)
spring

prison (n f)
prison

prix (n m)
prize, price

prix par jour (n m)
price per day

probablement (adv)
probably

prochain, prochaine (a)
before the noun: following; after the noun: next

professeur (n m)
professor, teacher

projeter (v)
to plan

promenade (n f)
walk

prononcer (v)
to pronounce

propre (a)
before the noun: own; after the noun: clean

propriétaire (n f)
owner

propriétaire (n m)
owner

provisions (f pl.)
supplies, groceries

prune (n f)
plum

public, publique (a)
public

publicité (n f)
a commercial

puis (conj)
then

pyjama (n m)
pajamas

quai (n m)
platform

quand (int)
when

quatrième (a)
fourth

que (pron)
that, which, what. ne only

quel (pron m)
what, which

quelle (pron f)
what, which

quelles (f pl.)
what, which

quelque part
somewhere

quelquefois
sometimes

quels (m pl.)
what, which

qui (pron)
who or whom

quitter (v)
to leave

quoi (pron)
what

quotidien, quotidienne (a)
daily

radio (n f)
radio

rafraîchir (v)
to refresh

raison (n f)
reason

râper (v)
to grate

rappeler (v)
to remind

rasoir (n m)
razor

rayer (v)
to delete, to scratch, to erase

réceptionniste (n f)
receptionist

réceptionniste (n m)
receptionist

recevoir (v irr)
to receive, to get; (past p.) reçu

réclamation (n f)
complaint

reçu (n m)
receipt

redescendre (v)
to come down again; (past p.) redescendu

réel, réelle (a)
real, actual, genuine

réfrigérateur (n m)
refrigerator

refuser (v)
to reject

regarder (v)
to watch

regretter (v)
to regret, to grieve

rejeter (v)
to reject, to throw again

religieuse (n f)
nun

remonter (v)
to go up again; (past p.) remonté

remplacer (v)
to replace

renaître (v)
to be born again. (past p.) rené

rendre (v)
to return, to restore, to give back, to repay

rentrer (v)
to return, to come back

rentrer à la maison
to come home, to go home

rentrer de l'école
to come back from school

rentrer du travail
to come back from work

renvoyer (v)
to return, to dismiss

repartir (v)
to go out again; (past p.) reparti

repas (n m)
meal

repasser (v)
to iron

replet, replète (a)
obese, stout

répondre (v)
to answer, to reply

reposer (v se)
to have a rest, to take a nap

réservation (n f)
booking, reservation

ressembler à (v)
to look like, to resemble

ressortir (v)
to come out again; (past p.) ressorti

restaurant (n m)
restaurant

rester (v)
to remain, to stay

retard (n m)
delay

retourner (v)
to return, to go back

retrait (n m)
withdrawal

réussir (v)
to be successful

réveil (n m)
alarm clock

réveiller (v se)
to wake up

revenir (v irr)
to come back

revolver (n m)
revolver

revue (n f)
magazine

rhum (n m)
rum

riche (a)
rich, wealthy, valuable

rideau (n m)
curtain

rincer (v)
to rinse

robe (n f)
dress

robe de chambre (n f)
robe, nightgown

roman (n m)
novel

rompre (v)
to break, to snap, to break off

rose (a)
pink

rôtie (a)
roasted

rôtir (v)
to roast

rouge (a)
red

roux, rousse (a)
reddish, red-haired

ruban (n m)
ribbon

russe (n m)
Russian

sac à dos (n m)
backpack

sac à main (n m)
purse, hand bag

saignant (a)
rare

saison (n f)
season

salade (n f)
salad

salaire (n m)
salary, wages

sale (a)
before the noun: bad; after the noun: dirty

salle à manger (n f)
dining room

salle d'attente (n f)
waiting room

salle d'embarquement (n f)
departure lounge

salle de bain (n f)
bathroom

salle de classe (n f)
classroom

salle de séjour (n f)
living room

salut !
Hi! Bye!

samedi
Saturday

sans (a)
without

sans (conj)
without

sans doute
probably

Santé !
Cheers!

sarcasme (n m)
sarcasm

sardine (n f)
sardine

saumon (n m)
salmon

savant (n m) (m only)
scholar, scientist

savoir (v irr)
to know; (past p.) su

savon (n m)
soap

science (n f)
science

se (pron)
him, her, they

se coiffer (v se)
to comb one's hair

se débrouiller (v se)
to get by, to manage

s'habiller (v se)
to get dressed

se lever (v se)
to get up

se maquiller (v se)
to put on makeup

se moquer de (v se)
to make fun of

se méfier de (v se)
to distrust

se raser (v se)
to shave (oneself)

se rendre compte de (v se)
to realize

se suicider (v se)
to kill oneself

se soucier de (v se)
to mind

se souvenir de (v se)
to remember

sec, sèche (a)
dry, arid, plain

sèche-cheveux (n m)
hair dryer

sécher (v)
to dry; (se) to dry (oneself)

secrétaire (n f)
secretary

secrétaire (n m)
secretary

s'amuser (v se)
to have a good time

s'écrouler (v se)
to collapse

s'efforcer de (v se)
to strive

sels de bain (n m pl.)
bath salts

semaine de quarante heures (n f)
forty-hour week

s'empresser de (v se)
to hasten

s'endormir (v se)
to fall asleep

s'enfuir (v se)
to flee

sentence (n f)
verdict

s'envoler (v se)
to fly away

septembre (n m)
September

septième (a)
seventh

serpent (n m)
snake

serveur (n m)
waiter

serveuse (n f)
waitress

service (n m)
service

service compris (n m)
tip included

service non compris (n m)
tip not included

serviette de toilette (n f)
towel

servir (v irr)
to serve

ses (pron)
his, hers

seul (a)
before the noun: only; after the noun: single

s'évanouir (v se)
to faint

s'habituer à (v se)
to get used to

shampooing (n m)
shampoo

si (conj)
so, so much, yes, but yes, if

signe (n m)
sign

signet (n m)
bookmark

silence (n m)
silence

s'il vous plaît
please

sixième (a)
sixth

slip (n m)
panties

smoking (n m)
tuxedo

s'occuper de (v se)
to look after

sœur (n f)
sister

soif (n f)
thirst

soir (n m)
evening

sol (n m)
floor

sole (n f)
sole

solitude (n f)
solitude

songer (v)
to dream, to imagine, to consider

sortie de secours (n f)
emergency exit

sortir (v irr)
to go out; (past p.) sorti

souffrir (v)
to suffer; (past p.) souffert

souhaiter (v)
to wish

soupe (n f)
soup

soupirail (n m)
basement window

sourire (n m)
smile

sourire (v)
to smile; (past p.) souri

souris (n f)
mouse

sous-sol (n m)
basement

sous-titres (n m)
subtitles

soutien-gorge (n m)
bra

souvent (adv)
often, frequently

station de métro (n m)
subway station

steward (n m)
steward

stylo (n m)
pen

sud (n m)
south

suivre (v)
to follow; (past p.) suivi

sujet (n m)
subject

supérieur, supérieure (a)
superior, upper, higher

sur (prep)
on, at, in, about

surprise (n f)
surprise

table (n f)
table

table basse (n f)
coffee table

tailleur (n m)
woman's suit

taire (v se)
to be silent

tant pis
never mind

tante (n f)
aunt

tapis (n m)
rug

tapis de bain (n m)
bath mat

tard (adv)
late

tartine (n f)
bread and butter

taxi (n m)
taxi

te (pron)
you

teinturerie (n f)
dry cleaners

tel, telle (a)
such

téléphone (n m)
telephone

téléphoner à (v)
to telephone

télévision (n f)
television

tendre (v)
to stretch, to strain

tenir (v irr)
to have, to hold; (past p.) tenu

tenir à
to be attached to

terminal (n m)
terminal

tête (n f)
head

thé (n m)
tea

théâtre (n m)
theatre

thon (n m)
tuna fish

toile d'araignée mondiale [TAM] (n f)
World Wide Web

toilettes (n f pl.)
restroom

toit (n m)
roof

tomate (n f)
tomato

tomber (v)
to fall; (past p.) tombé

tondre (v)
to shear, to clip, to crop, to cut

tordre (v)
to twist, to wring, to contort

tortue (n f)
tortoise

tôt (adv)
soon, quickly, early

toujours (adv)
always, ever, forever

tour de contrôle (n f)
control tower

tourisme (n m)
tourism

tous les matins
every morning

tout (a)
all, whole, every

tout de suite (adv)
immediately

tout droit
straight, straight ahead

toux (n f)
cough

traditionnel, traditionnelle (a)
traditional

traducteur (n m)
translator

traductrice (n f)
female translator

tragédie (n f)
tragedy

train (n m)
train

tranquille (a)
quiet, calm, tranquil, peaceful

transport (n m)
transportation

travail (n f)
work, job

travailler (v)
to work

tréma (n m)
umlaut (accent)

très (adv)
very, most, very much

troisième
third

tromper (v se)
to be wrong

trompeur, trompeuse (a)
deceitful, false, misleading

trop (adv)
too, too much, too many

trop cuit (a)
over done

trouver (v)
to find

trouver du travail
to find work

trouver un emploi
to find a job

truite (n f)
trout

tu (pron)
you

tuyau de plomb (n m)
lead pipe

uniforme (n m)
uniform

universel, universelle (a)
universal

usuel, usuelle (a)
usual

utile (a)
useful, beneficial

utiliser (v)
to use

vacance (n f)
vacancy

vacances (n f pl.)
vacation

valise (n f)
suitcase

valoir (v)
to be worth

vase (n f)
mud, slime

vase (n m)
vase

veau (n m)
veal

vedette (n f)
star

vendeur (n m)
clerk

vendeuse (n f)
female clerk

vendre (v)
to sell

vendredi (n m)
Friday

venir (v irr)
to come; (past p.) venu

verrouiller la porte (v)
to lock the door

vers (prep)
toward, around

vert, verte (a)
green

veste (n f)
jacket

veste sport (n f)
sport jacket

viande (n f)
meat

vidéo (n f)
video

vieil (a)
see vieux

vieux, vieil, vieille (a)
old, ancient, aged, advanced in years

vif, vive (a)
alive, live, living

ville (n f)
city

vin (n m)
wine

vin blanc (n m)
white wine

vin rouge (n m)
red wine

violet, violette (a)
purple

virement (n m)
transfer

virus (n m)
virus

visa (n m)
visa

visage (n m)
face

vite (adv)
quick, quickly, fast, rapidly

vitesse (n f)
speed

vitrail (n m)
stained-glass window

vocabulaire (n m)
vocabulary

vodka (n f)
vodka

voilà
there is, there are

voile (n f)
sail

voile (n m)
veil

voir (v)
to see (irr); (past p.) vu

voisin (n m)
neighbor

voisine (n f)
female neighbor

voiture (n f)
car

vol (n m)
flight

vol direct (n m)
direct flight

vol international (n m)
international flight

vol interne (n m)
domestic flight

volaille (n f)
poultry

voleur, voleuse (a)
thief, robber

vouloir (v irr)
to want, to wish, to will; (past p.) voulu

vous (pron)
you

voyage d'affaires (n m)
business trip

voyager (v)
to travel

vrai, vraie (a)
true, real, right

vraiment
truly, in truth, indeed, really

western (n m)
Western (movie)

whisky (n m)
whiskey

y (pron)
there, it

yeux (n m pl.)
eyes

English-to-French Glossary

about
sur

absolute
absolu

absolutely
absolument

accent
accent

accent (grave)
grave

accessory
accessoire

accident
accident

active
actif, active

actor
acteur

actress
actrice

acute
aigu, aiguë

acute (accent)
aigu

additional
nouveau, nouvel (before the noun)

adjoining
contigu, contiguë

admirer
admirateur, admiratrice

adventure
aventure

advertisement
annonce

Africa
Afrique

after
après

after
derrière

after all
enfin

afternoon
après-midi

again
encore

airline
compagnie aérienne

airport
aéroport

alarm clock
réveil

alcohol
alcool

alive
vif, vive

all
tout

alphabet
alphabet

already
déjà

also
aussi

altitude
altitude

always
toujours

ambiguous
ambigu, ambiguë

amusing
amusant, amusante

an Englishman
Anglais

an Englishwoman
Anglaise

ancient
vieux, vieil, vieille

ancient
ancien, ancienne (after the noun)

and
et

animal
animal

ankle
cheville

announcement
annonce

another
autre

anterior
antérieur

antique
ancien, ancienne (after the noun)

anxious
inquiet, inquiète

any
des

apartment
appartement

apartment building
immeuble

appetizer
hors d'oeuvre

apple
pomme

apple juice
jus de pomme

apricot
abricot

April
avril

architect
architecte

arm
bras

armchair
fauteuil

around
vers

arrival
arrivée

article
article

artist
artiste

as
aussi

as
en

Asia
Asie

assistance
assistance

astronaut
astronaute

at
à

at
sur

at last
enfin

at the home of
chez

at the office of
chez

at the right time
à propos

at the same time
en même temps

at which
où

attic
grenier

August
août

aunt
tante

Australia
Australie

autumn
automne

back
dos

backpack
sac à dos

bad
mauvais, mauvaise

bad
sale (before the noun)

badly
mal

bakery
boulangerie

balcony
balcon

banana
banane

bank
banque

bank card
carte bancaire

bar
bar

basement
sous-sol

basement window
soupirail

bath
baignoire

bath
bain

bath mat
tapis de bain

bath salts
sels de bain

bath towel
drap de bain

bathing suit
maillot de bain

bathroom
salle de bain

bathroom mirror
glace

bathroom scale
pèse-personne

bean
haricot

beautiful
beau, belle, bel

beauty
beauté

bed
lit

bedroom
chambre

bedspread
couvre-lit

beef
boeuf

beer
bière

before
avant

before
déjà

behind
derrière

behind
postérieur, postérieure

belt
ceinture

beret
béret

besides
aussi

better
meilleur, meilleure

bidet
bidet

bikini
bikini

bill
note

bill (bank note)
billet de banque

binder
classeur

bird
oiseau

birth
naissance

bizarre
drôle (before the noun)

black
noir, noire

black and white film
film en noir et blanc

blank
blanc, blanche

blanket
couverture

bless you (after someone sneezes)
à vos souhaits !

blouse
chemisier

blue
bleu, bleue

blue jeans
blue-jean

boarding
embarquement

boarding pass
carte d'embarquement

boat
bateau

body
corps

boiled
bouilli

book
livre

bookmark
signet

bookmark file
liste de signets

bookstore
librairie

boring
ennuyeux, ennuyeuse

bow tie
nœud papillon

boy
garçon

boyfriend
petit ami

bra
soutien-gorge

bracelet
bracelet

bread
pain

bread and butter
tartine

breaded
pané

breakfast
petit déjeuner

brief
court, courte

brief (concise)
bref, brève

briefly
brièvement

brilliantly
brillamment

broad
large

broccoli
brocolis

brooch
broche

brother
frère

brown
marron

brush
brosse

Brussels sprouts
choux de Bruxelles

bubble bath
bain moussant

building manager
concierge

bus
autobus

bus
bus

bus shelter
abribus

bus station
gare routière

bus stop
arrêt d'autobus

business trip
voyage d'affaires

busy
actif

but
mais

butcher
boucher, bouchère

butcher store
boucherie

butter
beurre

buttered bread with honey
tartine au miel

by
à

by
en

by accident
par hasard

by the way
à propos

Bye!
salut !

cabbage
chou

cake
gâteau

cake shop
pâtisserie

calm
calme

calm
doux, douce

calm
tranquille

Canada
Canada

Canadian
canadien, canadienne

canal
canal

canceled
annulé

candlestick
chandelier

car
auto

car
voiture

building manager
concierge

caretaker
concierge

carnival
carnaval

carpet
moquette

carry-on luggage
bagages à main

cartoon
dessin animé

cash machine
distributeur automatique des billets de banque

cash register
caisse

cat
chat

cauliflower
chou-fleur

cautious
discret, discrète

cedilla (accent)
cédille

ceiling
plafond

cellar
cave

chair
chaise

chambermaid
femme de chambre

chamomile tea
camomille

chain
chaîne

chance
chance

channel
chaîne

charter flight
charter

cheap
bon marché

check
chèque

check (bill)
addition

checkbook
carnet de chèques

checkbook
chéquier

cheek
joue

Cheers!
Santé !

cherry
cerise

chest
poitrine

chest of drawers
commode

chicken
poulet

child
enfant

Chinese
Chinois

choice
choix

church
église

circumflex (accent)
circonflexe

city
cité

city
ville

classified ads
petites annonces

classroom
salle de classe

clean
blanc, blanche

clean
propre (after the noun)

cleaning woman
femme de ménage

clerk
vendeur, vendeuse

closed
fermé, fermée

closet
armoire

coat
manteau

cod
morue

coffee
café

coffee table
table basse

coffee with milk
café au lait

coin
pièce

cold
froid, froide

comb
peigne

comedy
comédie

comfortable
confortable

comfortably
aisément

comforter
couette (n f)

comic strip
bande dessinée

commercial (advertisement)
publicité

commission
commande

complaint
réclamation

complete
complet, complète

computer
ordinateur

concise
court, courte

concrete
concret, concrète

conservative
conservateur, conservatrice

constantly
constamment

contiguous
contigu, contiguë

continually
constamment

contract
contrat

control tower
tour de contrôle

cook
chef

cooked
cuit

cool
frais, fraîche

coral
corail

corn
maïs

corner
coin

correctly
meilleur, meilleure

cough
toux

courageous
brave (after the noun)

course
cours

courteous
courtois, courtoise

cousin
cousin

cousin
cousine

creative
créateur, créatrice

credit card
carte de crédit

croissant
croissant

cruel
cruel, cruelle

cucumber
concombre

cufflink
bouton de manchette

cultural
culturel, culturelle

culture
culture

currency exchange outlet
bureau de change

current
actuel, actuelle

curtain
rideau

custom
mode

customer
client

customs
douane

customs officer
douanier

customs officer
douanière

daily
quotidien, quotidienne

dairy
crémerie

dangerous
dangereux, dangereuse

daughter
fille

dear
cher, chère (before the noun)

deceitful
menteur, menteuse

deceitful
trompeur, trompeuse

December
décembre

decently
convenablement

delay
retard

delayed
en retard

dentist
dentiste

deodorant
déodorant

departure
départ

departure lounge
salle d'embarquement

deposit account
compte sur livret

desk
bureau

dessert
dessert

detail
détail

dictionary
dictionnaire

difference
différence

different
autre

different
différent, différente (after the noun)

difficult
difficile

dining room
salle à manger

dinner
dîner

direct flight
vol direct

director
metteur en scène

dirty
sale (before the noun)

discreet
discret, discrète

dishwasher
lave-vaisselle

disk drive
lecteur de disquettes

distant
loin

divan
divan

diverse
différent, différente (before the noun)

doctor
docteur

doctor
médecin

documentary
documentaire

documentary
film documentaire

dog
chien

domain
domaine

domestic flight
vol interne

door, gate
porte

double bed
grand lit

double room
chambre pour deux personnes

down
en bas

downstairs
en bas

dress
robe

drink
boisson

drink, beverage
boire

dry
sec, sèche

dry cleaners
teinturerie

dry cleaning
nettoyage à sec

duck
canard

during
pendant

each
chaque

ear
oreille

earlier
antérieur

early
tôt

earring
boucle d'oreille

easily
aisément

east
est

easy
facile

egg
œuf

Egyptian
égyptien, égyptienne

eighth
huitième

elbow
coude

electric kettle
bouilloire électrique

electric stovetop
cuisinière électrique

electricity
électricité

elevator
ascenseur

e-mail
messagerie électronique, courriel,
e-mail

embassy
ambassade

emergency exit
issue de secours

emergency exit
sortie de secours

emergency landing
atterrissage forcé

employee
employé

employment contract
contrat de travail

enamel
émail

enamored
amoureux, amoureuse

enchanting
enchanteur, enchanteresse

energetic
actif

engagement ring
bague de fiançailles

engineer
ingénieur

England
Angleterre

English
anglais, anglaise

enjoy your meal
bon appétit

enjoyable
bon, bonne (before the noun)

enough
assez

entertaining
amusant, amusante

envelope
enveloppe

episode
épisode

eraser
gomme

error
erreur

essential
essentiel, essentielle

Europe
Europe

European
européen, européenne

evening
soir

ever
jamais

ever
toujours

every
chaque

every
tout

every morning
tous les matins

evidently
évidemment

evocative
évocateur, évocatrice

exact
même (after the noun)

excellence
excellence

exciting
passionnant

excuse me
excusez-moi

expense
dépense

expenses
frais

expensive
cher, chère (after the noun)

extensive
large

exterior
extérieur, extérieure

external
extérieur, extérieure

eye
œil

eyes
yeux

face
visage

fake
faux, fausse

false
faux, fausse

family
famille

fan
éventail

far from
loin de

farewell
adieu

farmer
agriculteur

fashion
mode

fat
gras, grasse

father
père

favorable
bon, bonne (after the noun)

favorite
favori, favorite

February
février

festival
festival

few
peu, petit peu

fewer
moins

fifth
cinquième

file
fichier

film
film

finally
enfin

fine
beau, belle, bel

fine
joli, jolie

finely
bien

finger
doigt

fingernail
ongle

fire
feu

fireplace
cheminée

first
premier, première

fish
poisson

flabby
mou, molle, mol

flattering
flatteur, flatteuse

flight
vol

flight attendant
hôtesse de l'air, steward

floor
sol

floor, story
étage

floppy disk
disquette

florist
fleuriste

flour
farine

following
prochain, prochaine (before the noun)

food
nourriture

foolish
fou, folle

foot
pied

for
depuis

for, during
pour

forearm
avant-bras

foreign
étranger, étrangère

forest
forêt

forever
toujours

former
ancien, ancienne (before the noun)

former
antérieur, antérieure

forty-hour week
semaine de quarante heures

fourth
quatrième

franc (monetary unit)
franc

France
France

free
gratuit

freely
aisément

freezer
congélateur

French
français, française

French bread
baguette

French fries
frites

Frenchman
Français

Frenchwoman
Française

frequently
fréquemment

fresh
doux, douce

fresh
frais, fraîche

Friday
vendredi

fridge
frigo

fried
frit, frite

fried egg
œuf sur le plat

friend
ami, amie

friend
copain

friend
copine

friend of
copain

friendship
amitié

frogs' legs
cuisses de grenouille

from which
où

fruit
fruit

fruit juice
jus de fruit

funny
drôle (after the noun)

furniture
meuble

game
jeu

garage
garage

garden
jardin

gas
gaz

gas stovetop
cuisinière à gaz

gasoline
essence

Geneva
Genève

gentle
doux, douce

gentle
gentil, gentille

genuine
réel, réelle

German
Allemand

Germany
Allemagne

gift
cadeau

girl
fille

girlfriend
petite amie

glad
content, contente

glasses
lunettes

gloves
gants

good
bon, bonne (after the noun)

good afternoon
bonjour

good evening
bonsoir

Good luck!
Bonne chance !

good morning
bonjour

Good night (sleep well)
Bonne nuit

goodbye
au revoir

gracefully
gentiment

grammar
grammaire

grandfather
grand-père

grandfather clock
pendule

grandmother
grand-mère

grandparents
grand-parents

grapefruit
pamplemousse

gray
gris, grise

greasy
gras, grasse

great
grand, grande (before the noun)

Grecian
grec, grecque

Greek
grec, grecque

green
vert, verte

grocery store
épicerie

groceries
provisions

guaranteed
certain, certaine (after the noun)

habit
habitude

habitual
habituel, habituelle

hair
cheveux

hair dryer
sèche-cheveux

hairdresser
coiffeur

half
à moitié

half
moitié

half-brother
demi-frère

half-sister
demi-sœur

hall
couloir

ham
jambon

ham and eggs
œufs au jambon

hamster
hamster

hand
main

handbags
bagages à main

handkerchief
mouchoir

handle
manche

handsome
beau, belle, bel

happy
heureux, heureuse

hard disk
disque dur

hat
chapeau

he
il

head
tête

hello
bonjour

help, home care
aide ménagère

her
elle

here
ici

Hi!
salut !

high
haut, haute

higher
supérieur, supérieure

high-heeled shoes
chaussures à talons hauts

him
se

his, hers
ses

historical film
film historique

homework devoirs	**husband** mari	**in, during** dans
honey miel	**hypertext** hypertexte	**included** compris
hope espoir	**I** je	**inferior** inférieur, inférieure
horror film film d'horreur	**icon** icone	**information** informations
horse cheval	**if** si	**inside** dedans
hospital hôpital	**immediately** tout de suite	**intelligent** intelligent, intelligente
hot chaud	**important** important, importante	**interesting** intéressant
hot chocolate chocolat chaud	**in** à	**interior** intérieur, intérieure
hot water eau chaude	**in** en	**international flight** vol international
hotel hôtel	**in** sur	**Internet** Internet
hour heure	**in back of** en arrière de	**inventive** créateur, créatrice
house maison	**in front of** en avant de	**invoice, bill** facture
housewife ménagère	**in front, ahead** devant	**Ireland** Irlande
how comment	**in love** amoureux, amoureuse	**is it that** est-ce que
how many combien de	**in short** brièvement, enfin	**Israeli** israélien, israélienne
how much combien	**in the long run** à la longue	**it** y
hunger faim	**in the meantime** en attendant	**Italian** italien, italienne
hurting douloureux, douloureuse	**in which** où	**jacket** blouson

jacket
veste

jam
confiture

January
janvier

Japanese
japonais

jealous
jaloux, jalouse

jeans
jean

jet
jet

jewel
bijou

jeweler
bijoutier

jeweler
bijoutière

jewelry store
bijouterie

job application
demande d'emploi

job offer
offre d'emploi

journalist
journaliste

July
juillet

June
juin

keen
aigu

keyboard
clavier

kind
bon, bonne (after the noun)

kind
gentil, gentille

kitchen
cuisine

kitchen sink
évier

knee
genou

knife
couteau

lamb
agneau

lamp
lampe

landing
atterrissage

large
grand, grande

large
gros, grosse

last
dernier, dernière

late
tard

later
postérieur, postérieure

latest
dernier, dernière

laundromat
lavomatic

laundry room
buanderie

lawyer
avocat(e)

lead pipe
tuyau de plomb

lease
bail

leases
baux

left
à gauche

leg
jambe

lemon
citron

lemonade
limonade

less
moins

lesser, minor
mineur, mineure

lesson
leçon

letter
lettre

letter carrier
facteur

lettuce
laitue

liberty
liberté

library
bibliothèque

like
en

likewise
aussi

limited
court, courte

limp
mou, molle, mol

liquor store
magasin de vins et spiritueux

little
petit

live
en direct

live
vif, vive

living
vif, vive

living room
salle de séjour

lobster
homard

London
Londres

long (time)
long, longue

long while
longtemps

loving
amoureux, amoureuse

low, inferior
bas, basse

luck
chance

lunch
déjeuner

magazine
magazine

magazine
revue

magician
magicien

maid
bonne

mail
poste

main
majeur, majeure

main course
plat principal

malicious
malin, maligne

manager
directeur

manner
façon

manner
mode

many
beaucoup

March
mars

margarine
margarine

market
marché

mathematics
mathématiques

mattress
matelas

May
mai

me
me

meal
repas

meat
viande

medicine cabinet
armoire de toilette

medium rare
à point

melon
melon

memory
mémoire

menu
carte

microwave oven
four à micro-ondes

middle
moyen, moyenne

milk
lait

mineral water
eau minérale

miniskirt
minijupe

minister
pasteur

mirror
miroir

mischievous
malin, maligne

Miss
mademoiselle, mesdemoiselles
(pl.)

mode
mode

model
mannequin

modern
moderne, moderne

Monday
lundi

money
argent

more comfortably
meilleur, meilleure

morning
matin

Moscow
Moscou

most
très

mother
mère

mouse
souris

mouth
bouche

movie theater
cinéma

Mr.
monsieur, messieurs (pl.)

Mrs.
madame, mesdames (pl.)

much
beaucoup

mud, slime
vase

museum
musée

music shop
disquaire

musician
musicien

mussel
moule

mustard
moutarde

nationality
nationalité

natural
naturel, naturelle

naturally
naturellement

near to
près de

near, by
près

nearly
à peu près

neat
joli, jolie

neck
cou

necklace
collier

neighbor
voisin

neighbor
voisine

neither
ni

nephew
neveu

never
ne . . . jamais

never mind
tant pis

new
frais, fraîche

new
neuf, neuve

newsgroup
forum

newspaper
journal

next
ensuite

next
prochain, prochaine (after the noun)

next to
à côté de

nice
brave (before the noun)

nice
gentil, gentille

nice
joli, jolie

niece
nièce

night guard
gardien de nuit

nightgown
chemise de nuit

nightgown
robe de chambre

ninth
neuvième

no
non

no longer
ne . . . pas . . . non plus

no longer
ne . . . plus

no one
ne . . . aucun

no one
ne . . . nul

no vacancies
complet

noble
gentil, gentille

nobody
ne . . . personne

noise
bruit

non smoking
non fumeur

none
ne . . . point

north
nord

North America
Amérique du Nord

nose
nez

not
ne . . . pas

not at all
ne . . . aucunement

not at all
ne . . . nullement

not at all
ne . . . pas du tout

not even one
ne . . . pas un

not much
ne . . . guère

not one
ne . . . aucun

not yet
ne . . . pas encore

not yet
ne . . . toujours pas

notebook
cahier

nothing
ne . . . rien

novel
roman

November
novembre

now
ici

now
maintenant

nowhere
ne . . . nulle part

numerous
nombreux, nombreuse

nun
religieuse

nurse
infirmier

nurse
infirmière

obese, stout
replet, replète

object
objet

October
octobre

of
à

of course
bien sûr

of, from
de

office
bureau

often
souvent

old
vieux, vieil, vieille

omelet
omelette

on
en

on
sur

on sale
en solde

one-way ticket
billet simple

only
ne . . . que

only
seul (before the noun)

optimism
optimisme

or
ou

orange
orange

orange juice
jus d'orange

other
autre

other
différent, différente (after the noun)

out
dehors

outside (out of doors)
dehors

oven
four

overdone
trop cuit

overcoat
pardessus

owl
hibou

own
propre (before the noun)

owner
propriétaire

oyster
huître

painful
douloureux, douloureuse

pajamas
pyjama

pal
copain

panties
slip

pants
pantalon

pantyhose
collant

paper
papier

parade
parade

pardon me?
pardon?

parent
parent

Paris
Paris

Parisian
parisien, parisienne

park
parc

parking lot
parking

passenger
passagère

passport
passeport

password
mot de passe

patiently
patiemment

pavement
pavé

pay raise
augmentation

pay, wages
paye

payment
paiement

pea
pois

peaceful
tranquille, tranquille

peach
pêche

pear
poire

peas
petits pois

pen
stylo

pencil
crayon

pendant
pendentif

penniless
pauvre (after the noun)

people
gens

perhaps
peut-être

person
personne

pessimism
pessimisme

pharmacist
pharmacien

pharmacy
pharmacie

photograph
photo

photography
photographie

piano
piano

picnic
pique-nique

pillow
oreiller

pilot
pilote

pin
épingle

pineapple
ananas

pink
rose

pity
pitié

plain
sec, sèche

plane
avion

platform
quai

please
s'il vous plaît

pleased
content, contente

pleased to meet you
enchanté, enchantée

pleasing
joli, jolie

plum
prune

pocket money
argent de poche

poem
poème

poetry
poésie

pointed
aigu

police officer
gendarme

police station
commissariat

polite
courtois, courtoise

pork
porc

Portuguese
portugais

position
poste

post office
poste

postal service
poste

poster
affiche

posting
contribution

potato
pomme de terre

poultry
volaille

pound
livre

precious
cher, chère (after the noun)

preserving
conservateur, conservatrice

pretty
beau, belle, bel

pretty
gentil, gentille

pretty
joli, jolie

previous
antérieur

previously
déjà

price
prix

price per day
prix par jour

priest
prêtre

prison
prison

prize
prix

probably
probablement, sans doute

propeller
hélice

public
public, publique

purchase
achat

purple
violet, violette

purse
porte-monnaie

purse (handbag)
sac à main

quickly
tôt

quickly
vite

quiet
calme

quiet
tranquille, tranquille

rabbit
lapin

radio
radio

rain coat
imperméable

rare
saignant

raspberry
framboise

razor
rasoir

readily
aisément

reason
raison

receipt
reçu

recent
nouveau, nouvel (after the noun)

receptionist
réceptionniste

red
rouge, rouge

red wine
vin rouge

reddish
roux, rousse

red-haired
roux, rousse

refrigerator
réfrigérateur

rent
loyer

request
demande

reservation
réservation

restaurant
restaurant

revolver
revolver

ribbon
ruban

right
à droite

rightly
bien

ring
bague

roasted
rôti

rocking chair
fauteuil à bascule

roof
toit

rope
corde

round trip ticket
billet aller-retour

rug
tapis

rum
rhum

runway
piste

Russian
russe

sail
voile

salad
salade

salmon
saumon

same
même (before the noun)

sarcasm
sarcasme

sardine
sardine

satisfied
content, contente

Saturday
samedi

savings
économies

savings account
compte d'épargne

scale
balance

scarf
foulard

scholar
savant

school
école

science
science

science fiction film
film de science-fiction

scientist
savant

scrambled eggs
œufs brouillés

screen
écran

seafood
fruits de mer

season
saison

seat
place

seat belt
ceinture

second
deuxième

secondhand
d'occasion

secretary
secrétaire

see you later
à tout à l'heure

see you soon
à bientôt

see you tomorrow
à demain

September
septembre

serene
calme

service
service

set-price meal
prix fixe

seventh
septième

shampoo
shampooing

sharp
aigu

shawl
châle

she
elle

sheet
drap

shelf
étagère

shirt
chemise

shoe size
pointure

shoes
chaussures

shop
magasin

short
court, courte

short
petit, petite

shoulder
épaule

shower
douche

shrimp
crevette

shy
discret, discrète

side
côté

side order
à la carte

sideboard
buffet

sign
signe

silence
silence

silent
muet

similar, equal
pareil, pareille

since
depuis

single
seul (after the noun)

single room
chambre pour une personne

sinning
pécheur, pécheresse

sister
sœur

sixth
sixième

skim milk
lait écrémé

skirt
jupe

sleeve
manche

small
petit

small shop
boutique

smile
sourire

smoker
fumeur

snack
casse-croûte

snack
goûter

snails
escargots

snake
serpent

so
donc, si

soap
savon

social worker
assistant social

social worker
assistante sociale

socks
chaussettes

sofa
canapé

soft
mou, molle, mol

soft-boiled egg
œuf à la coque

software
logiciel

sole
sole

solid
concret, concrète

solitude
solitude

some
des

sometimes
quelquefois

somewhere
quelque part

son
fils

song
chanson

soon
tôt

sore
douloureux, douloureuse

soup
soupe, potage

south
sud

South America
Amérique du Sud

Spanish
espagnol

speed
vitesse

spicy
épicé

spinach
épinards

sponge
éponge

sport jacket
veste sport

spring
printemps

stained-glass window
vitrail

stairs
escalier

star
vedette

station
gare

steadily
constamment

steak
biftek

step
marche

stepfather
beau-père

stepmother
belle-mère

steward
steward

stomach
estomac

stopover
escale

stovetop
cuisinière

straight ahead
tout droit

strange
étranger, étrangère

strawberry
fraise

student
étudiant, étudiante

study
bureau

study
étude

stuffed
farci

subject
sujet

subtitles
sous-titres

subway
métro

subway station
station de métro

such
tel, telle

suit
costume

suitably
convenablement

suitcase
valise

summer
été

Sunday
dimanche

sunglasses
lunettes de soleil

superior
supérieur, supérieure

supermarket
supermarché

supersonic plane
avion supersonique

supplies
provisions

surprise
surprise

sweet
doux, douce

Swiss franc
franc suisse

table
table

take-off
décollage

tall
grand, grande (after the noun)

tall
haut, haute

taxi
taxi

tea
thé

teacher
professeur

tedious
long, longue

telephone
téléphone

television
petit écran

television
télévision

tenant
locataire

tenth
dixième

terminal
terminal

test
examen

thank you
merci

thank you very much
merci beaucoup

that
lequel, lesquelles, lesquels

that
que

the back
arrière

the front
avant

theatre
théâtre

their
leur

then
donc, puis

there
y, là

there is (are)
il y a

there is (are)
voilà

therefore
donc

these
ces

they
elles

they
ils

they
se

thick,
épais, épaisse

thief
voleur, voleuse

third
troisième

thirst
soif

this
ce, cet

this
cette

thumb
pouce

Thursday
jeudi

ticket
billet

ticket office
guichet

ticket-dispensing machine
distributeur de tickets

tie
cravate

tie-clip
fixe-cravate

tights
collant

tip
pourboire

tip included
service compris

tip not included
service non compris

tired
las, lasse

to
à

to
en

to accept
accepter

to accomplish
accomplir

to act
agir

to advise
conseiller

to allow
permettre

to announce
annoncer

to appear on TV
passer à la télé

to applaud
applaudir

to arrive
arriver

to ask for
demander

to attain
parvenir

to be
être

to be able
pouvoir

to be afraid
avoir peur de

to be ambitious
avoir de l'ambition

to be an age
avoir . . . ans

to be angry
être fâché

to be ashamed of
avoir honte de

to be attached to
tenir à

to be born
naître

to be born again
renaître

to be happy
être heureux

to be hungry
avoir faim

to be interested in
intéresser à

to be lucky
avoir de la chance

to be named
s'appeler

to be necessary
falloir

to be pleased
être content

to be right
avoir raison

to be silent
se taire

to be sleepy
avoir sommeil

to be sorry
être désolé

to be successful
réussir

to be surprised
être surpris

to be thirsty
avoir soif

to be unemployed
être sans emploi

to be worth
valoir

to be wrong
avoir tort

to be wrong
tromper

to become
devenir

to begin
commencer

to believe
croire

to belong
être à

to bite
mordre

to blossom
fleurir

to boil
bouillir

to bore
ennuyer

to break
rompre

to broadcast
diffuser

to brush
brosser

to build
bâtir

to buy
acheter

to call
appeler

to carry
porter

to celebrate
célébrer

to change
changer

to check
enrayer

to choose
choisir

to clean
nettoyer

to clear the table
débarrasser la table

to climb
monter

to close
fermer

to close the curtains
fermer les rideaux

to close the door
fermer la porte

to collapse
s'écrouler

to comb one's hair
se coiffer

to come
venir

to come back
revenir

to come back from school
rentrer de l'école

to come back from work
rentrer du travail

to come down again
redescendre

to come home
rentrer à la maison

to come out again
ressortir

to construct
bâtir

to cook
faire la cuisine

to correct
corriger

to corrupt
corrompre

to cost
coûter

to cut
couper

to defend, to protect
défendre

to delete
rayer

to die
mourir

to discover
découvrir

to dismiss
renvoyer

to distrust
se méfier de

to do
faire

to do the dishes
faire la vaisselle

to do the shopping
faire les courses

to dream
songer

to drink
boire

to drive
conduire

to drown
noyer

to dry
sécher

to dry (oneself)
se sécher

to dust
épousseter

to earn
gagner

to earn a living
gagner sa vie

to eat
manger

to employ
employer

to enter
entrer

to erase
effacer

to exchange
échanger

to exclaim
s'écrier

to expect
espérer

to fail
faillir

to faint
s'évanouir

to fall
tomber

to fall asleep
s'endormir

to feel cold
avoir froid

to feel hot
avoir chaud

to feel like
avoir envie de

to find
trouver

to find a job
trouver un emploi

to find work
trouver du travail

to finish
finir

to flee
s'enfuir

to fly away
s'envoler

to follow
suivre

to frighten
effrayer

to fry
frire

to furnish
fournir

to get along
s'entendre

to get bored
s'ennuyer

to get by (manage)
se débrouiller

to get dressed
s'habiller

to get off
descendre

to get up
se lever

to get used to
s'habituer à

to give a hand
donner un coup de main

to give back
rendre

to go
aller

to go away
en aller

to go down
descendre

to go out
sortir

to go out again
repartir

to go shopping
faire des achats

to go shopping
faire du shopping

to go to the restroom
aller aux toilettes

to go to work
aller travailler

to go up again
remonter

to grate
râper

to grieve
regretter

to grill
griller

to guarantee
garantir

to hang
pendre

to hasten
accourir

to hasten
s'empresser de

to hate
détester

to have
avoir

to have
tenir

to have a good time
s'amuser

to have a nap
faire la sieste

to have an ache
avoir mal

to have breakfast
prendre son petit déjeuner

to have experience
avoir de l'expérience

to have the opportunity
avoir l'occasion de

to have to
devoir

to hear
entendre

to help
aider

to hold
tenir

to hope
espérer

to hurry
dépêcher

to imagine
songer

to insert
insérer

to insult
agonir

to intend to
avoir l'intention de

to interrupt
interrompre

to iron
repasser

to irritate
agacer

to kill oneself
se suicider

to know
savoir

to lack experience
manquer d'expérience

to lay (as in eggs)
pondre

to lay off
licencier

to leave
partir, quitter

to like
aimer

to listen
écouter

to live
habiter

to load
charger

to lock the door
verrouiller la porte

to look
chercher

to look after
s'occuper de

to look for a job
chercher un emploi

to lose
perdre

to love
aimer

to make
faire

to make fun of
se moquer de

to make one's bed
faire son lit

to make the beds
faire les lits

to melt
fondre

to mind
se soucier de

to mix
mélanger

to need
avoir besoin de

to obey
obéir à

to obtain
obtenir

to offer
offrir

to open
ouvrir

to order
commander

to owe
devoir

to parcel
morceler

to pay
payer

to pay attention to
faire attention à

to peel
éplucher

to place
mettre, placer

to plan
projeter

to please
plaire

to please (someone)
plaire à

to prefer
préférer

to prepare
préparer

to prepare a meal
faire à manger

to pronounce
prononcer

to put
mettre

to put in one's contact lenses
mettre ses verres de contact

to put in one's false teeth
mettre son dentier

to put on makeup
se maquiller

to rain
pleuvoir

to read
lire

to realize
se rendre compte de

to receive
recevoir

to refresh
rafraîchir

to regret
regretter

to reject
refuser, rejeter

to remain
rester

to remember
se souvenir de

to remind
rappeler

to rent
louer

to repay
rendre

to replace
remplacer

to reply
répondre

to resemble
ressembler à

to resign
démissionner

to restore
rendre

to retire
prendre sa retraite

to return
rentrer, rendre, retourner

to rinse
rincer

to roast
rôtir

to run
courir

to say
dire

to scatter
épandre

to see
voir

to seem
avoir l'air

to sell
vendre

to send
envoyer

to serve
servir

to set the alarm clock
mettre son réveil

to set the table
mettre la table

to shave (oneself)
se raser

to shear, to clip, to crop, to cut
tondre

to sleep
dormir

to slice
couper en tranches

to smile
sourire

to speak
parler

to speak to someone
parler à

to spend
dépenser

to spice
épicer

to split
fendre

to stammer
bégayer

to stay
rester

to stretch
étirer, tendre

to strive
s'efforcer de

to study
étudier

to succeed
parvenir

to suffer
souffrir

to support
appuyer

to suspend
pendre

to sweep
balayer

to swim
nager

to take
prendre

to take a day off
prendre un jour de congé

to take a nap
reposer

to take a vacation
prendre des vacances

to take place
avoir lieu

to telephone
téléphoner à

to tell
dire

to think
penser

to think about someone
penser à

to throw
jeter

to throw again
rejeter

to travel
voyager

to try
essayer

to turn off
éteindre

to turn off the radio
éteindre la radio

to turn off the television
éteindre la télévision

to turn on
allumer

to turn on the radio
allumer la radio

to turn on the television
allumer la télévision

to twist
tordre

to understand
comprendre

to undress (oneself)
déshabiller

to use
utiliser

to wait
attendre

to wait in line
faire la queue

to wake up
réveiller

to want
vouloir

to want, to desire
désirer

to wash
laver

to wash oneself
se laver

to wash up
faire sa toilette

to waste
gaspiller

to watch
regarder

to water the plants
arroser les plantes

to wear
porter

to welcome
accueillir

to will
vouloir

to wipe
essuyer

to wish
espérer

to wish
souhaiter

to wonder
se demander

to work
travailler

to write
écrire

to yawn
bâiller

toast
pain grillé

toaster
grille-pain

today
aujourd'hui

toe
orteil

together (at the same time)
ensemble

restroom
toilettes

toilet paper
papier hygiénique

tomato
tomate

tomorrow
demain

too
aussi

too
trop

too much
trop

toothbrush
brosse à dents

toothpaste
dentifrice

tortoise
tortue

tourism
tourisme

toward
vers

towel
serviette de toilette

traditional
traditionnel, traditionnelle

tragedy
tragédie

train
train

tranquil
calme

tranquil
tranquille

transfer
virement

translator
traducteur, traductrice

transportation
transport

travel agency
agence de voyages

traveler's check
chèque de voyage

trout
truite

truck
camion

true
vrai, vraie

truly
vraiment

Tuesday
mardi

tuna fish
thon

turkey
dinde

tuxedo
smoking

twin room
chambre à deux lits

umbrella
parapluie

umlaut (accent)
tréma

uncle
oncle

undershirt
maillot de corps

unfortunate
malheureux, malheureuse

unfortunate
pauvre (before the noun)

unhappy
malheureux, malheureuse

uniform
uniforme

Uniform Resource Locator (URL)
adresse universelle

United States
États-Unis

universal
universel, universelle

unknown
étranger

untrue
faux, fausse

up, upstairs
en haut

upper
haut, haute

upper
supérieur, supérieure

useful
utile

usual
usuel, usuelle

vacancy
vacance

vacation
vacances

valuable
riche

vase
vase

veal
veau

vegetable
légume

vegetable merchant
marchand de légumes

veil
voile

verdict
sentence

very
très

very young
petit

video
vidéo

virus
virus

visa
visa

vocabulary
vocabulaire

vodka
vodka

wages
salaire

waiter
serveur

waiting room
salle d'attente

waitress
serveuse

walk
promenade

wall
mur

wallet
portefeuille

wardrobe
armoire

sink
lavabo

watch
montre

water
eau

way
mode

we, us
nous

weak
mou, molle, mol

wealthy
riche

Web browser
logiciel de navigation, navigateur

wedding ring
alliance

Wednesday
mercredi

well
bien

well done
bien cuit

well done
bravo

west
ouest

Western (movie)
western

what
que

what
quel, quelle, quels, quelles

what
quoi

wheat
blé

when
où

when
quand

when (at what time)
à quelle heure

where
où

which
lequel, lesquelles, lesquels

which
que

which
quel, quelle, quels, quelles

which, that
laquelle

while
pendant

whiskey
whisky

white
blanc, blanche

white wine
vin blanc

who
qui

whole
complet, complète

whole
tout

why
pourquoi

wife
femme

window
fenêtre

window (plane, boat)
hublot

wine
vin

wine merchant
marchand de vin

wing
aile

winter
hiver

with
avec

with melted cheese
au gratin

withdrawal
retrait

without
sans

woman's suit
ensemble

woman's suit
tailleur

work (job)
travail

World Wide Web
toile d'araignée mondiale [TAM]

wrench
clé anglaise

wrist
poignet

writer
écrivain

wrong
faux, fausse

yellow
jaune

yes
oui

yes, but
si

yesterday
hier

you
te

you
tu

you
vous

youthful
frais, fraîche

Verb Conjugation Tables

-er Verbs

Parler (to speak); past participle, parlé

Subject	Present	Imperfect	Future	Conditional	Subjunctive
je	parle	parlais	parlerai	parlerais	parle
tu	parles	parlais	parleras	parlerais	parles
il	parle	parlait	parlera	parlerait	parle
nous	parlons	parlions	parlerons	parlerions	parlions
vous	parlez	parliez	parlerez	parleriez	parliez
ils	parlent	parlaient	parleront	parleraient	parlent

-ir Verbs

Finir (to finish; past participle, fini

Subject	Present	Imperfect	Future	Conditional	Subjunctive
je	finis	finissais	finirai	finirais	finisse
tu	finis	finissais	finiras	finirais	finisses
il	finit	finissait	finira	finirait	finisse
nous	finissons	finissions	finirons	finirions	finissions
vous	finissez	finissiez	finirez	finiriez	finissiez
ils	finissent	finissaient	finiront	finiraient	finissent

-re Verbs

Attendre (to wait for); past participle, attendu

Subject	Present	Imperfect	Future	Conditional	Subjunctive
je	attends	attendais	attendrai	attendrais	attende
tu	attends	attendais	attendras	attendrais	attendes
il	attend	attendait	attendra	attendrait	attende
nous	attendons	attendions	attendrons	attendrions	attendions
vous	attendez	attendiez	attendrez	attendriez	attendiez
ils	attendent	attendaient	attendront	attendraient	attendent

Irregular Verbs

Aller (to go); past participle, allé

Subject	Present	Imperfect	Future	Conditional	Subjunctive
je	vais	allais	irai	irais	aille
tu	vas	allais	iras	irais	ailles
il	va	allait	ira	irait	aille
nous	allons	allions	irons	irions	allions
vous	allez	alliez	irez	iriez	allies
ils	vont	allaient	iront	iraient	aillent

Avoir (to have); past participle, eu

Subject	Present	Imperfect	Future	Conditional	Subjunctive
j'	ai	avais	aurai	aurais	aie
tu	as	avais	auras	aurais	aies
il	a	avait	aura	aurait	ait
nous	avons	avions	aurons	aurions	ayons
vous	avez	aviez	aurez	auriez	ayez
ils	ont	avaient	auront	auraient	aient

Devoir (to have to); past participle, dû

Subject	Present	Imperfect	Future	Conditional	Subjunctive
je	dois	devais	devrai	devrais	doive
tu	dois	devais	devras	devrais	doives
il	doit	devait	devra	devrait	doive
nous	devons	devions	devrons	devrions	devions
vous	devez	deviez	devrez	devriez	deviez
ils	doivent	devaient	devront	devraient	doivent

Dire (to say, tell); past participle, dit

Subject	Present	Imperfect	Future	Conditional	Subjunctive
je	dis	disais	dirai	dirais	dise
tu	dis	disais	diras	dirais	dises
il	dit	disait	dira	dirait	dise
nous	disons	disions	dirons	dirions	disions
vous	dites	disiez	direz	diriez	disiez
ils	dissent	disaient	diront	diraient	disent

Être (to be); past participle, été

Subject	Present	Imperfect	Future	Conditional	Subjunctive
je	suis	étais	serai	serais	sois
tu	es	étais	seras	serais	sois
il	est	était	sera	serait	soit
nous	sommes	étions	serons	serions	soyons
vous	êtes	étiez	serez	seriez	soyez
ils	sont	étaient	seront	seraient	soient

Faire (to make, do); past participle, fait

Subject	Present	Imperfect	Future	Conditional	Subjunctive
je	fais	faisais	ferai	ferais	fasse
tu	fais	faisais	feras	ferais	fasses
il	fait	faisait	fera	ferait	fasse
nous	faisons	faisions	ferons	ferions	fassions
vous	faites	faisiez	ferez	feriez	fassiez
ils	font	faisaient	feront	feraient	fassent

Mettre (to put); past participle, mis

Subject	Present	Imperfect	Future	Conditional	Subjunctive
je	mets	mettais	mettrai	mettrais	mette
tu	mets	mettais	mettras	mettrais	mettes
il	met	mettait	mettra	mettrait	mette
nous	mettons	mettions	mettrons	mettrions	mettions
vous	mettez	mettiez	mettrez	mettriez	mettiez
ils	mettent	mettaient	mettront	mettraient	mettent

Pouvoir (to be able to, can); past participle, pu

Subject	Present	Imperfect	Future	Conditional	Subjunctive
je	peux	pouvais	pourrai	pourrais	puisse
tu	peux	pouvais	pourras	pourrais	puisses
il	peut	pouvait	pourra	pourrait	puisse
nous	pouvons	pouvions	pourrons	pourrions	puissions
vous	pouvez	pouviez	pourrez	pourriez	puissiez
ils	peuvent	pouvaient	pourront	pourraient	puissant

Recevoir (to receive); past participle, reçu

Subject	Present	Imperfect	Future	Conditional	Subjunctive
je	reçois	recevais	recevrai	recevrais	reçoive
tu	reçois	recevais	recevras	recevrais	reçoives
il	reçoit	recevait	recevra	recevrait	reçoive
nous	recevons	recevions	recevrons	recevrions	recevions
vous	recevez	receviez	recevrez	recevriez	receviez
ils	reçoivent	recevaient	recevront	recevraient	reçoivent

Savoir (to know); past participle, su

Subject	Present	Imperfect	Future	Conditional	Subjunctive
je	sais	savais	saurai	saurais	sache
tu	sais	savais	sauras	saurais	saches
il	sait	savait	saura	saurait	sache
nous	savons	savions	saurons	saurions	sachions
vous	savez	saviez	saurez	sauriez	sachiez
ils	savent	savaient	sauront	sauraient	sachent

Vouloir (to want); past participle; voulu

Subject	Present	Imperfect	Future	Conditional	Subjunctive
je	veux	voulais	voudrai	voudrais	veuille
tu	veux	voulais	voudras	voudrais	veuilles
il	veut	voulait	voudra	voudrait	veuille
nous	voulons	voulions	voudrons	voudrions	voulions
vous	voulez	vouliez	voudrez	voudriez	vouliez
ils	veulent	voulaient	voudront	voudraient	veuillent

Index

THE EVERYTHING SERIES!

BUSINESS & PERSONAL FINANCE

Everything® Accounting Book
Everything® Budgeting Book, 2nd Ed.
Everything® Business Planning Book
Everything® Coaching and Mentoring Book, 2nd Ed.
Everything® Fundraising Book
Everything® Get Out of Debt Book
Everything® Grant Writing Book, 2nd Ed.
Everything® Guide to Buying Foreclosures
Everything® Guide to Fundraising, $15.95
Everything® Guide to Mortgages
Everything® Guide to Personal Finance for Single Mothers
Everything® Home-Based Business Book, 2nd Ed.
Everything® Homebuying Book, 3rd Ed., $15.95
Everything® Homeselling Book, 2nd Ed.
Everything® Human Resource Management Book
Everything® Improve Your Credit Book
Everything® Investing Book, 2nd Ed.
Everything® Landlording Book
Everything® Leadership Book, 2nd Ed.
Everything® Managing People Book, 2nd Ed.
Everything® Negotiating Book
Everything® Online Auctions Book
Everything® Online Business Book
Everything® Personal Finance Book
Everything® Personal Finance in Your 20s & 30s Book, 2nd Ed.
Everything® Personal Finance in Your 40s & 50s Book, $15.95
Everything® Project Management Book, 2nd Ed.
Everything® Real Estate Investing Book
Everything® Retirement Planning Book
Everything® Robert's Rules Book, $7.95
Everything® Selling Book
Everything® Start Your Own Business Book, 2nd Ed.
Everything® Wills & Estate Planning Book

COOKING

Everything® Barbecue Cookbook
Everything® Bartender's Book, 2nd Ed., $9.95
Everything® Calorie Counting Cookbook
Everything® Cheese Book
Everything® Chinese Cookbook
Everything® Classic Recipes Book
Everything® Cocktail Parties & Drinks Book
Everything® College Cookbook
Everything® Cooking for Baby and Toddler Book
Everything® Diabetes Cookbook
Everything® Easy Gourmet Cookbook
Everything® Fondue Cookbook
Everything® Food Allergy Cookbook, $15.95
Everything® Fondue Party Book
Everything® Gluten-Free Cookbook
Everything® Glycemic Index Cookbook
Everything® Grilling Cookbook
Everything® Healthy Cooking for Parties Book, $15.95
Everything® Holiday Cookbook
Everything® Indian Cookbook
Everything® Lactose-Free Cookbook
Everything® Low-Cholesterol Cookbook

Everything® Low-Fat High-Flavor Cookbook, 2nd Ed., $15.95
Everything® Low-Salt Cookbook
Everything® Meals for a Month Cookbook
Everything® Meals on a Budget Cookbook
Everything® Mediterranean Cookbook
Everything® Mexican Cookbook
Everything® No Trans Fat Cookbook
Everything® One-Pot Cookbook, 2nd Ed., $15.95
Everything® Organic Cooking for Baby & Toddler Book, $15.95
Everything® Pizza Cookbook
Everything® Quick Meals Cookbook, 2nd Ed., $15.95
Everything® Slow Cooker Cookbook
Everything® Slow Cooking for a Crowd Cookbook
Everything® Soup Cookbook
Everything® Stir-Fry Cookbook
Everything® Sugar-Free Cookbook
Everything® Tapas and Small Plates Cookbook
Everything® Tex-Mex Cookbook
Everything® Thai Cookbook
Everything® Vegetarian Cookbook
Everything® Whole-Grain, High-Fiber Cookbook
Everything® Wild Game Cookbook
Everything® Wine Book, 2nd Ed.

GAMES

Everything® 15-Minute Sudoku Book, $9.95
Everything® 30-Minute Sudoku Book, $9.95
Everything® Bible Crosswords Book, $9.95
Everything® Blackjack Strategy Book
Everything® Brain Strain Book, $9.95
Everything® Bridge Book
Everything® Card Games Book
Everything® Card Tricks Book, $9.95
Everything® Casino Gambling Book, 2nd Ed.
Everything® Chess Basics Book
Everything® Christmas Crosswords Book, $9.95
Everything® Craps Strategy Book
Everything® Crossword and Puzzle Book
Everything® Crosswords and Puzzles for Quote Lovers Book, $9.95
Everything® Crossword Challenge Book
Everything® Crosswords for the Beach Book, $9.95
Everything® Cryptic Crosswords Book, $9.95
Everything® Cryptograms Book, $9.95
Everything® Easy Crosswords Book
Everything® Easy Kakuro Book, $9.95
Everything® Easy Large-Print Crosswords Book
Everything® Games Book, 2nd Ed.
Everything® Giant Book of Crosswords
Everything® Giant Sudoku Book, $9.95
Everything® Giant Word Search Book
Everything® Kakuro Challenge Book, $9.95
Everything® Large-Print Crossword Challenge Book
Everything® Large-Print Crosswords Book
Everything® Large-Print Travel Crosswords Book
Everything® Lateral Thinking Puzzles Book, $9.95
Everything® Literary Crosswords Book, $9.95
Everything® Mazes Book
Everything® Memory Booster Puzzles Book, $9.95

Everything® Movie Crosswords Book, $9.95
Everything® Music Crosswords Book, $9.95
Everything® Online Poker Book
Everything® Pencil Puzzles Book, $9.95
Everything® Poker Strategy Book
Everything® Pool & Billiards Book
Everything® Puzzles for Commuters Book, $9.95
Everything® Puzzles for Dog Lovers Book, $9.95
Everything® Sports Crosswords Book, $9.95
Everything® Test Your IQ Book, $9.95
Everything® Texas Hold 'Em Book, $9.95
Everything® Travel Crosswords Book, $9.95
Everything® Travel Mazes Book, $9.95
Everything® Travel Word Search Book, $9.95
Everything® TV Crosswords Book, $9.95
Everything® Word Games Challenge Book
Everything® Word Scramble Book
Everything® Word Search Book

HEALTH

Everything® Alzheimer's Book
Everything® Diabetes Book
Everything® First Aid Book, $9.95
Everything® Green Living Book
Everything® Health Guide to Addiction and Recovery
Everything® Health Guide to Adult Bipolar Disorder
Everything® Health Guide to Arthritis
Everything® Health Guide to Controlling Anxiety
Everything® Health Guide to Depression
Everything® Health Guide to Diabetes, 2nd Ed.
Everything® Health Guide to Fibromyalgia
Everything® Health Guide to Menopause, 2nd Ed.
Everything® Health Guide to Migraines
Everything® Health Guide to Multiple Sclerosis
Everything® Health Guide to OCD
Everything® Health Guide to PMS
Everything® Health Guide to Postpartum Care
Everything® Health Guide to Thyroid Disease
Everything® Hypnosis Book
Everything® Low Cholesterol Book
Everything® Menopause Book
Everything® Nutrition Book
Everything® Reflexology Book
Everything® Stress Management Book
Everything® Superfoods Book, $15.95

HISTORY

Everything® American Government Book
Everything® American History Book, 2nd Ed.
Everything® American Revolution Book, $15.95
Everything® Civil War Book
Everything® Freemasons Book
Everything® Irish History & Heritage Book
Everything® World War II Book, 2nd Ed.

HOBBIES

Everything® Candlemaking Book
Everything® Cartooning Book
Everything® Coin Collecting Book
Everything® Digital Photography Book, 2nd Ed.

Everything® Drawing Book
Everything® Family Tree Book, 2nd Ed.
Everything® Guide to Online Genealogy, $15.95
Everything® Knitting Book
Everything® Knots Book
Everything® Photography Book
Everything® Quilting Book
Everything® Sewing Book
Everything® Soapmaking Book, 2nd Ed.
Everything® Woodworking Book

HOME IMPROVEMENT

Everything® Feng Shui Book
Everything® Feng Shui Decluttering Book, $9.95
Everything® Fix-It Book
Everything® Green Living Book
Everything® Home Decorating Book
Everything® Home Storage Solutions Book
Everything® Homebuilding Book
Everything® Organize Your Home Book, 2nd Ed.

KIDS' BOOKS

All titles are $7.95
Everything® Fairy Tales Book, $14.95
Everything® Kids' Animal Puzzle & Activity Book
Everything® Kids' Astronomy Book
Everything® Kids' Baseball Book, 5th Ed.
Everything® Kids' Bible Trivia Book
Everything® Kids' Bugs Book
Everything® Kids' Cars and Trucks Puzzle and Activity Book
Everything® Kids' Christmas Puzzle & Activity Book
Everything® Kids' Connect the Dots
    Puzzle and Activity Book
Everything® Kids' Cookbook, 2nd Ed.
Everything® Kids' Crazy Puzzles Book
Everything® Kids' Dinosaurs Book
Everything® Kids' Dragons Puzzle and Activity Book
Everything® Kids' Environment Book $7.95
Everything® Kids' Fairies Puzzle and Activity Book
Everything® Kids' First Spanish Puzzle and Activity Book
Everything® Kids' Football Book
Everything® Kids' Geography Book
Everything® Kids' Gross Cookbook
Everything® Kids' Gross Hidden Pictures Book
Everything® Kids' Gross Jokes Book
Everything® Kids' Gross Mazes Book
Everything® Kids' Gross Puzzle & Activity Book
Everything® Kids' Halloween Puzzle & Activity Book
Everything® Kids' Hanukkah Puzzle and Activity Book
Everything® Kids' Hidden Pictures Book
Everything® Kids' Horses Book
Everything® Kids' Joke Book
Everything® Kids' Knock Knock Book
Everything® Kids' Learning French Book
Everything® Kids' Learning Spanish Book
Everything® Kids' Magical Science Experiments Book
Everything® Kids' Math Puzzles Book
Everything® Kids' Mazes Book
Everything® Kids' Money Book, 2nd Ed.
**Everything® Kids' Mummies, Pharaoh's, and Pyramids
    Puzzle and Activity Book**
Everything® Kids' Nature Book
Everything® Kids' Pirates Puzzle and Activity Book
Everything® Kids' Presidents Book
Everything® Kids' Princess Puzzle and Activity Book
Everything® Kids' Puzzle Book

Everything® Kids' Racecars Puzzle and Activity Book
Everything® Kids' Riddles & Brain Teasers Book
Everything® Kids' Science Experiments Book
Everything® Kids' Sharks Book
Everything® Kids' Soccer Book
Everything® Kids' Spelling Book
Everything® Kids' Spies Puzzle and Activity Book
Everything® Kids' States Book
Everything® Kids' Travel Activity Book
Everything® Kids' Word Search Puzzle and Activity Book

LANGUAGE

Everything® Conversational Japanese Book with CD, $19.95
Everything® French Grammar Book
Everything® French Phrase Book, $9.95
Everything® French Verb Book, $9.95
Everything® German Phrase Book, $9.95
Everything® German Practice Book with CD, $19.95
Everything® Inglés Book
Everything® Intermediate Spanish Book with CD, $19.95
Everything® Italian Phrase Book, $9.95
Everything® Italian Practice Book with CD, $19.95
Everything® Learning Brazilian Portuguese Book with CD, $19.95
Everything® Learning French Book with CD, 2nd Ed., $19.95
Everything® Learning German Book
Everything® Learning Italian Book
Everything® Learning Latin Book
Everything® Learning Russian Book with CD, $19.95
Everything® Learning Spanish Book
Everything® Learning Spanish Book with CD, 2nd Ed., $19.95
Everything® Russian Practice Book with CD, $19.95
Everything® Sign Language Book, $15.95
Everything® Spanish Grammar Book
Everything® Spanish Phrase Book, $9.95
Everything® Spanish Practice Book with CD, $19.95
Everything® Spanish Verb Book, $9.95
Everything® Speaking Mandarin Chinese Book with CD, $19.95

MUSIC

Everything® Bass Guitar Book with CD, $19.95
Everything® Drums Book with CD, $19.95
Everything® Guitar Book with CD, 2nd Ed., $19.95
Everything® Guitar Chords Book with CD, $19.95
Everything® Guitar Scales Book with CD, $19.95
Everything® Harmonica Book with CD, $15.95
Everything® Home Recording Book
Everything® Music Theory Book with CD, $19.95
Everything® Reading Music Book with CD, $19.95
Everything® Rock & Blues Guitar Book with CD, $19.95
Everything® Rock & Blues Piano Book with CD, $19.95
Everything® Rock Drums Book with CD, $19.95
Everything® Singing Book with CD, $19.95
Everything® Songwriting Book

NEW AGE

Everything® Astrology Book, 2nd Ed.
Everything® Birthday Personology Book
Everything® Celtic Wisdom Book, $15.95
Everything® Dreams Book, 2nd Ed.
Everything® Law of Attraction Book, $15.95
Everything® Love Signs Book, $9.95
Everything® Love Spells Book, $9.95
Everything® Palmistry Book
Everything® Psychic Book
Everything® Reiki Book

Everything® Sex Signs Book, $9.95
Everything® Spells & Charms Book, 2nd Ed.
Everything® Tarot Book, 2nd Ed.
Everything® Toltec Wisdom Book
Everything® Wicca & Witchcraft Book, 2nd Ed.

PARENTING

Everything® Baby Names Book, 2nd Ed.
Everything® Baby Shower Book, 2nd Ed.
Everything® Baby Sign Language Book with DVD
Everything® Baby's First Year Book
Everything® Birthing Book
Everything® Breastfeeding Book
Everything® Father-to-Be Book
Everything® Father's First Year Book
Everything® Get Ready for Baby Book, 2nd Ed.
Everything® Get Your Baby to Sleep Book, $9.95
Everything® Getting Pregnant Book
Everything® Guide to Pregnancy Over 35
Everything® Guide to Raising a One-Year-Old
Everything® Guide to Raising a Two-Year-Old
Everything® Guide to Raising Adolescent Boys
Everything® Guide to Raising Adolescent Girls
Everything® Mother's First Year Book
Everything® Parent's Guide to Childhood Illnesses
Everything® Parent's Guide to Children and Divorce
Everything® Parent's Guide to Children with ADD/ADHD
Everything® Parent's Guide to Children with Asperger's
    Syndrome
Everything® Parent's Guide to Children with Anxiety
Everything® Parent's Guide to Children with Asthma
Everything® Parent's Guide to Children with Autism
Everything® Parent's Guide to Children with Bipolar Disorder
Everything® Parent's Guide to Children with Depression
Everything® Parent's Guide to Children with Dyslexia
Everything® Parent's Guide to Children with Juvenile Diabetes
Everything® Parent's Guide to Children with OCD
Everything® Parent's Guide to Positive Discipline
Everything® Parent's Guide to Raising Boys
Everything® Parent's Guide to Raising Girls
Everything® Parent's Guide to Raising Siblings
**Everything® Parent's Guide to Raising Your
    Adopted Child**
Everything® Parent's Guide to Sensory Integration Disorder
Everything® Parent's Guide to Tantrums
Everything® Parent's Guide to the Strong-Willed Child
Everything® Parenting a Teenager Book
Everything® Potty Training Book, $9.95
Everything® Pregnancy Book, 3rd Ed.
Everything® Pregnancy Fitness Book
Everything® Pregnancy Nutrition Book
Everything® Pregnancy Organizer, 2nd Ed., $16.95
Everything® Toddler Activities Book
Everything® Toddler Book
Everything® Tween Book
Everything® Twins, Triplets, and More Book

PETS

Everything® Aquarium Book
Everything® Boxer Book
Everything® Cat Book, 2nd Ed.
Everything® Chihuahua Book
Everything® Cooking for Dogs Book
Everything® Dachshund Book
Everything® Dog Book, 2nd Ed.
Everything® Dog Grooming Book

Everything® Dog Obedience Book
Everything® Dog Owner's Organizer, $16.95
Everything® Dog Training and Tricks Book
Everything® German Shepherd Book
Everything® Golden Retriever Book
Everything® Horse Book, 2nd Ed., $15.95
Everything® Horse Care Book
Everything® Horseback Riding Book
Everything® Labrador Retriever Book
Everything® Poodle Book
Everything® Pug Book
Everything® Puppy Book
Everything® Small Dogs Book
Everything® Tropical Fish Book
Everything® Yorkshire Terrier Book

REFERENCE

Everything® American Presidents Book
Everything® Blogging Book
Everything® Build Your Vocabulary Book, $9.95
Everything® Car Care Book
Everything® Classical Mythology Book
Everything® Da Vinci Book
Everything® Einstein Book
Everything® Enneagram Book
Everything® Etiquette Book, 2nd Ed.
Everything® Family Christmas Book, $15.95
Everything® Guide to C. S. Lewis & Narnia
Everything® Guide to Divorce, 2nd Ed., $15.95
Everything® Guide to Edgar Allan Poe
Everything® Guide to Understanding Philosophy
Everything® Inventions and Patents Book
Everything® Jacqueline Kennedy Onassis Book
Everything® John F. Kennedy Book
Everything® Mafia Book
Everything® Martin Luther King Jr. Book
Everything® Pirates Book
Everything® Private Investigation Book
Everything® Psychology Book
Everything® Public Speaking Book, $9.95
Everything® Shakespeare Book, 2nd Ed.

RELIGION

Everything® Angels Book
Everything® Bible Book
Everything® Bible Study Book with CD, $19.95
Everything® Buddhism Book
Everything® Catholicism Book
Everything® Christianity Book
Everything® Gnostic Gospels Book
Everything® Hinduism Book, $15.95
Everything® History of the Bible Book
Everything® Jesus Book
Everything® Jewish History & Heritage Book
Everything® Judaism Book
Everything® Kabbalah Book
Everything® Koran Book
Everything® Mary Book
Everything® Mary Magdalene Book
Everything® Prayer Book

Everything® Saints Book, 2nd Ed.
Everything® Torah Book
Everything® Understanding Islam Book
Everything® Women of the Bible Book
Everything® World's Religions Book

SCHOOL & CAREERS

Everything® Career Tests Book
Everything® College Major Test Book
Everything® College Survival Book, 2nd Ed.
Everything® Cover Letter Book, 2nd Ed.
Everything® Filmmaking Book
Everything® Get-a-Job Book, 2nd Ed.
Everything® Guide to Being a Paralegal
Everything® Guide to Being a Personal Trainer
Everything® Guide to Being a Real Estate Agent
Everything® Guide to Being a Sales Rep
Everything® Guide to Being an Event Planner
Everything® Guide to Careers in Health Care
Everything® Guide to Careers in Law Enforcement
Everything® Guide to Government Jobs
Everything® Guide to Starting and Running a Catering
    Business
Everything® Guide to Starting and Running a Restaurant
**Everything® Guide to Starting and Running
    a Retail Store**
Everything® Job Interview Book, 2nd Ed.
Everything® New Nurse Book
Everything® New Teacher Book
Everything® Paying for College Book
Everything® Practice Interview Book
Everything® Resume Book, 3rd Ed.
Everything® Study Book

SELF-HELP

Everything® Body Language Book
Everything® Dating Book, 2nd Ed.
Everything® Great Sex Book
**Everything® Guide to Caring for Aging Parents,
    $15.95**
Everything® Self-Esteem Book
Everything® Self-Hypnosis Book, $9.95
Everything® Tantric Sex Book

SPORTS & FITNESS

Everything® Easy Fitness Book
Everything® Fishing Book
Everything® Guide to Weight Training, $15.95
Everything® Krav Maga for Fitness Book
Everything® Running Book, 2nd Ed.
Everything® Triathlon Training Book, $15.95

TRAVEL

Everything® Family Guide to Coastal Florida
Everything® Family Guide to Cruise Vacations
Everything® Family Guide to Hawaii
Everything® Family Guide to Las Vegas, 2nd Ed.
Everything® Family Guide to Mexico
Everything® Family Guide to New England, 2nd Ed.

Everything® Family Guide to New York City, 3rd Ed.
**Everything® Family Guide to Northern California
    and Lake Tahoe**
Everything® Family Guide to RV Travel & Campgrounds
Everything® Family Guide to the Caribbean
Everything® Family Guide to the Disneyland® Resort, California
    Adventure®, Universal Studios®, and the Anaheim
    Area, 2nd Ed.
Everything® Family Guide to the Walt Disney World Resort®,
    Universal Studios®, and Greater Orlando, 5th Ed.
Everything® Family Guide to Timeshares
Everything® Family Guide to Washington D.C., 2nd Ed.

WEDDINGS

Everything® Bachelorette Party Book, $9.95
Everything® Bridesmaid Book, $9.95
Everything® Destination Wedding Book
Everything® Father of the Bride Book, $9.95
Everything® Green Wedding Book, $15.95
Everything® Groom Book, $9.95
Everything® Jewish Wedding Book, 2nd Ed., $15.95
Everything® Mother of the Bride Book, $9.95
Everything® Outdoor Wedding Book
Everything® Wedding Book, 3rd Ed.
Everything® Wedding Checklist, $9.95
Everything® Wedding Etiquette Book, $9.95
Everything® Wedding Organizer, 2nd Ed., $16.95
Everything® Wedding Shower Book, $9.95
Everything® Wedding Vows Book, 3rd Ed., $9.95
Everything® Wedding Workout Book
Everything® Weddings on a Budget Book, 2nd Ed., $9.95

WRITING

Everything® Creative Writing Book
Everything® Get Published Book, 2nd Ed.
Everything® Grammar and Style Book, 2nd Ed.
Everything® Guide to Magazine Writing
Everything® Guide to Writing a Book Proposal
Everything® Guide to Writing a Novel
Everything® Guide to Writing Children's Books
Everything® Guide to Writing Copy
Everything® Guide to Writing Graphic Novels
Everything® Guide to Writing Research Papers
Everything® Guide to Writing a Romance Novel, $15.95
Everything® Improve Your Writing Book, 2nd Ed.
Everything® Writing Poetry Book